£20 (3 vols)

b
c

THE LONDON BRIGHTON
AND SOUTH COAST RAILWAY:
III. COMPLETION AND MATURITY

The London Brighton and South Coast Railway:

III. COMPLETION AND MATURITY

JOHN HOWARD TURNER

B. T. BATSFORD LTD
London

ISBN 0 7134 1389 1

Photoset in Great Britain by
Bristol Typesetting Co Ltd
Barton Manor, St Philips, Bristol
Printed and Bound in Great Britain by
Redwood Burn Limited
Trowbridge & Esher
for the Publishers
B. T. Batsford Ltd
4 Fitzhardinge Street
London W1H 0AH

CONTENTS

LIST OF PLATES

FOREWORD

Although the main basis of the LBSC Rly system had largely been completed by 1869, as dealt with in Volumes I and II of this account, a number of additional lines were built during the succeeding 20 years. Further, the continuing overall increase in traffic from the 1890s onwards eventually made it essential to undertake extensive improvements to lines already open, both by quadrupling various sections and by rebuilding stations to give more extensive and up-to-date accommodation than already provided.

Early in the twentieth century the LBSC Rly obtained powers to work traffic electrically, and from 1909 onwards the London suburban area was progressively electrified. This work would probably have been completed by about 1917 or 1918 but for the outbreak of the First World War, which brought extensions to the electrification to a standstill. When, in due course, it became possible to restart, the company was nearing the end of its separate existence, since on and from 1 January 1923 it formed part of the Southern Railway. Just before this extremely important event, the Brighton decided to extend electrification to the coast, but nothing came of this as the Southern as a whole had other, and even more urgent, matters needing attention. Hence parts, only, of the LBSC Rly London suburban area were actually electrified by that company; and although other parts of the scheme were completed under the aegis of the Southern Railway, some sections of the Brighton's London area scheme never came to fruition. To enable the whole of the LBSC Rly electrification picture to be seen in perspective, therefore, the account of the Brighton's scheme is taken just over two years into the Southern Railway period, to 1 April 1925.

Electrification was the most important single factor in the final development of the LBSC Rly, but must be seen against the even larger background of traffic conditions at the time. The Author so presents it in this, the final book of his three-volume account of the company.

To deal with the whole period 1870–1922 (in many ways one of the most important in the whole of the LBSC Rly's separate existence) in one volume has been exceptionally difficult, and has necessitated frequent re-drafting so as to retain only what is essential in order that the overall position may be understood. As in the case of Volumes I and II, virtually all the information given in the present Volume has been taken from the Author's private records (mostly official data), interpreted by his own exceedingly detailed personal knowledge of the entire system which has accumulated over some 60 years of direct acquaintance. The Author's great regret is that space limitations are such that he has had to omit a large proportion of the information that he has in his records.

The pattern set by Volumes I and II has been continued, the final development of the LBSC Rly system being shown by a series of specially drawn maps and diagrams. As in the earlier Volumes, the maps have been prepared to show the main topographical characteristics of the areas concerned, and are not intended to take the place of detailed maps showing contours, small rivers and streams, and other features; nor do they show towns and villages not particularly associated with LBSC Rly lines.

Once again I wish to express my deep appreciation to those who have continued to give me help when I have asked for it. My numerous friends on the Southern Region of British Railways have, as always, assisted when necessary, and I must again express my appreciation to the Keeper of the National Railway Museum—with whom I have a close professional association as a consultant in another capacity—for permission to use some of the Museum's photographs. Other photographs are acknowledged individually on the plates concerned.

Again I wish to express my deepest thanks to my wife, Eleanor Howard Turner; to my research partner, Joan Eastland; and to my illustrator, Patrick Piper. My wife is a station master's daughter, and her support and interest just cannot be measured. Joan comes of a railway family (all on the LBSC Rly) and spent virtually her whole working life on the Southern Railway and on British Railways (Southern Region); her help and support cannot be put into words. Patrick's drawings speak for themselves, and without his assistance it would have been very difficult for me to have illustrated this work so well.

In conclusion, I also wish to repeat my thanks to Messrs. Batsford, and especially to William (Bill) Waller, for publishing this three-volume account—originally it was to consist of two volumes, only, but the fact that the great majority of the information in it has not been published before, caused Messrs. Batsford to decide that three volumes were needed.

I hope that these three volumes will be of help to historians in general as well as to those more particularly interested in the LBSC Rly.

JOHN HOWARD TURNER

ABBREVIATIONS

The following abbreviations are used from time to time in this Volume.

Abbreviations

EL Rly	East London Railway
GE Rly	Great Eastern Railway
GN Rly	Great Northern Railway
GW Rly	Great Western Railway
LBSC Rly	London, Brighton & South Coast Railway
LCD Rly	London, Chatham & Dover Railway
LNW Rly	London & North Western Railway
LSW Rly	London & South Western Railway
Rly	Railway
SE Rly	South Eastern Railway
SEC Rly	South Eastern & Chatham Railway (the working union of the SE Rly and the LCD Rly, from 1899)
WL Rly	West London Railway
WLE Rly	West London Extension Railway
£ s. d.	Pound, Shillings, and Pence (old British currency). There were 12 pence to 1 shilling, and 20 shillings to £1. At the time of the change of currency, 1s. was represented by 5p. in new (present) currency.

Second Supplement to Volume I

Several of the matters which had still to be left open when Volume I was sent to the publishers in 1976, were cleared up by the Author soon afterwards. Hence he included the necessary clarification at the beginning of Volume II, in the form of a Supplement to Volume I. That Supplement appears as pp. xi–xiii of Volume II, the latter volume having been sent to the publishers in 1977.

Since then, the Author has completed his investigations on certain further matters that had to be left open in Volume I. Moreover, he has now explored all known surviving records of Shoreham Viaduct, in the light of the conflicting evidence referred to on p. xii of Volume II in the course of the Supplement to Volume I.

These, and certain other matters, are, the Author hopes, cleared up finally in the following paragraphs. These should therefore be read in conjunction both with Volume I itself and with the original Supplement to Volume I (printed as pp. xi–xiii of Volume II).

Arun Bridge (Original)
(Vol. I, p. 211, lines 6–11; and Vol. II, p. xi). The Author has been unable to find any further information which would enable him finally to clarify the matter reported in the Supplement to Volume I (p. xi of Volume II). It is, however, not impossible that, after the original bridge had been brought into use, a new east sub-structure was constructed north of the line of the bridge, in replacement of that on the south side of the bridge; and that the replacement sub-structure was that indicated on the 1860–62 drawing referred to on p. xi of Volume II.

Bricklayers Arms station
(Vol. I, p. 204, Note 1 (referring to p. 194, line 9 of the text)). The Author wishes to emphasize that the report of an alleged irregularity in the way in which land for Bricklayers Arms station was acquired, appeared (as printed as Note 1 on p. 204 of

Volume I) on 12 May 1944—i.e., nearly 111 years after the Act for building the station and line. Descendants of those named in that Note, attempted to 're-possess' what they called 'their' land, in 1944. That date is *not* a misprint for 1844, as suggested to the Author by one historian, and the book is correct in showing 1944.

Croydon Canal Relics
(Vol. I, p. 48, lines 14–18). The Author has been informed by Mr. A. Hughes that a short stretch of the former Croydon Canal still exists to the east of the railway between Forest Hill and Sydenham stations, in addition to the length in Betts Park, Penge, referred to on p. 49 of Volume I and illustrated by the Author's photograph in Plate I, facing p. 160 of that Volume. The length reported by Mr. Hughes is a short distance south of the footbridge over the railway between Forest Hill and Sydenham stations; it generally only holds water after a time of heavy rain.

Greenwich station
(Vol. I, p. 43, 14th line from foot). The date of opening should read 24 December 1838, and obviously not 1938.

Lewes–Newhaven Line
(Vol. I, p. 227, 8th line from foot, and p. 231, line 4). Although this line was opened on Monday 6 December 1847, the Author has been informed by his friend and fellow historian Mr. H. V. Borley that contemporary local Sussex newspapers reported that, due to violent storms, no trains were able to run either on that day or on the following day. This may well explain why the opening date has hitherto usually been given as Wednesday 8 December 1847. The two days' delay in actually starting train services has already been explained in Note 6 on p. 25 of Volume II.

London & Brighton Railway contracts
(Vol. I, p. 132, lines 21–25, and pp. 143–144). The Author has been informed by Mr. Peter McGow that data on various contracts for building the main line of the London & Brighton Railway, had been marked on a survey originally held by Thomas Wood, the Secretary of the London & Brighton. That survey was made by Mr. J. U. Rastrick, then the London &

Brighton's Resident Engineer, in November 1837, and Mr. Wood's copy is now in the possession of Mr. McGow.

Wood's copy of the survey has been annotated to show contract lengths, the names of contractors, and the values of their contracts. Whilst some of the information on the survey, which has been extracted and sent to the Author by Mr. McGow, is additional to that given by the Author on pp. 143-144 of Volume I, in certain other cases the information forwarded by Mr. McGow is somewhat at variance with that given by the Author. The latter took his data direct from all the surviving contracts themselves, and he is therefore satisfied that those contracts (and hence the data on pp. 143-144 of Volume I) were what was finally agreed.

In the Author's opinion, the contract data quoted by Mr. McGow from the London & Brighton Railway's Secretary's copy of Rastrick's survey, was what was originally intended by the firms of contractors named on that copy of the survey. He (the Author) therefore thinks it likely that in certain instances either variations were agreed before the contracts were let, or else that, for one reason or another, other changes were made, and even different contractors employed.

The following data relating to contracts which no longer exist in the Southern Region's Chief Civil Engineer's records, are shown on Wood's copy of Rastrick's survey. The Author gives this information in geographical order, in accordance with the method that he used on p. 144 of Volume I:

NO.	WORKS	CONTRACTOR AND SUM INVOLVED
1	Croydon–Sanderstead	Samuel Briggs (£29,300)
2	Sanderstead–Coulsdon	Thomas Green (£37,500)
5	South end of Merstham Tunnel–Earlswood Common	Treadwell (£73,800)

Wood's copy of Rastrick's survey also shows No. 3 as being for 74 chains in the Parish of Merstham, at a figure of £28,500, whilst no annotation is given for No. 4 (Merstham Tunnel) As will be noted from p. 144 of Volume I, no formal contracts were let for Nos. 3 and 4, and it seems to the Author that this may well have been because Hoof, the contractor for Merstham Tunnel itself, may have wished to excavate the long and very deep chalk cutting to the north of that tunnel, in addition to building the tunnel itself—see pp. 133–134 and 221 of Volume I.

London and Portsmouth Railway (proposed)
(Vol. I, p. 260, 9th line from foot). The date of publication of the prospectus of the above line, should read 12 October 1844, and obviously not 1884.

London Bridge station
(Vol. I, pp. 32 (last line), 41 (penultimate line), 43 (15th line from foot), and 183 (line 24)). The following amplification is given of the somewhat unusual circumstances associated with the opening of London Bridge station.

A committee of three London & Greenwich Railway directors had been appointed on 19 November 1836, to supervise the arrangements for opening the railway, on which public services started some time before the formal ceremony on Wednesday 14 December 1836. In connection with the latter, the Secretary of the Greenwich company announced on 13 December that the usual train service would be interrupted between 10 00 and 14 00 on 14 December to enable the ceremonial trains to be run. The tone of this announcement was such as to give a clear impression that public services had then already been operating for some little time, and not merely for a day or two. The first public announcements of the formal opening appeared on 3 December, and stated that the Lord Mayor would attend on 13 December. The latter date was later put back to 14 December, probably because the Lord Mayor had had to change his programme. It is very difficult to imagine that the announcements on 3 December would have been made in advance of the station being at least in a condition for trains to be operated, and without some running having taken place (even if only by trial trains). The directors of the London & Greenwich Railway would not have taken the risk of the formal ceremony being a fiasco due to incompleteness and lack of experience.

In this connection, traffic returns published on pp. 36–38 of the July 1837 issue of Herapath's *The Railway Magazine and Annals of Science*, introduced what must surely be a measure of confusion into the matter. The figures published show, on a weekly basis, numbers of passengers and receipts; and the first two entries read as follows:

WEEK ENDING	NUMBERS CONVEYED	RECEIPTS £ s. d.		
14 December 1836	1,387	39	11s.	0d.
21 December 1836	19,086	549	14s.	7d.

There are two matters of special note in the above statistics.

In the first place, it seems a very odd action to 'close' a week's figures on the day of formal opening (and on a Wednesday at that), and to continue henceforth to regard that day as the last in each week (the Author only quotes above, the first two entries of a period taken up to the printing date of Herapath for July 1837). Presumably the records concerned, commenced on 14 December 1836 after the formal opening had taken place, so that the very low figures for the first 'week' in fact refer to the traffic on the late afternoon and evening of 14 December.

In the second place, and still more important, the returns published in Herapath and cited above, are bound to have been read (and could still be read) as implying that public working with fare-paying passengers only commenced after the line was formally opened to London Bridge by the Lord Mayor. The London & Greenwich line had been opened to the public on 8 February 1836 as between Spa Road and Deptford; and the length 'north' of Spa Road as far as Bermondsey Street underbridge, not far from London Bridge station, had been brought into use on 10 October 1836 (see Volume I, pp. 41 40) Passengers had certainly not been carried free from 8 February until 14 December. Even if a new account had been started on 14 December—which would seem to be very unlikely—the returns prior to that date ought surely to have been included in a statement indicating the use being made of the line and the receipts earned.

The Author is continuing to seek positive evidence of when public services from and to London Bridge actually commenced, but in the meantime he reiterates that the likely date seems to have been Thursday 1 December 1836, as stated on pp. 32, 41, 43, and 183 of Volume I.

Merstham (original station)
(Vol. I, pp. 165 (11th-10th lines from foot), and 183 (last line)-184 (lines 1-27)). The dates of opening and closing of the

original Merstham station, some $\frac{3}{4}$ mile south of the present one, are given in the above references. However, although that station had an extremely short life (less than two years, from 1 December 1841 to 1 October 1843), there seems to have been a period in 1842 when it was closed and then reopened. A statement to that effect was included on p. 10 of Mr. Jeoffry Spence's book entitled *The Caterham Railway*, which was published by the Oakwood Press in 1952. The Author has discussed this matter with his friend and fellow historian Mr. Spence, who cannot, unfortunately, now point to the source of his information. The Author has not so far come across any contemporary evidence on the matter, and is inclined to the feeling that if the reopening followed legal action (as reported by Mr. Spence), it seems odd that that station could again be closed (this time finally) in the following year unless in the meantime the legal position had been altered.

The Author is continuing to seek evidence that will help to establish the facts on this matter. Whatever occurred was primarily of concern to the South Eastern Railway (who assumed ownership of the line from Coulsdon to Redhill when the South Eastern opened their own line east of Redhill on 26 May 1842, although the London & Brighton continued to work the Coulsdon–Redhill length until the SE Rly completed the purchase in 1844). The Author therefore hopes to be in a position to clarify matters in time for publication of his companion account of the South Eastern & Chatham Railway, on which he is now engaged.

Shoreham-Chichester Line
(Vol. I, p. 211, 7th–5th line from foot, and Vol. II, p. xii). The Author has been unable to find any further information which would enable him to clarify the matter of the provision of crossing loops when the above line was still single (see Supplement to Volume I, at p. xii of Volume II). This line, after being opened in 1845–1846, was doubled as between Shoreham and the east end of the Arun Bridge as early as 1847, although doubling from west of that bridge to Chichester was not done until 1857—see Volume II, p. 105. It therefore seems likely that crossing loops may well have been initially provided more extensively at the Shoreham end of the line (as a forerunner to early doubling), than at the Chichester end.

Shoreham Viaduct

(Vol. I, p. 210, line 1, and Vol. II, p. xii, lines 28 *et seq.*). The Author's statement on p. 210 of Volume I, that the original viaduct contained 14 spans, was (in the absence of drawings of the original bridge) made on the basis of the 1889 drawings for the reconstruction scheme, since (as explained on p. xii of Volume II) the plan and elevation of 1889 would surely have indicated the positions of any piers of the existing viaduct if the new piers were not to coincide with them.

Following Fowler's 1891 report on the state of the cast-iron underbridges on the LBSC Rly, in which Shoreham Viaduct is referred to as having 36 spans, the Author again studied the 1889 drawings for the reconstruction, and also requested that a close search be made for any drawings of Shoreham Viaduct as originally built.

The latter search proved fruitless—there are no surviving drawings of the 1846 viaduct, in the records of the Chief Civil Engineer of the Southern Region. The Author's second personal study of the reconstruction drawings enables him to confirm that these give no indication that there were any other foundations or piers that would have to be removed, and hence fully supports his original statement on the number of spans (i.e., 14—there were (and are) also two side spans).

The Author is therefore at a loss to explain how Fowler's 1891 report could have referred to Shoreham Viaduct as having 36 spans, when no indication of the large number of piers that would be redundant after reconstruction, appears on the drawings for that reconstruction.

Spa Road station

(Vol. I, p. 41, 4th and 3rd lines from foot). The day of opening for the date 8 February 1836 was a Monday and not a Friday.

Volumes II and III

It was originally agreed between the publishers and the Author, before the latter had written much more than one half of the first part of the book, that the work would require two volumes. Hence, in what became Volume I (covering events up to the formation of the LBSC Rly in 1846), there are certain references to matters to be gone into in more detail in what was then to be Volume II. In the event, the publishers decided that the very long typescript that the Author had had to prepare in order to give reasonable coverage to the whole life-span of the LBSC Rly in one volume, should be divided into Volumes II and III.

The result of this alteration in plan, made after Volume I had been published, is that various allusions in Volume I which at present cite Volume II, must now be read as references to Volume III. Particulars are as follow:

PAGE NO. IN VOL. I	POSITION ON PAGE	REMARKS
Preface, ix	5th line from foot of text	Read as 'The three volumes'
Foreword, xi	Line 22	Read as three-volume
xiii	Lines 15–17 of text	Vol. II covers period 1846–1869
		Vol. III covers period 1870–1922
166	Line 22	Read as Vol. III
182	Line 21	Read as Vol. III
187	Line 10	Vol. II covers period 1846–1869
		Vol. III covers period 1870–1922
238	Last line of text	Read as Vol. III
280	3rd line from foot	Vol. II covers period 1846–1869
		Vol. III covers period 1870–1922

Supplement to Volume II

Two matters which are referred to in Volume II are amplified below. The first of these is linked with a matter also referred to in the Second Supplement to Volume I, on p. xii of the present volume. The second has been included to emphasize the importance of the effects on the LBSC Rly of the LCD Rly traffic at Victoria.

Additionally, the Author has now been advised of the likely date of doubling the Polegate–Eastbourne line, a matter to which he had been unable to refer when Volume II was sent to the publishers.

Lewes–Newhaven Line

(Vol. II, p. 25, Note 6). As recorded in the Second Supplement to Volume I, on p. xi of the present volume, the occurrence of violent storms on 6 December 1847 (the opening day for the Lewes–Newhaven line), and again on 7 December, prevented trains from running until Wednesday 8 December. This delay no doubt gave rise to statements that the line was not opened until 8 December 1847. The date of 6 December as given in Volume I (p. 227, 8th line from foot) and in Volume II (p. 25, Note 6) stands as the date of opening, the Volume II reference giving a brief explanation, only (see p. 25, Note 6), of the date on which services were able to begin.

Polegate–Eastbourne Line

When this line was opened, on 14 May 1849 (Volume II, p. 11 (penultimate line of tabular statement), and also Volume I, p. 231 (penultimate line of tabular statement)), only a single road was provided. At some later date the branch was made a double line, but the Author could not find any record of the date of doubling when he finally had to send Volume II to the publishers. Just before Volume III was sent for publication, the Author was advised that a study of deposited plans suggested that the date of doubling was about 1859–1860—i.e., that the work was done before the resiting of Eastbourne station, itself probably completed in 1866 (see Volume II, p. 245 (14th–7th lines from foot)).

Victoria station (London)

(Vol. II, pp. 124 (14th line from foot), 175 (5th line from foot)—186 (line 6), and 201–202 (lists of dates)). Passing reference, only, to that part of Victoria station which was originally intended for LCD Rly traffic was made on p. 124 of Volume II, in a paragraph which was otherwise concerned with LBSC Rly interests at Victoria: to have given detail concerning LCD Rly interests would have been out of place in the present account. Similarly, no mention of what in later years became known colloquially as the 'Chatham' part of Victoria, was made when giving a brief historical build-up of the LCD Rly lines in the South London area (see pp. 185–186 of Volume II). In amplification of the data referred to above, it is desirable to note that the second part of Victoria station was opened on 25 August 1862, coincidentally with the opening of the LCD Rly's own line from Stewarts Lane to Herne Hill; on and from that date the LBSC Rly became the sole user of 'their' part of Victoria station, which was to the west of the 'Chatham's' part. However, this complete relief did not continue, as, after the opening of the West London Extension Railway on 2 March 1863 (Volume II, p. 121, 11th line from foot), Great Western and London & North Western Railway trains eventually reached Victoria— North Western trains using the 'Brighton' side of the terminus. Agreement between the London, Chatham & Dover and the Great Western resulted in the latter company becoming part 'owner' of the Chatham side of Victoria, and hence Great Western trains used the 'Chatham' part of the station.

Congestion over the river itself was not, of course, relieved by the opening of the 'Chatham' side of Victoria, and was increased with the introduction of services over the West London Extension Railway. It was not until the widening on 20 December 1866 of Victoria Bridge (the present title of Grosvenor Bridge had not then come into use) and its approach lines, as recorded on p. 202 of Volume II, that there was a complete separation of the train services using the two parts of Victoria station.

CHAPTER ONE

The LBSC Rly at the start of 1870

EVENTS LEADING to the formation of the LBSC Rly in 1846 are covered in Volume I, and the rapid expansion of the company, ending in near bankruptcy, is described in Volume II. Before beginning to deal with the years from 1870 onwards—which are covered in Chapters II *et seq* in the present volume—it is desirable to stress that, in broad terms, the company's system of lines was already nearing completion at the close of 1869.

It was, in fact, only to the east of the main line to Brighton that there were commercial pressures to build new lines, improved access to Eastbourne being an important factor behind much of the planning. To the west of the main line to Brighton, it was mainly in the Portsmouth area that important developments had still to take place, in conjunction with the London & South Western Railway.

Block signalling was normal practice by 1869, and inter-locking of levers to prevent dangerous movements was becoming customary. Rules and Regulations had been revised from time to time to take account of altered conditions, but it must be remembered that even the London & Croydon Railway—the oldest of the five companies forming the LBSC Rly—had only been open for some 30 years in 1869. Hence the Brighton, in common with many other railway companies, was in a state of transition when that year drew to a close.

On the one hand was the fact that most of the Brighton's system was in existence although the financial position of the company was very weak. On the other hand, equipment was being frequently improved, and better methods of working were being introduced from time to time, these factors allowing controlled expansion in certain directions and consolidation and improved returns in others. The succeeding chapters therefore not only give particulars of the completion of the Brighton company's system from 1870 onwards, and of the extensive rebuilding and modernization works found necessary to provide for the steady build-up of traffic. They also cover new methods of working which were introduced to take account of altered circumstances, some of which, at least, could not have been foreseen at earlier periods.

CHAPTER TWO

Tunbridge Wells-Eastbourne (1870-1881)

IT WAS recorded in Volume II, Chapter IX, that work on a number of new lines east of the original main line to Brighton had been stopped when financial conditions started to become precarious early in 1866. The mounting difficulties of 1866–67, and the final crisis in the latter year (Volume II, Chapter XIV) were such that two schemes were abandoned and a third was shelved. Those that were abandoned were the Ouse Valley line and its St. Leonards extension, and the Surrey & Sussex Junction. A fair amount of work had been done on the Ouse Valley line itself, and a considerable amount on the Surrey & Sussex Junction, when the contracts were terminated. The line that was shelved was one that would provide a direct means of communication between Tunbridge Wells and Eastbourne, for use by the SE Rly as well as by the LBSC Rly; under 27 & 28 Vic. cap. 172 of 14 July 1864, the LBSC Rly was required to apply in the next session for authority to build such a line; as recorded in Volume II (Note 8 to Chapter IX), nothing was done up to the end of the period covered by the latter chapter (i.e., 1869).

In the present chapter, attention is given to the provision of a connection between Tunbridge Wells and Eastbourne, as required by the 1864 Act, and also to certain other developments associated with Eastbourne. In the next chapter, attention will be given to the various other lines and work which were authorized and built through East Sussex up to the year 1899.

In chronological order, the first development was to provide improved communications between Eastbourne and Hastings. Eastbourne was the terminus of a branch from Polegate, north-west of Eastbourne, the junction being so orientated that traffic between Eastbourne and the Hastings direction had to reverse at Polegate. Under section 7 of 33 & 34 Vic. cap. 154 dated 1 August 1870, authority was given for a spur to enable through running to be possible between Eastbourne and towns to the east. This double-track spur, originally called the Eastbourne branch but later officially known as the Willingdon Loop, started 2 miles 36 chains north of Eastbourne, at Willingdon Junction, and curved right at 44/39 chains for almost ½ mile, this section being level. There were then about 8 chains of straight, after which the line entered another right-hand curve (35 chains radius), also nearly ½ mile long, to join the Hastings line at Stone Cross Junction 20 chains west of Pevensey. A fall at 1 in 660 started at the beginning of the short straight, and continued for some 25 chains, beyond which the line rose at 1 in 125 to Stone Cross Junction. The Loop was 1 mile 8 chains long, and had three brick-arch underbridges and a farm crossing, none of them of interest. The line was opened on 1 August 1871. Eastbourne station was improved in 1872.

As the Brighton company's finances were still such that they took no action regarding the link with Tunbridge Wells that they were to seek authority to build, a local company, the Tunbridge Wells & Eastbourne Railways (sic) Company, was formed for the purpose.[1] Prospective LBSC Rly action had naturally been primarily concerned with through running, both by its own trains, and by those of the SE Rly as required by the Brighton's 1864 Act. The Tunbridge Wells & Eastbourne company, as a local concern, had, however, to base its finances on the assessment of local traffic, and therefore that company's route was selected to serve as many intermediate places as possible consistent with avoiding heavy expenditure on earthworks. Within the general area concerned were, roughly from north to south, Rotherfield (with Mark Cross over 2 miles to the east-north-east), Mayfield, Cross in Hand (with Waldron about 1½ mile to the south and Heathfield some 2–3 miles to the east-south-east), and Hellingly (with Horsebridge about a mile to the south). Of these, Cross in Hand and Heathfield were on part of the Wealden ridge which rises to over 500 ft. above sea level, and which in this vicinity forms the watershed between the Medway to the north and the (east) Rother to the south. Several of the towns mentioned had been sizeable places for many years: for instance in 1835 the population figures were recorded as follows:[2]

Rotherfield	3,085	Waldron	997
Mayfield	2,738	Hellingly	1,504
Heathfield	1,801		

The district was essentially agricultural, with considerable emphasis in hop growing. The Archbishop of Canterbury had a mansion at Mayfield before the Reformation, which later became the property of Sir Thomas Gresham and at which Queen Elizabeth stayed in 1573. Heathfield had two connections with history: in 1450 the rebel Jack Cade was killed at nearby Cade Street, whilst in Heathfield Park is a tower erected in 1792–93 by Sir Francis Newbery to commemorate the successful defence of Gibraltar by British and Hanoverian troops from 1779 to 1783, against Spanish and French forces. General George Augustus Elliott, then in command of the defence, was made KCB in recognition, and was created Lord Heathfield in 1787. He had then owned Heathfield Park for some years, and died in 1790.[3]

From the foregoing, it will be seen that the railway had to cross the Wealden ridge, and that a circuitous course would be needed to enable it to serve the various towns in the district. Hence a steeply-graded line, with many curves, was inevitable. The Tunbridge Wells & Eastbourne company received their Act as 36 & 37 Vic. cap. 226 on 5 August 1873. This allowed the construction of a line from Rotherfield to Mayfield 7 miles 32 chains long, and another from Mayfield to Hailsham via Hellingly (13 miles 10 chains long in all). Despite the effort involved in forming the company and obtaining an Act of Parliament to enable it to be built, little happened as the necessary capital could not be raised. However, by the early 1870s the LBSC Rly's financial position had improved and so the latter company was again in a position to take an interest in local schemes within their territory. Hence a second Act was obtained in 1876 to enable the Tunbridge Wells & Eastbourne company to be vested in the Brighton company, and for a different route, more suitable for a main-line company, to be followed between Rotherfield and Hellingly. This Act was 39 & 40 Vic. cap. 55 of 27 June 1876. The new line was to be 12 miles 20 chains long between Rotherfield and Hellingly, beyond which the 1873 route was to be followed to Hailsham.

The 1876 Act also authorized the construction of a line to connect the Brighton's Hailsham branch direct to the East-bourne line, in order to save a reversal at Polegate. This line would have curved left out of the Hailsham branch as it approached Polegate and crossed under the Polegate-Pevensey-Hastings line to join the Polegate-Eastbourne line a short distance east of Polegate. This connecting line would have been 42¼ chains long (Figure 1). Among other requirements of the 1876 Act, were, in section 22, that passenger and goods stations were to be provided at or near Rotherfield, Mayfield, Cross in Hand, Horeham (to serve Waldron), and Hellingly, and that two passenger trains each way were to stop daily at Cross in Hand between 08 00 and 22 00. Cross in Hand was (and still is) a small place west of Heathfield, as already explained, and no doubt the requirement for two passenger trains each way to call was to serve Heathfield. Section 23 required that certain provisions in the Brighton company's Tunbridge Wells & Eastbourne Act of 1864, were to be revived and made effective.

As things were moving at last, the SE Rly made an agreement dated 29 March 1877, with the LBSC Rly, for a share of the receipts from the Eastbourne traffic when the line was brought into use.[4] However, progress was still slow, and in 1878 it was decided that a distinct improvement could be made in the Polegate area. Instead of the Polegate avoiding line authorized by the 1876 Act, it was decided that Polegate station should be resited some 400 yds. to the east of its existing position, thus enabling the line from Hailsham to enter Polegate from the west into the new station instead of from the east into the existing station. To do this meant a complete realignment of the Hailsham line at its south end, which instead of curving right to join the main line, would now curve sharply right nearer to Hailsham, and then swing left across its former route to join the main line nearly ¼ mile east of its former junction. Resiting Polegate station meant that the Eastbourne branch had to be realigned, to start further east than hitherto and to curve more sharply right than before in order to rejoin its former route.

Powers were obtained under section 4 of 42 Vic. cap. 31 of 23 May 1879, this being the LBSC Rly (various Powers) Act, 1879. Polegate Railway No. 1, 46 chains long, was to form the new

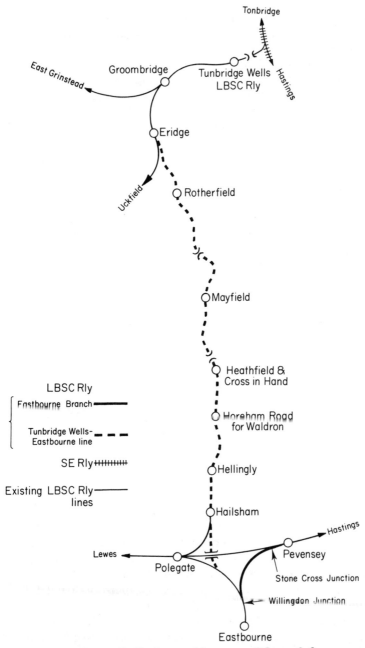

Figure 1. Tunbridge Wells–Eastbourne Line, as at 28 June 1876

connection to the Hailsham branch; Polegate Railway No. 2, 32.45 chains long, was to form the re-routed Eastbourne line (Figure 2).

The new line from the Tunbridge Wells direction, single, started from Eridge, and ran parallel with the Uckfield line (also single) on the east side of the latter for about 1¼ miles on the same

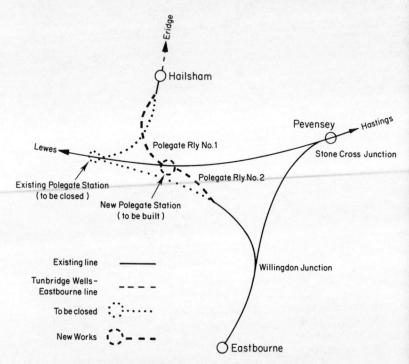

Figure 2. Polegate Alterations for Tunbridge Wells–Eastbourne Line, as at 24 May 1879

gradient as the Uckfield line (i.e., rising at 1 in 176 and then a 1 in 80). To this point the new line ran almost straight, but it now curved left at 38 chains radius for some 35 chains to bring the general route round to the east-south-east. For the next 13½ miles the line was a succession of curves, many of them joined by only very short straights and with a considerable number of reversals of curvature. After a short level as the line curved away from that to Uckfield, a very steep rise commenced which took the line over the high ground between Rotherfield and Mayfield;

this bank was over $2\frac{1}{2}$ miles long and most of it was at 1 in 50, preceded by lengths of 1 in 88 and 1 in 56. Near the summit there was a short tunnel, Argos Hill. Beyond the summit the line fell for $2\frac{3}{4}$ miles at 1 in 52/1 in 50, passing through a long bridge, at a skew under the main road from the south to Tunbridge Wells. This bridge, which was almost a short tunnel but had no official name, was some $\frac{1}{2}$ mile down the bank beyond the summit. Rotherfield, the first station, was 3 miles 11 chains from Eridge, and was situated on a short level, specially created for the purpose, between the end of the 1 in 56 rise and the start of the 1 in 50. Mayfield, the second station, was 2 miles 60 chains beyond Rotherfield; it was on a short length of level put in for the purpose, where the 1 in 52 falling gradient ended and the 1 in 50 fall started. Some $7\frac{1}{4}$ miles after Eridge, and about $1\frac{3}{8}$ mile after Mayfield, the 1 in 50 fall ended where the line crossed the (east) River Rother, and the 1 in 50 ascent started again, to continue for some $2\frac{1}{4}$ miles to the second summit. Once over this, the line fell for about $6\frac{1}{2}$ miles, but although there was a $1\frac{3}{4}$ mile length at 1 in 50, most of the descent was easier. Just before the bottom of the bank the sinuous course came to an end, and the rest of the line to Hailsham was formed of considerable straight lengths with only two curves, one of 76 chains $\frac{1}{2}$ mile long to the left, and the other very short at 56 chains to the right. The gradients over this stretch were undulating but with two lengths at 1 in 80, one up and the other down.

Heathfield and Cross in Hand, the third station, was placed just south of Heathfield Tunnel, itself on a 1 in 304 descent immediately after the $2\frac{1}{4}$ mile rise to the second summit and before the second long descent really started. Heathfield station was 3 miles 62 chains south of Mayfield. Heathfield Tunnel, partly on a 34-chain left-hand curve approaching the station, was 266 yds. long. Beyond Heathfield, the next station was Horeham Road for Waldron, 2 miles 41 chains to the south and situated on a short rise of 1 in 264 after the 1 in 50 descent had eased to 1 in 80 and before the general fall at 1 in 68/1 in 300/1 in 66 was resumed.

The next station was at Hellingly, 3 miles 48 chains beyond Horeham Road. It was virtually at the bottom of the bank from Heathfield. The line continued for 1 mile 63 chains beyond Hellingly to Hailsham, where it made an end-on connection with the existing branch from Polegate. Between Hellingly and

Hailsham there was the minor hump of 1 in 80 rising, and later 1 in 80 falling, already mentioned. Nearly 50 bridges had to be built, but there were no road crossings.

At Polegate, the new left-hand curve off the Heathfield line entered the station at a radius of 10 chains. The new curve on to the Eastbourne line was at 17/20 chains right-hand for about 20 chains, and, following a very short straight, the new line curved left at 52 chains radius for a few chains to join the alignment of the existing line. There was a fall at 1 in 110/1 in 126 into the existing line, whilst the new Hailsham line rose at 1 in 377 to enter Polegate.

There is only space in this account to refer to one of the stations in any detail—Heathfield and Cross in Hand. This was sited immediately south of the overbridge carrying the Lewes–Hawkhurst road (now A265) over the line. Cross in Hand village lay about a mile west of the station, whilst Heathfield itself was about 1½ miles south-east of the station, which was at an altitude of some 500 feet. The ridge concerned started east of Uckfield and ran towards Mountfield and Battle. It contained iron-ore deposits. The Lewes–Hawkhurst road overbridge was itself only a short distance from the south end of Heathfield Tunnel. The latter, and also the overbridges on the line, were constructed to take two roads. The single running road in the tunnel was on the east side, and a siding was later laid on the west side. There can be few other instances where a siding extended right through a tunnel (other, of course, than on underground railways).[5] The station was supplied with water from a 370-ft. borehole at the north end. There was, as already inferred, a passing loop, each line having its own side platform. The yard was south-east of the station, on the down side.

All other stations on the line were also provided with passing loops and two platforms, except for Hellingly which had a single platform on the west side, Rotherfield and Mayfield each had a yard on the down side north of the station, whilst at Horeham Road the yard was on the up side south of the station. The yard at Hellingly was not brought into use until 1 March 1890; it was on the up side, south of the station. Lighting of all stations was by oil, the well-known natural gas lighting at Heathfield not being introduced until 1896 (see later). The line was originally officially called the Tunbridge Wells and Polegate branch, and was later officially known as the Heathfield line, but colloquially it was referred to as 'the Cuckoo line' on account of Heathfield Cuckoo Fair, held annually on 14 April.

The new Polegate station was provided with two island platforms, giving Down Loop and Down Main, and Up Main and Up Loop respectively. A small yard was provided on the down side west of the station, in the fork between the Hailsham branch and the Down Main line from Lewes.

The works were brought into use in three stages, as follows:

Hailsham–Heathfield .... 5 April 1880
Heathfield–Eridge .... 1 September 1880
Polegate: New station and curves .... 3 October 1881

Rotherfield station, on the Tunbridge Wells–Uckfield line, was renamed Crowborough on 1 August 1880, a month before the Heathfield line station of Rotherfield was opened.

Although provision for the South Eastern to reach Eastbourne had, as already recorded in Volume II (Chapter IX), been the original factor in the decision that led to the building of the Heathfield line, the South Eastern had really obtained their objective through their Agreement with the Brighton dated 29 March 1877.[6] This, as already explained, entitled the South Eastern to a share in the receipts from the Eastbourne traffic. Hence, although the South Eastern could run through to and from Eastbourne as from 3 October 1881 (the connecting line at Tunbridge Wells had been opened to passenger traffic on 1 February 1876 (Volume II, Chapter IX)), that company did not institute a train service as soon as they might have done. It was not, in fact, until 1 April 1884 that South Eastern trains ran regularly to and from Eastbourne. Moreover, the South Eastern service (between Charing Cross and Eastbourne, not calling at stations on the Heathfield line) only lasted until 31 December 1885 since the SE Rly found that the returns from their 1879 arrangement with the LBSC Rly generally yielded a sum of some £29,000 per year[7] without their having to run any trains to earn it.

Later developments on the Heathfield line included a change of station name: Horeham Road for Waldron was renamed Horeham Road & Waldron on 1 June 1890. Of more general interest, however, was that when the borehole at Heathfield, used to supply water for the station, was being deepened in 1896 a reservoir of natural gas was tapped. The supply was 96% pure methane, and a small gasholder and other equipment was installed to enable the station to be lit by this natural gas, in replacement of the previous oil lighting. The plant for the purpose was installed on the down side immediately north of the overbridge carrying the Lewes–Hawkhurst road across the line, that bridge being itself immediately north of the station platforms.

Due to its purity, Heathfield gas was of great value in research in aid of safety in mines, and bottled supplies were later regularly used for this purpose. In passing, it may be added that all the available gas was later to be taken for research purposes, and hence in 1934 the station lighting was converted to use ordinary town's gas.

When the new station at Polegate was opened, it was laid down not only that all trains put into the Loop roads must stop at the station, but also that all trains to and from the Hailsham line must stop at the station.[8] To facilitate the working of Up S E Rly traffic, a splitting distant signal for Polegate West box was provided under Polegate East box's Up Home signals (then known as Rear signals) from the Eastbourne line, this new distant signal reading to the Hailsham line whereas the existing distant signal read only to the Main line towards Lewes. It was removed after the S E Rly withdrew their train services. All L BSC Rly trains of all types, and light engines, had to call at each station on the Heathfield line.

The 1867 Agreement between the LBSC Rly and the SE Rly had been drawn up on the basis of a life of 10 years, and in 1870 it had been approved by Parliament (Volume II, p. 172). Its tenure would therefore, in the ordinary course, have expired during the period covered by the present chapter. However, as both companies favoured its continued existence, extensions of the Agreement were made as necessary so as to retain its validity (see also Chapters III and VII).

NOTES

1. It has been stated [White, H. P. *A Regional History of the Railways of Great Britain, Vol. 2 (Southern England)*, Phoenix, 1961, 93] that there was a local proposal to build a 3 ft. gauge line from Hailsham northwards to Tunbridge Wells. The Act for the line as actually

constructed, i.e., 36 & 37 Vic. cap. 226 of 5 August 1873, authorized a standard-gauge line: not only was there no mention of the gauge in that Act (after the Gauge Commissioner's investigations in the 1840s, authority had to be obtained to depart from 4 ft. 8½ in. gauge); but sections 47 and 48 of the Act referred specifically to through working of carriages and trucks from LBSC Rly lines.

2. Lewis, Samuel, *A Topographical Dictionary of England*, S. Lewis & Co., London, 1835.

3. Sobey, T. H., 'Gibraltar Tower Restored', *Sussex Life*, 10 (January 1974), 30.

4. Sekon, G. A., *The History of the South Eastern Railway*, Railway Press, London, 1895, 23.

5. The Author can find no support for any suggestion that the second road through Heathfield Tunnel was a running line until after World War II [Stones, H. R., End of the 'Cuckoo Line', *Railway Magazine*, 115 (1969) 67]. LBSC Rly diagrams of Heathfield prepared in 1922, supported by a photograph published in 1935 [*Southern Railway Magazine*, 1935, 12] show clearly that the road on the west side through the tunnel was a siding, as stated by the Author.

6. As from 6 July 1879, the arrangement was that 50 per cent of the Eastbourne receipts would go to the LBSC Rly, and that the other 50 per cent would be divided between the LBSC Rly and the SE Rly, this second 50 per cent being itself subject to an allowance of 25 per cent to the company providing the trains.

7. Sekon, G. A. *Ibid.*, 23.

8. LBSC Rly Notice No. 46, dated 29 September 1881.

CHAPTER THREE

The System completed in the East (1877-1899)

CONSIDERATION MUST now be given to the various lines and works which were authorized and built through East Sussex between 1877 and 1889 and to changes to them over the succeeding 10 years. Some of these lines were, in effect, revivals of lines previously abandoned, whilst others were entirely new.

Since 1 October 1866, East Grinstead had been in railway communication with Tunbridge Wells, and hence, with the line to Three Bridges (opened on 9 July 1855), was on an east–west route. It had, however, no ready means by which Lewes, the County Town of East Sussex, could be reached, whilst communications with Croydon and London left something to be desired. Local interests therefore suggested in 1875 the formation of a company to build lines south towards Lewes and north towards Croydon, and as a start an approach was made to the LBSC Rly to ascertain their reactions to the submission of Bills to build such lines. The Brighton was sympathetic to a line between East Grinstead and Lewes, although it could not undertake to offer any financial support; but it was against the idea of a line northwards from East Grinstead towards Croydon because the Brighton itself was about to apply for authority to build such a line as a joint undertaking with the South Eastern. The Brighton was, of course, free to take what it deemed were appropriate steps in the case of any line(s) southwards from East Grinstead, since these would in any case be solely within the LBSC Rly's territory and would not be competitive with any SE Rly lines. For the LBSC Rly themselves, however, to build, or even themselves to support another company in building, a line north of East Grinstead to the Croydon area would be asking for a renewal of hostilities with the South Eastern and would, not unreasonably, be regarded by the S E Rly as a breach of faith by the L BS C Rly.

Dealing first with the developments south of East Grinstead, the L BS C Rly's non-financial support of the proposals caused the local interests to direct their efforts towards the provision of lines to Lewes and also to Haywards Heath, to place East Grinstead in communication not only with Lewes but also with the main line to Brighton and along the west coast. Eventually the Lewes & East Grinstead Railway Company was formed and received its Act on 10 August 1877 under 40 & 41 Vic. cap. 218. This authorized the construction of lines towards Lewes and to Haywards Heath, with a connection to the existing line at East Grinstead. All these lines were to to be single (Figure 3).

The promotion of any line from East Grinstead to the Croydon area raised difficult 'political' questions, as already stated. Under the 1848 and 1854 L BS C Rly/S E Rly Agreements (Volume II, Chapter II), the Brighton was not expected to build any lines of its own to the east of the main line through Croydon, as far south as Redhill, or to the north of the South Eastern's Redhill–Tonbridge line; or to support any other company wishing to build any such line. Under the L BS C Rly's 1864 Agreement with the S E Rly for the Eastbourne traffic (Volume II, Chapter IX), the South Eastern understandably considered that the railways serving Tunbridge Wells and Eastbourne should not be added to except for the provision of the connecting line at Tunbridge Wells itself and the direct line between that town and Eastbourne; in each case, those new lines were to be built by the L BS C Rly but were to be available for use by the S E Rly. It was, of course, on the grounds that the Brighton was acting entirely contrary to the spirit, if not to the actual legal implications, of these Agreements, in promoting their Ouse Valley line and its St. Leonards extension, and in being behind the Surrey & Sussex Junction Railway, that had caused such a flare-up between the South Eastern and the Brighton in 1865-1867 (Volume II, Chapter IX). At that time, the L BS C Rly had taken the first steps to reduce the tension between the two companies, which resulted in the 1867 Agreement and the restoration of peace between them (Volume II, Chapter IX). Hence the L BS C Rly was undoubtedly wise to have discussions with the S E Rly on the former's 1875 proposals for a line between Croydon and East Grinstead.

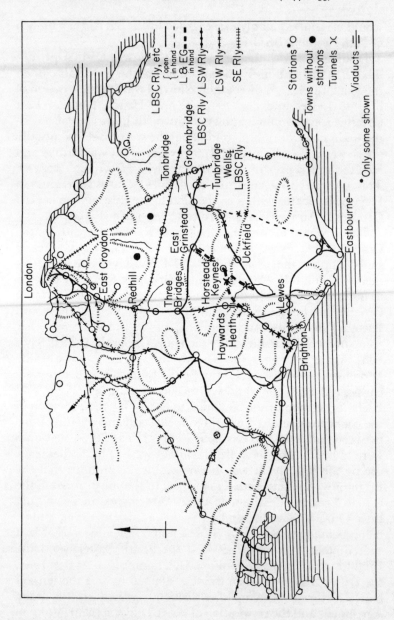

Figure 3. LBSC Rly as at 11 August 1877. Showing Lewes & East Grinstead
Lines Just Authorized
London Area detail omitted

The Brighton's plan was to make as much use as possible of the route of the abandoned Surrey & Sussex Junction Railway, which followed the north side of the Caterham Valley for some distance and then went up the Marden valley. The route was, in fact, generally similar to various earlier schemes, including that put forward by the SE Rly for their original lines to Dover and Brighton, which were to divide in the vicinity of Oxted (see Volume I). With South Eastern agreement, the Brighton prepared the scheme and sought Parliamentary approval, which was granted under 41 Vic. cap. 72 dated 17 June 1878. This authorized the construction of a line from Croydon to Oxted and from there to East Grinstead with a spur to the SE Rly west of Edenbridge, where the new line to East Grinstead was to pass under the old SE Rly main line from Redhill to Tonbridge. It also authorized the construction of a spur west of Groombridge, in order that there could be direct running between the East Grinstead-Groombridge (and Tunbridge Wells) line and the Tunbridge Wells-Groombridge-Eridge (and Uckfield and Heathfield) line. A spur at this point had formed part of the Surrey & Sussex Junction scheme (Volume II, Chapter IX) (Figure 4). At East Grinstead, the line from Croydon and Oxted was to form an end-on junction with the Lewes and East Grinstead Railway, authorized 10 August 1877 as already recorded. All the lines authorized by the 1878 Act were to be double.

The 1878 Act (entitled the LBSC Rly (Croydon, Oxted, East Grinstead Railways) Act, 1878), contained three other provisions of great importance:

Section 6 stated that the railways concerned were all to be considered part of the LBSC Rly, subject to Section 18 *et seq.*

Section 18 stated that if within two months of the passing of this Act the SE Company were formally to request to become joint owner of the line from Croydon to Oxted, and on to the junction with the SE Rly, the SE Company was to be admitted to joint ownership.

Section 32 stated that the Lewes & East Grinstead Railway, on completion and having been opened for passenger traffic, was to be amalgamated with the LBSC Rly.

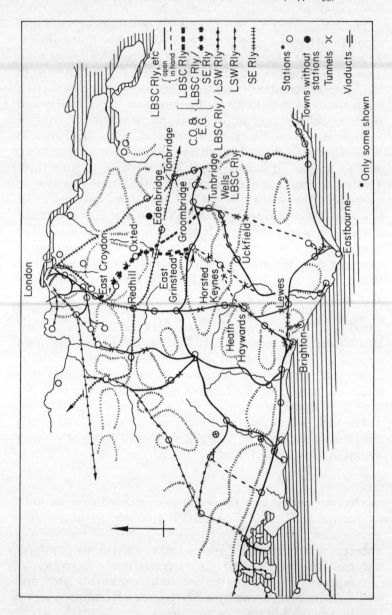

Figure 4. LBSC Rly as at 24 August 1879, Showing Croydon, Oxted & East
Grinstead Lines (Partly joint with SE Rly) & Works at East
Grinstead
London Area detail omitted

Additionally, section 35 required that a service of four trains each way should be provided between East Grinstead and Lewes, daily (including Sundays), and calling at West Hoathly, Horsted Keynes, Fletching & Sheffield Park, and Newick & Chailey, which therefore had to have stations.

The S E Rly did invoke Section 18 of the Act. As a result of Section 32 of the 1878 Act, it was decided that the Lewes & East Grinstead company's line from East Grinstead to Haywards Heath should be made a double track from the start, so as to form part of a through route from Croydon (and London); and that structures on the line to Lewes should be capable of allowing that line to be doubled if necessary. A further result of the two Acts was that it was seen to be very desirable for passengers to be able to change easily at East Grinstead, between trains on the Oxted–Lewes/Haywards Heath line and those on the Three Bridges/Groombridge and Tunbridge Wells line. This could best be achieved if the station on the latter line were removed from its 1866 position to one above that for the new north–south line from Croydon and Oxted to Lewes/Haywards Heath: the two lines would be more or less at right angles to one another, and a 'double-deck' station would not present much difficulty in design and construction.

While work was proceeding on the lines north and south of East Grinstead, yet further improvements were decided upon to facilitate the working at that town. The principal addition was the construction of a spur line to enable through running movements to be made between the Croydon, Oxted & East Grinstead line and the East Grinstead–Groombridge line. To achieve this, the spur line was to run between the Oxted line some ½ mile north of the low-level part of the new East Grinstead station, and, curving right and then left on a rising gradient, enter the high-level part of the new station at its west end. A loop line west of the high-level station was to run between the spur and the line to Three Bridges, so that there could be through running between trains to and from the Oxted and Three Bridges lines. These lines, together with a deviation at Lingfield on the Oxted line north of East Grinstead, were authorized by section 4 of 42 Vic. cap. 31 of 23 August 1879 (the LBSC Rly (Various Powers) Act, 1879) (Figure 4). The west loop at East Grinstead was never made. Finally, under section 4 of 43 & 44 Vic. cap. 71, dated 19 July 1880, the Horsted

Keynes–Hayward Heath line was to be taken, as an independent double track, right through to the latter town instead of joining the Main line to Brighton at Copyhold some $1\frac{1}{4}$ miles to the north of Haywards Heath (Figure 3).

As has already been explained, the Croydon, Oxted & East Grinstead line was to follow the course of the former Surrey & Sussex Junction Railway until the latter reached a point beyond the head of the Caterham Valley. This involved a continuous climb from South Croydon (where the Oxted line left the main Brighton line), including the construction of a $\frac{1}{2}$ mile tunnel. Near the top of the incline, the line approached the final heights of the North Downs, to the south of which the ground fell away steeply towards the Weald. East Grinstead is situated on one of the hills of the Wealden Ridge.

The country between East Grinstead and Lewes may be divided into two sections, separated by the course of the River Ouse. South and west of the river (that is, away from the right bank) there are gentle undulations. North and east of the river lies the Wealden Ridge, the Ouse flowing from west to east along the southern slopes of the Ridge until, some 9 miles north of Lewes, the river turns towards the south to flow past Isfield and Lewes to Newhaven and the sea. East Grinstead itself is on a hill divided from the rest of the Ridge by a valley, also running east and west immediately south of the town. Lewes lies roughly south from East Grinstead, and hence the general southerly direction of the Lewes & East Grinstead Railway would take it more or less at right angles over the Wealden Ridge and the valley south of East Grinstead town. The route was, in fact, broadly similar to those of the 1863 and 1864 schemes for the Beckenham, Lewes & Brighton line, and to that of the 1866 London, Lewes & Brighton line (joint SE Rly/LCD Rly)—see Volume II.

Finally, a decision was taken to build a line from south of Oxted to join the East Grinstead–Groombridge and Tunbridge Wells line in the parish of Withyham, west of the spur that had been authorized in 1878 under 41 Vic. cap. 72, to give direct running between the East Grinstead–Groombridge line and the Groombridge–Eridge line. As recorded earlier in this chapter, this 1878 spur was itself a re-incarnation of part of the 1865 Surrey & Sussex Junction line, and the Oxted–Withyham line was also a revival, on only a slightly different route, of the southern portion of the main Surrey & Sussex Junction line.

Both the L BS C Rly and the S E Rly supported this line (Figure 5).

Authority was granted under 44 & 45 Vic. cap. 189 of 11 August 1881, for the construction of the Oxted–Withyham line, under the title of the Oxted & Groombridge Railway Act, 1881. The new line was to start 1 mile 10 chains south-east of Oxted, just north of where the Croydon, Oxted & East Grinstead line entered a right-hand 44-chain curve to turn south towards East Grinstead. The CO & EG was joint L BS C Rly/S E Rly until 3 miles 4 chains south of Oxted, where a spur was to lead up to the S E Rly Redhill–Tonbridge line (as will be explained in detail later), so that the Oxted & Groombridge led off the CO & EG where the latter was still joint. The Oxted & Groombridge, itself also to be under at least joint benevolence, was to continue the general south-easterly alignment of the CO & EG north-west of the 44-chain curve already alluded to, and was to pass under the S E Rly Redhill–Tonbridge line nearly $1\frac{3}{4}$ miles east of where the CO & EG would pass under the S E Rly. A spur from the Oxted & Groombridge line was to lead up to the S E Rly, to give similar facilities for running as the corresponding spur from the CO & EG line. The line to Withyham, described in the Act as Railway No. 1, was to be 12 miles 25 chains long. The spur up to the S E Rly, described as Railway No. 2, was to be 62.55 chains long.

Section 28 of the Act gave a time limit of three years for the completion of the Oxted & Groombridge Railway, but although much had been done by the former Surrey & Sussex Junction company, progress was so slow that an arrangement was made for the line to be taken over by the L BS C Rly. Authority for this was given by section 12 of the L BS C Rly (Various Powers) Act of 1884, dated 3 July, the Brighton company being given five years from the date of the 1881 Act to complete the works. With-drawal of S E Rly concern for the line meant that Railway No. 2, the spur up to the S E Rly, was dropped, and the Oxted & Groombridge became purely a Brighton line. Even extension to 1886 was later found insufficient, and under the L BS C Rly (Various Powers) Act of 1886, dated 4 June, the time was further extended to 30 September 1887. Once again, more time was needed, and under the L BS C Rly (Various Powers) Act of 1887, dated 29 May, an extension to 30 September 1888 was granted.

As all the foregoing lines were under construction more or less

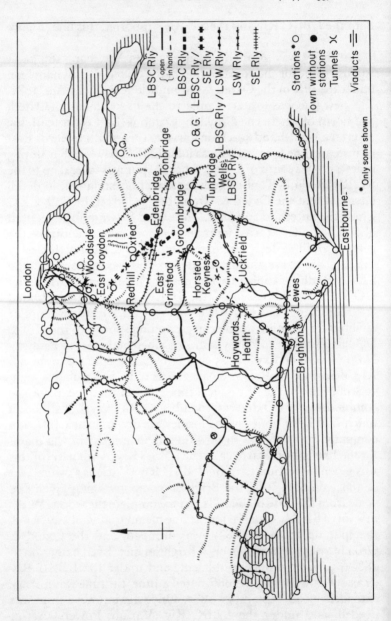

Figure 5. LBSC Rly as at 12 August 1881, Showing Oxted & Groombridge
Line as Authorized (Partly joint with SE Rly)
London Area detail omitted

simultaneously, it has been considered best to treat them as a group (which of course they were) and to describe them as an entity. Attention will first be given to the line from Lewes to East Grinstead as it was authorized and completed first, and this will be followed by the Haywards Heath line. The Croydon, Oxted & East Grinstead line, works at East Grinstead, and the Oxted & Groombridge line, will be dealt with last.

Concerning the Lewes line (Figure 3), planned and built by the Lewes & East Grinstead company, for the first 3 miles or so from Lewes use was to be made of the Lewes & Uckfield line (see Volume II), the Lewes end of which had been completely altered on and from 3 August 1868 (Volume II). At what was originally known as Barcombe Junction, some ½ mile south of Barcombe station, the East Grinstead line turned left by a compound 29/20 chain curve some 30 chains long. This changed the general direction from the north-easterly course of the Uckfield line, to a more or less north-westerly direction towards East Grinstead. For the next 7½ miles the line was basically straight, although there was a ½ mile long 56/76 chain compound right-hand curve starting less than a mile from Barcombe Junction, and about 1¾ miles of curvature (52 chains to the left, a short straight, 39 chains to the right, another short straight, and 39 chains to the left), starting about 4 miles from Barcombe Junction. The remaining curvature along this length, extending to nearly 8 miles from Barcombe Junction, was in relatively short lengths and of radii of 44 chains or more. Barcombe (new), the first station on the line, served that place better than the original Barcombe station on the Uckfield line as it was nearer to the village; it was 1 mile 8 chains from Barcombe Junction. The second station was built 3 miles 37 chains beyond Barcombe (new), and was named Newick & Chailey as it was sited where the line was taken between those two places. Newick & Chailey was just beyond the start of the 39-chain right-hand curve of the sequence of three curves already noted. As far as here, there was a broken rise, the steepest lengths being at 1 in 75 and 1 in 80, but intermediately there were falls at 1 in 80 and 1 in 600. Just before Newick & Chailey there was a 63-yd. tunnel, Cinder Hill, on the 52-chain left-hand curve preceding the right-hand curve on which the station was situated. The rising gradient of 1 in 75 eased to 1 in 115 about half way through the tunnel.

After Newick & Chailey the line fell for $\frac{3}{4}$ mile at 1 in 280, followed by almost a mile at 1 in 82 before the third station, originally called Fletching & Sheffield Park, was built. This was placed between the short first and second 44-chain left-hand curves already noted. Fletching village was some 2 or 3 miles to the east of the station, and there was no direct road to the village because Sheffield Park lay between the station and Fletching. The line then crossed over the Ouse, and began to climb at 1 in 75 for $\frac{3}{4}$ mile before it reached the end of the largely-straight length from Barcombe Junction. For the next $5\frac{1}{4}$ miles the line climbed almost continuously, much of it at 1 in 75 and with a considerable amount of curvature which eventually, some $2\frac{3}{4}$ miles after the start of the bank and some 4 miles 35 chains beyond Fletching, brought the general direction to north as the line climbed the southern slopes of the Wealden Ridge. The fourth station, Horsted Keynes, was where the northerly direction was assumed, 4 miles 35 chains beyond Fletching. The village was about $1\frac{1}{4}$ mile to the south-east of Horsted Keynes station.

The fifth station was placed 2 miles 25 chains north of Horsted Keynes. It was named West Hoathly, after the village a short way to the west of the line. It was placed on a short level following the 1 in 75 rise from Horsted Keynes, at the top of which there was West Hoathly Tunnel, 730 yds. long and straight. The north portal of the tunnel was not a great way south of the station. There was a series of short curves for the first $1\frac{1}{2}$ miles beyond Horsted Keynes, but the rest of the bank was mainly straight.

After West Hoathly, the line fell for some 2 miles at 1 in 122 and 1 in 150, with some curvature, but then resumed the 1 in 75 climb for over $1\frac{1}{4}$ miles before becoming level for some 50 chains and then descending at 1 in 200 to East Grinstead. At a distance of 1 mile 68 chains beyond West Hoathly was placed the sixth (and last) intermediate station, Kingscote for Turner's Hill. The latter, an important village on the old coaching road to Brighton, was some 2 miles west of the line.

Close to East Grinstead, the line crossed the valley already noted, by the 10-arch Imberhorne Viaduct, named after the estate to the west of East Grinstead. East Grinstead station was 2 miles 20 chains beyond Kingscote. Curvature north of Kingscote was down to 29 chains, but there were several lengths of straight.

The line from Barcombe Junction to Horsted Keynes was only intended for passenger traffic, and hence there were no yards at the three stations concerned (Barcombe (New), Newick & Chailey, and Fletching & Sheffield Park). Barcombe, in fact, had no passing loop and was only a single-platform station, the actual platform being on the east (or Down) side. Newick & Chailey, and Fletching & Sheffield Park, each had passing loops with two side platforms.

Horsted Keynes was provided with two island platforms, one between the two roads of the passing loop on the Lewes line and the other between the Down and Up roads of the Haywards Heath line; a normal double line was resumed north of the station.[1] The station buildings were on the Down side, east of the Down Lewes line, but the platform there (giving a face each side of the Down Lewes line) does not seem to have been used when the station was originally opened.[2]

Horsted Keynes had a yard on the Down side, south of the station. To reach it involved the use of the single line towards Fletching.

West Hoathly had a sizeable yard on the Up side north of the station, and Kingscote was generally similar.

East Grinstead Low Level had a yard on the Down side south of the station, outside which was the connecting line (non passenger) to the High-Level yard south of the old (1866) station. That line was therefore east of the new High-Level station and on the Up side of the High Level lines

Barcombe Junction does not seem to have been renamed Culver Junction until several years after the line to Horsted Keynes had been opened.

There were no road crossings on the line, but about 40 bridges. One, at least, of the latter, taking the high embankment north of Kingscote across the Handcross –Turner's Hill–East Grinstead road (now B 2110), was built to the shape normally adopted for LBSC Rly tunnels (Plate 1).

The Haywards Heath line (Figure 3), also planned and built by the Lewes & East Grinstead company, had to be taken from the south slopes of the Wealden Ridge, across the Ouse Valley and then up to the high ground beyond the south end of the Ouse Viaduct on the main line to Brighton. The line left that to Lewes at Horsted Keynes, and curved right at 32 chains radius for about 20 chains, this length being succeeded by a mile-long straight. Over the next 1½ miles there were, in order, about 15 chains of left-hand 96-chain radius curve, about 55 chains of straight, and a short length of 44-chain right-hand curve. After that, a short straight led into a 32-chain left-hand curve some 50 chains long to bring the line along the Down side of the main line about 1¼ miles north of Haywards Heath. The line away from Horsted Keynes was on a falling gradient for about ½ mile, part of it as steep as 1 in 70. On the descent the line crossed Sherriffs Mill Road bridge, in the form of a 6-arch viaduct. There was then a short rise at 1 in 280/1 in 115 to a local summit, followed by a further mile down, part of it at 1 in 76. Immediately past the local summit there was a 218-yd. tunnel, Lywood, which was straight although the 96-chain left-hand curve already mentioned started shortly after the line left the tunnel. Ardingly, the only intermediate station on the line, was placed on the 44-chain right-hand curve at the foot of the descent from Lywood Tunnel. It had a yard behind the Down platform at the west end. The line crossed over the River Ouse just before Ardingly, and then rose steeply at 1 in 100/1 in 85 to come alongside the main line to Brighton just after the latter entered Copyhold Cutting (which had of course to be widened on the Down (east) side for the purpose). The bank up from Ardingly to Copyhold was nearly 1¼ miles long, and shortly before the Horsted Keynes line reached the main line it crossed the partly-completed route of the Ouse Valley line (Volume II). Ardingly was 2 miles 22 chains from Horsted Keynes, and Haywards Heath was 2 miles 39 chains beyond Ardingly. There were about eight bridges on the line, but no road crossings. Some of the bridges, at any rate at the Horsted Keynes end, were built of rather soft bricks, which had a strong red colour. They did not weather well.

The Croydon, Oxted & East Grinstead line must now be described (Figure 4). This started at South Croydon by left-hand/right-hand reverse curves, each of 38 chains radius and totalling some 15 chains long in all, on a rising gradient of 1 in 83. After the reverse curves, there was a straight about 30 chains long, followed by nearly a mile of right-hand 116-chain radius curve and then, after a short straight, by over ¾ mile of 63-chain left-hand curve. The large-radius right-hand curve brought the line nearly parallel with the main line (and to the east of it), but the 63-chain left-hand curve finally established the general direction as south-east. The first station, Sanderstead, was placed 1 mile 2 chains beyond South Croydon, and was half-way round the 116-chain radius curve. The village was about a mile south-east of the station, and some hundreds of feet above it on the top of the Downs. As the population of Sanderstead as late as 1896 was only 267,[3] one wonders if the station saw much traffic!

At the end of the 63-chain curve, there was rather over $\frac{1}{2}$ mile of straight, on which was Riddlesdown Tunnel, 836 yds. long with two shafts, but starting immediately at the end of the tunnel was a succession of curves for over $3\frac{3}{4}$ miles, mostly of 76 chains radius. Upper Warlingham, the second station, was 3 miles 10 chains beyond Sanderstead and was on an 84-chain left-hand curve. After the initial rise at 1 in 83, the line rose steadily for some 6 miles as it climbed as high as possible into the North Downs. Most of the rise was at 1 in 100, but there were short breaks through the two stations and beyond Riddlesdown Tunnel. Upper Warlingham station was, in fact, high above Whyteleafe, which is in the Caterham Valley. The bank continued for over 2 miles beyond Upper Warlingham, past the Marden Park estate and reached its summit some 6 miles 30 chains beyond South Croydon.

Until just before the summit, the route was that of the erstwhile Surrey & Sussex Junction Railway, and in fact use was made of part-finished earthworks. A modified alignment was followed from just south of the summit, the Oxted line curving right at 42/32 chains radius into about a 12-chain straight before entering an 80-chain left-hand curve some 70 chains long. Oxted Tunnel started at the end of the compound right-hand curve, and continued for some $\frac{3}{4}$ mile beyond the end of the 80-chain left-hand curve, which was thus wholly within the tunnel. The later was 2266 yds. long, with seven shafts, and the line started to fall at 1 in 132 after a short level at the summit and continued at that descent for over $\frac{1}{2}$ mile beyond the southern portal, some 8 miles 30 chains south of South Croydon. The fall continued for about $3\frac{3}{4}$ miles, much of it at 1 in 100, and there were long lengths of straight broken by limited curvature.

Oxted, the third station, was 4 miles 74 chains from Upper Warlingham, and was on a $\frac{3}{4}$-mile long right-hand curve with a local easement of gradient to 1 in 300. At a distance of 1 mile 10 chains beyond Oxted, and on an alignment somewhat east of that of the Surrey & Sussex Junction line, the general direction of the latter towards Groombridge ceased to be followed and a half-mile long 44-chain right-hand curve took the line virtually due south towards East Grinstead. Between Oxted station and that 44-chain curve, there was the third tunnel on the line, Limpsfield, 550 yds. long and straight. There was one shaft, later closed up. Although that tunnel might be mistaken for the corresponding tunnel on the Surrey & Sussex Junction, it must not be confused with it. Limpsfield Tunnel, as built, was to the east of the Surrey & Sussex Junction one, which had been partially completed by the contractors for that line and which was later marked on the records of the Brighton lines as having partly fallen in.

After the 44-chain curve, the line continued straight for almost 3 miles, in the course of which it passed under the SE Rly's Redhill–Tonbridge line some $3\frac{1}{4}$ miles beyond Oxted, where the steep descent from north of Oxted Tunnel gave way to easier undulations, with a falling tendency, for a further $3\frac{1}{2}$ miles. About half-way along this undulating length, the long straight gave way to a series of curves, mostly with intervening straights.

Lingfield, the fourth station, was 5 miles 79 chains beyond Oxted. The station served a village with historical origins, Celtic and Roman relics having been found. Crowhurst Place, south-south-west of that village lies to the north of Lingfield, whose population in 1881 approached 3000. At Lingfield, the undulating fall changed abruptly to a nearly-continuous rise at 1 in 70 for all but $3\frac{1}{4}$ miles as the line ascended the northern slopes of the Wealden Ridge. Dormans, the fifth station, was 1 mile 39 chains beyond Lingfield; it was named after Dormans Park, to the south-west of the station, and not after the village of Dormans Land, to the north-east.

Near the top of the steep rise, where the gradient eased to 1 in 132, was St. Margaret's Junction, where the spur to the High-Level station at East Grinstead turned off to the right. The actual junction was 1 mile 59 chains beyond Dormans. The main line continued for 44 chains to East Grinstead Low Level station, where it made an end-on connection with the line from Lewes (into which the line from Haywards Heath came at Horsted Keynes, as already explained).

Engineering works on the line were heavy. Apart from

Riddlesdown, Oxted, and Limpsfield Tunnels, which have already been referred to, several viaducts were needed. The first of these was Riddlesdown, half-way between the south end of Riddlesdown Tunnel and Upper Warlingham station; it comprised five spans of wrought-iron girders on brick piers, and was on a 76-chain right-hand curve on a section of the line which, rising at 1 in 264, was easier than the general inclination of 1 in 100. There was then a four-arch brick viaduct to carry the line across Woldingham Road (by which name it is known), just over 1¼ miles south of Upper Warlingham station. The third viaduct was Oxted, just south of that station and having three main wrought-iron spans on brick piers (Plate 2). Finally, there was Cook's Pond Viaduct, some way south of Dormans; it carried the line over the stretch of water concerned, and had five main wrought-iron spans on brick piers.

The spur from St. Margaret's Junction to East Grinstead High Level, left the main line by a short 60-chain right-hand curve on the 1 in 132 rising gradient at the top of the bank from Lingfield, and immediately started to climb at 1 in 69. After a short straight, it curved left at 10 chains radius to enter the High Level station. The spur was 56 chains long. One feature of considerable interest on it was that, where it crossed under the London road as the latter entered the town of East Grinstead, the line was very close to the garden of Dr. John Whyte's house. To avoid encroachment, a heavy retaining wall had to be built beside the Up line of the spur, immediately south of London Road bridge (Plate 3).

Over 50 other bridges were needed on the Oxted and East Grinstead line, apart from the viaducts already listed. There were no road crossings. The line was double track from the start, and most of the stations were of straightforward design. Sanderstead had a small yard behind the Up platform, whilst Upper Warlingham also had an up-side yard but arranged at the country end and reached from the Down road by a slip from the south-end crossover. Oxted had an extensive yard on the up side at the south end, one road therein being particularly reserved for South Eastern traffic and being named accordingly. Lingfield had a small yard on the Up side north of the platforms and some Down sidings, whilst Dormans only had a single siding behind the Up platform, worked from the north (or Lingfield) end. The freight facilities at East Grinstead have already been described when dealing with the Lewes and Haywards Heath lines; the Low Level station comprised the usual two side platforms, but the High Level one was provided with two island platforms, the southern one between the two roads of the crossing loop of the Three Bridges–Groombridge line and the northern one between the Down and Up lines of the St. Margaret's Junction spur. East of East Grinstead High Level station, all running roads converged on to the single track to Groombridge.

The spur to the S E Rly south of Oxted, left at a point 3 miles 4 chains beyond the latter, and curved left at 15 chains radius on a rising gradient 1 in 162/1 in 232. It was 26 chains long. The two junctions were named Crowhurst Junction North (where the spur left the East Grinstead line) and Crowhurst Junction East (where the spur joined the S E Rly Redhill–Tonbridge line). The latter was, of course, purely a S E Rly box. In passing it may be noted that Crowhurst Junction East was renamed Crowhurst Junction South in January 1886. Crowhurst village lies to the west of the East Grinstead line, and to the south of the Redhill–Tonbridge line).

While construction of the Oxted and East Grinstead line was in hand, a further joint LBSC Rly/SE Rly line was under discussion at the Croydon end. This, the Woodside and South Croydon Railway, was intended to enable South Eastern traffic to reach the Oxted line off the S E Rly's Mid-Kent line, as an alternative route to running via New Cross (LBSC Rly), East Croydon, and South Croydon. Authority was given under 43 & 44 Vic. cap. 150 of 6 August 1880. It was essentially a 'London Area' development, and as such will be dealt with in a subsequent chapter, but is noted here in order to emphasize the interest that the South Eastern was taking in the Oxted line.

Finally, reference must be made to the main features of the Oxted & Groombridge line, and the Withyham spur (as it was then known) (Figure 5). The Oxted & Groombridge left the Croydon, Oxted & East Grinstead 1 mile 10 chains south of Oxted by means of an 88/82-chain left-hand curve about ¼ mile before the line to East Grinstead curved to the right at 44 chains radius. The junction, known as Hurst Green, was on a falling gradient of 1 in 157/1 in 110, the descent continuing on broken gradients (some easy, but the steepest at 1 in 103) for about 4¾ miles. The general south-easterly direction was followed for nearly 2¾ miles, there being only two large-radius curves on that length, to the right at 1 in 150 and 1 in 110 respectively. Here the line approached the SE Rly's Redhill–Tonbridge line where the latter was in a cutting through a slight eminence. The Oxted & Groombridge line was to pass through this eminence by a tunnel, but the respective levels were such that there was insufficient headroom to construct a tunnel under the SE Rly. An easement for a tunnel beneath the SE Rly had, in fact, been granted by the latter company on 12 November 1886, but in the event two separate tunnels were made for the Oxted & Groombridge line, one north of the SE Rly and the other south of the latter, which was carried by a wrought-iron bridge over the line between the two tunnels. The SE Rly line was straight, but the O & G curved left through the tunnels at 76 chains radius on a falling gradient at 1 in 132/1 in 264, on its way down from Hurst Green Junction. The two tunnels and the overbridge between them were officially regarded as one tunnel, its length being 319 yards and its name Edenbridge (Plate 4).[4]

Beyond the tunnel, the 76-chain left-hand curve sharpened slightly to 72 chains radius as the line continued to turn towards the east, until the general direction was east-south-east. After the long curve, which extended in all for over 70 chains, there was a short straight and then a ½-mile long 66-chain right-hand curve. These two curves enabled the railway to avoid going through the centre of Edenbridge itself, and instead took the line close to the north and east of that town. The first station on the Oxted & Groombridge was built here, to serve Edenbridge. It was 5 miles 22 chains from Oxted, and 4 miles 12 chains from Hurst Green Junction. It was named (plain) Edenbridge, and was placed towards the end of the 66-chain right-hand curve about ½ mile before the bottom of the descent from Hurst Green Junction.

The line now entered a straight over 2 miles long after which there was a 61/72 chain compound curve to the right, over ½ mile long, followed by ½ mile straight and nearly a mile at 63 chains left hand. These two curves had the effect of bringing the general direction of the line back to that from which it left Edenbridge Tunnel; it enabled the railway to pass to the west and south of a local hill and beauty spot, Mark Beech, but a tunnel was still needed at this location. This started at the end of the 61/72-chain curve, and was straight except for the last 20 chains or so, as the 63-chain left-hand curve, already noted, started at this point. The tunnel was named Mark Beech and was 1338 yds. long; it had three shafts. The south entrance is shown in Plate 5.

As already recorded, the descent from Hurst Green Junction ended some ½ mile beyond Edenbridge. There followed about 2½ miles rising, mainly at 1 in 100/1 in 120, but easing to 1 in 264 as it approached a short level at the summit; there was then a fall over 3 miles long, with nearly a mile at 1 in 100 but much of it easier, to take the line down into the Medway Valley. The end of the rise and the summit level were within Mark Beech Tunnel, and the descent, initially at 1 in 264, started nearly half-way through the tunnel and before the 63-chain left-hand curve started.

Hever, the second station on the line, was 1 mile 61 chains beyond Edenbridge, on a short length of 1 in 330 rising that was specially inserted between lengths of 1 in 100 and 1 in 120 on the climb from Edenbridge to Mark Beech Tunnel. Cowden, the third station, was 1 mile 79 chains beyond Hever, some ¼ mile beyond the southern portal of the tunnel and about half-way around the 63-chain left-hand curve which started in the tunnel. After the latter curve, there was a short straight and then some 2 miles of practically continuous curvature, a short 64-chain right-hand curve being followed, after a short straight, by an 88-chain/88-chain reverse curve, left/right respectively; and the second part of this curve then sharpened to 74 chains. The total length of this reverse curve was some 2½ miles.

The remainder of the Oxted & Groombridge line followed a fairly direct course, there being a very short right-hand 74-chain curve, a 35-chain long 78-chain left-hand curve, and finally about 35 chains of 102-chain left-hand all joined by fair-length straights; the 102-chain curve took the line into the East Grinstead, Groombridge & Tunbridge Wells line 1 mile 43 chains east of Withyham station on the East Grinstead line, and within the parish of Withyham. The junction was 73 chains west of Groombridge station on the East Grinstead line, but only 53 chains west of the junction between the East Grinstead and the Uckfield lines west of Groombridge.

The remaining station on the Oxted & Groombridge line was built 2 miles 61 chains beyond Cowden, and was named Ashurst, the name being associated with the small village to the east of the line, and with Ashurst Park beyond the village.

Shortly before reaching Ashurst station the line crossed over the River Medway, here forming the county boundary between Surrey and Kent. The junction at Withyham, was named Ashurst Junction (on Engineer's diagrams, Ashurst West Junction). Between Ashurst and Ashurst Junction the line entered Sussex.

The Withyham spur left Ashurst East Junction (Engineer's description, this junction being 11 chains east of Ashurst West Junction) by a 39-chain right-hand curve, nearly ½ mile long, and then ran straight for about 30 chains to join the Groombridge–Uckfield line, 1 mile 3 chains north of Eridge. That junction was then referred to as Eridge Junction.[5] From Ashurst East Junction to Eridge Junction was 67 chains. For a short distance the spur fell at 1 in 159, but then rose at 1 in 189/1 in 290/1 in 300 to Eridge Junction.

There were some 50 bridges on the Oxted & Groombridge line, and about 6 on the Withyham spur. There were no road crossings, but a considerable number of other crossings. Three of the latter, all between Hurst Green Junction and the north end of Edenbridge Tunnel, were needed to preserve the rights of the Old Surrey and Burstow Hunt.

As already explained, the Croydon, Oxted & East Grinstead line was joint with the SE Rly from South Croydon to Crowhurst Junction North, whilst the Woodside & South Croydon was also joint with the SE Rly. Maintenance arrangements were on the basis of the northern half being allocated to the SE Rly and the southern half to the LBSC Rly. The SE Rly therefore maintained the line (including the Woodside & South Croydon line) to south of Upper Warlingham, where the LBSC Rly became responsible. The demarcation point was 69 chains south of Upper Warlingham. There was a City Post (i.e., a Coal Dues monument) on the Down side some way north of that station.

Edenbridge, Hever, Cowden and Ashurst were all simple two-platform stations. Edenbridge had a yard on the up side at the south end, whilst Hever and Cowden each had a small yard on the down side, north of the respective stations. Ashurst had a small yard on the down side, south of the station.

The line from South Croydon to Groombridge Junction became officially known as the South Croydon–Tunbridge Wells line, whilst the line from Hurst Green Junction to East

Grinstead, Horsted Keynes and Haywards Heath, became known officially as the Oxted, East Grinstead, and Ardingly line. Both became known semi-officially as 'the Oxted lines' (and often, for shortness of describing the route—leaving the main line at South Croydon—as 'the Oxted '). The Crowhurst Junction connection to the SE Rly was termed the Crowhurst Spur. The Horsted Keynes–Barcombe Junction (Culver Junction) line, originally called the Lewes and East Grinstead line, later became officially known as the Sheffield Park line.[6] The Withyham Spur did not receive an official name because, although the earthworks were completed and the track laid, the line was not brought into use when the Oxted & Groombridge section was opened. This seems to have been as a result of the satisfactory agreement with the SE Rly regarding the Eastbourne traffic, and the withdrawal of that company's short-lived Eastbourne service (Chapter II). The opening dates of 'the Oxted lines' and of the other lines associated with them, which together completed the LBSC Rly to the east of the main line to Brighton, were as follows:

Culver Junction (formerly Barcombe Junction)–East
Grinstead Low Level . . . . 1 August 1882
(with non-passenger connecting line at East Grinstead
to 1866 station yard on Groombridge line)
Horsted Keynes–Haywards Heath . . . . 3 September 1883
South Croydon Junction–East Grinstead Low Level ⎫
Crowhurst Junction North–Crowhurst Junction East[†] ⎬ 10 March 1884
St. Margaret's Spur at East Grinstead . . . . ⎭
East Grinstead High Level station
Woodside–Selsdon Road (on Oxted line) . . . . 10 August 1885
Hurst Green Junction–Edenbridge . . . . 2 January 1888
Edenbridge—Ashurst Junction . . . . 1 October 1888*
Ashurst Junction–Eridge Junction . . . . Not opened during
                                                             period of this
                                                             chapter

†For freight trains only. Opened for passenger trains on
1 August 1884
*Ashurst Junction had been opened on 21 March 1888
for contractor's work on the new line.

New stations were opened as follows:

Marden Park . . . . 1 July 1885
(1 mile 61 chains south of Upper Warlingham, and
between there and Oxted Tunnel)

Selsdon Road .... 10 August 1885
(in fork of junction of new Woodside line with Oxted
line, 29 chains south of South Croydon and 53 chains
north of Sanderstead)

Stations were renamed as follows:

Fletching & Sheffield Park renamed Sheffield Park .. 1 January 1883
Barcombe (New) renamed Barcombe .... 1 January 1885
[Barcombe, on the Uckfield line, renamed
Barcombe Mills on same date]
Marden Park renamed Woldingham .... 1 January 1894
Upper Warlingham renamed Upper Warlingham &
Whyteleafe .... 1 January 1894
Edenbridge renamed Edenbridge Town .... 1 May 1896

All lines and spurs were opened as double track with two
exceptions: Horsted Keynes–Culver Junction line (the Sheffield
Park line): and the non-passenger connecting line at East
Grinstead between the High Level goods yard and the line from
East Grinstead southwards. Both these lines were built as single
track, and remained so.

The line from East Grinstead through Horsted Keynes to
Haywards Heath was selected for a trial of Saxby & Farmer's
Union Lock signalling equipment. This type of apparatus had
been invented by James Hodgson, who was a member of Saxby
& Farmer's staff and who later became that firm's managing
director (and, finally, chairman until his death). The design was
intended for use with Saxby & Farmer's type of rocker frame
with gridiron locking, which was the LBSC Rly's standard for
many years. Visually, the block instruments looked like Tyers
two-position semaphore instruments (also the Brighton's standard at the time), but their operation was by means of drop-
handles, each instrument having such a drop-handle combined
with a concentric bell-plunger. The drop handle, which had
three positions, was mounted on a shaft which ran from front to
back through the instrument and which, at the back end, was
rod-connected to the locking of the signal frame. When the
drop-handle was in the normal ('line blocked') position, levers
in the frame were free to be operated. To accept a train from the
box in the rear, the drop-handle had to be moved right across to
the 'line clear' position, which could only be done if the road
were properly set. With the drop handle in this position, use of

the bell plunger lowered the semaphore block indicator at the box in the rear as well as that on the accepting signalman's own instrument. When 'Train entering Section' was belled from the box in the rear, the drop-handle was moved to its central ('train on line') position, use of the bell plunger then again raising the relevant semaphore block indicators. Operation of a treadle beyond the home signal of the receiving box, by the arriving train, then enabled the drop-handle to be replaced to its normal position, so again freeing the lever frame. Use of the bell-plunger to send 'train out of section' then had no effect on the block indicators.

The section or leading signal at the box in the rear, was electrically released by receiving 'line clear' from the box in advance; and that signal was replaced automatically, either by the operation of a treadle beyond it or by the signalman in advance acknowledging 'train entering section' after having placed his drop-handle to the 'train on line' position. Once acceptance had been given to the box in the rear, a second train could not be accepted until the first one had operated the treadle on its arrival.

This design of apparatus was thus intended to give broadly similar safeguards to those provided by Sykes Lock and Block (to which signal replacers could be added), but using block instruments which gave similar indications to the LBSC Rly's existing standard Tyer's instruments. It was commonly called Hodgson's block, after the name of its inventor. On the East Grinstead and Haywards Heath line, it started at East Grinstead South Box and finished at Ardingly box. The installation remained into Southern Railway days, but the Author has no record of any other use of this equipment on the LBSC Rly. There was certainly no other installation on the Brighton company at the end of 1922, when the latter's separate existence ceased.

One further event associated with the Oxted group of lines must be mentioned. Lingfield racecourse had been opened in 1890, on a site east-south-east of the town and west-south-west of the station, from which it was distant by over a mile. Lingfield station seems to have been provided with its down loop line, making the Down platform into an island, about this time, and horse-dock facilities were provided in the yard on the Up side. Finally, under section 9 of 61 & 62 Vic. cap. 111, dated 25 July

1898, authority was granted for the construction of a spur to the racecourse itself. This was, however, never built.

By about 1880 the facilities at Lewes had become inadequate, and an entire rearrangement of all lines in the area was seen to be necessary in order that traffic could be handled satisfactorily. Not only did the London–Newhaven, Eastbourne, and Hastings traffic, via the Keymer line and Southerham Junction, have to cross Brighton–Tunbridge Wells traffic by flat junctions, but the Keymer and Southerham Junction lines on each side of the station were so sharply curved that the inevitable slow running held up traffic on the nominally straight Brighton–Tunbridge Wells line through the 1857 station. Hence thought was given to lowering the Brighton–Tunbridge Wells line and raising the Keymer–Southerham Junction line, so that the latter would be able to pass over the former more or less at right angles, on a new alignment having easier curves than those then existing. A two-level station of a similar type to that planned for East Grinstead, but of course much larger than the latter, was envisaged. The general alignment of the proposed lines was shown on the plans deposited in Parliament for the 1883 session.

As existing rail level at Lewes was only a few feet above that of the River Ouse at high tide, any lowering of one of the lines could have involved potential flood risk. This may well have been one of the reasons why the foregoing scheme was modified to obviate the two-level station. Under the revised proposals, a new one-level station was planned for a site somewhat south-east of the 1857 station. The Brighton and Tunbridge Wells lines were to reach the new station by deviations south and north of the latter. The Keymer line was to leave the tunnel by an easier left-hand curve than that leading into the existing (1857) station, in order to join the Brighton–Tunbridge Wells line immediately north of the proposed new station, which was to be in the fork of the junction in a similar manner to the existing (1857) station. The Southerham Junction line was to turn to the right out of the Tunbridge Wells line, and to curve round to rejoin its existing alignment on to Southerham Junction. The existing 'straight' section of the Brighton–Tunbridge Wells line through the 1857 station was to be closed and its site largely used for part of the new station. The existing sharply-curved Keymer and Southerham Junction lines were to be retained for freight traffic, thus keeping Keymer line freight traffic clear of the new station. The diverted Tunbridge Wells line was to rise as it left the new station, so as to be able to pass over the old Southerham Junction line (now freight), and then to drop down again to its former level. Whilst the new station would give much more accommodation than the old one, it would not eliminate the flat crossings of the east–west and north–south traffic flows.

Authority for the work was given under section 5 of the LBSC Rly's Various Powers Act, 1884 (47 & 48 Vic. cap. 97, dated 3 July 1884). The new passenger station included a Down Loop ('Bay') line as well as a Down Main and an Up Main for the Keymer line, which by this time was known as the London line. On the Brighton side, there was a loop ('Bay') line as well as a Main line in each direction, trains from Brighton being designated 'Down' and those to Brighton being described as 'Up'. The whole job was expensive and difficult, and naturally involved stage-works.

The first section to be completed was part of the Brighton side of the station and the diverted Tunbridge Wells line. In the station itself, this section consisted of the Up island platform embraced by the two roads to Brighton, and the Down island platform with the Down Brighton Main line only. This section was brought into use on Monday 4 March 1889.[7]

The second section consisted of the London side of the station and the main buildings. The work comprised the Down island platform, embraced by the Down London Loop ('Bay') and the Down London Main lines; the Up London line; and the wedge-shaped platform with the main buildings on it, serving the Up London line and the outside of the Down Brighton Loop ('Bay') line then also brought into use. This section was brought into use on Monday 17 June 1889,[8] the remainder of the 1857 station being closed on the same day. The new arrangements are shown in Figure 6. The original route between Lewes West and Lewes East Junction, became 'freight only' on 3 October 1889. A recent view from the site of the north-east end of the second (1857) station, looking towards the remains of the first (1846) station, is given as Plate 6. The footbridge in the photograph connects the abutments of the relevant road overbridge shown in the diagram included in Volume II (see Figure 18 on page 75 therein).

As will shortly be explained, the results of many years'

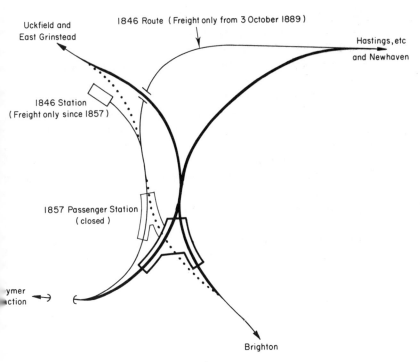

Figure 6. Lewes: 1889 Passenger Station

improvements at Newhaven had at last enabled the Newhaven–Dieppe steamer service to be operated at regular times irrespective of the state of the tide, this important step being possible from 1889 (as referred to later in this chapter). To improve the working of the connecting trains and also to enable similar steps to be taken with the main Eastbourne and Hastings trains, consideration was given to the provision of means for keeping the London traffic clear of the passenger platforms at the new station at Lewes. Deposits in Parliament for the 1890 session show relief London lines, passing north of the new station between the mouth of the tunnel and Lewes East Junction (where the 1889 Southerham line from the Lewes new station joined the original (1846) route). The Author has not yet found any detailed proposals, but the relief lines would have passed over the Tunbridge Wells lines as the latter were starting to rise before themselves passing over the 1846 line to Southerham. No further action seems to have been taken on this scheme.[9]

The sharp left-hand curve by which the original Keymer line entered the line from Brighton as originally laid out, and as retained in the 1857 station, started just inside the southern portal of Lewes Tunnel (see Volume I, Chapter XII). The junction leading to the new station, left the original line a short distance east of the tunnel mouth, although there was some realignment. Provided that only 4-wheeled or 6-wheeled stock was used, the commencement of the curve within the tunnel gave no trouble. Some sluing was however necessary in connection with the introduction of bogie stock, to maintain sufficient clearance. This had the result of reducing the 6 ft. space between the Down and the Up lines just within the tunnel, but did not form a restriction on the free use of the stock of all types then in use.

Insufficient space is available for detailed information to be given of the improvements at Newhaven that have already been mentioned. However brief references must be made to certain particularly important points. The first of these concerned the Newhaven–Dieppe shipping route as a whole: under the Continental Communication (Newhaven and Dieppe) Act, 1872, referenced 35 & 36 Vic. cap. 177 of 6 August, there were to be a widening, deepening, and improvement of the River Ouse, and improved railway facilities; and the LBSC Rly was to enter into an Agreement with the Government of France regarding the port of Dieppe. The use of train ferries was also authorized.

Six years later the Newhaven Harbour Improvement Act 1878 was passed as 41 Vic. cap. 71 dated 17 June. This gave authority for the enlargement and improvement of the harbour, and for the construction of a dock. The Wharf station opened with the line from Lewes on 6 December 1847 (Volume I, p. 227), was closed on 17 May 1886 and replaced by the Harbour station.

Finally, as already noted, in 1889 it became possible for the cross-Channel steamers to use the port at any state of the tide. Improvements at Calais, where the harbour facilities were made suitable for cross-Channel vessels to enter and leave at all times, had been completed in that year, and the forthcoming elimination of tidal working of boat trains to and from Dover had no doubt been a spur to the LBSC Rly and the Newhaven Harbour authorities, to keep the Newhaven–Dieppe route competitive by the elimination of tidal working. Similar improvements were made at Boulogne, thus enabling the S E Rly Folkestone services also to be at regular times. In France, a curve at Tintilleries, outside Boulogne, enabling Calais to be reached direct from the Paris direction, had been opened in 1888.

A number of other matters must now receive attention.

A new private siding was installed about 1880 between Barcombe (old) and Isfield on the line from Lewes to Uckfield. This siding was built to serve Billiter's mill on the east (or Up (to Lewes)) side of the line about $1\frac{1}{4}$ miles south of Isfield, and a short distance south of Anchor Crossing. The siding was connected with the Up (to Lewes) line, and a crossover road was provided between the two running lines to make the siding accessible to Down trains. Distant, rear (i.e., home), and starting signals were provided for each running line, with a covered ground frame on the Down (west) side. The ground frame was named Billiter's Siding Signal Box, this style of nomenclature being used by various railway companies under similar circumstances. The box was not a block post as later understood, and was opened when required for the siding to be worked, a man being sent from Barcombe (old) for this purpose.

When the Hastings line was extended from its temporary terminus at Bulverhithe to St. Leonards in 1846 (see Volume I), only a single platform was provided at the new station of Hastings & St. Leonards—perhaps because, with the forthcoming further extension to join the S E Rly at Bopeep Junction en route to Hastings, alterations would be needed. In the event, the single-platform station remained for 23 years, the platform having to be used by trains in both directions. This station was renamed St. Leonards on 13 February 1851 when the connecting line to Bopeep Junction was opened, and was again renamed St. Leonards (West Marina) on 5 December 1870. Finally, a new station, with Down and Up platforms, was opened on 1 June 1889. Strengthening of Bopeep Tunnel by the S E Rly in the late 1870s necessitated a reduced '6 ft.' between the two roads. Hence an instruction was issued that one train was not to pass another in that tunnel.

A passing loop was opened at Rotherfield (later Crowborough), with a second platform, on 6 January 1879;[10] and the Groombridge Junction—Eridge length was doubled about 1888. Finally the line between Eridge and Uckfield was doubled in 1894, giving two roads throughout to Brighton via Tunbridge

Wells/Groombridge. South of Eridge, the Heathfield single line ran parallel with the Uckfield single line for about 1¼ miles, as stated in Chapter II. Hence the Heathfield line was made the Down line to Uckfield over this length, the original Uckfield line then becoming the Up line into Eridge. A new junction, named Redgate Hill, was established where the Heathfield line left the Uckfield line, the single road of the Heathfield line starting at the new junction.

As also recorded in Chapter II, the first station beyond Eridge on the Uckfield line, opened as Rotherfield, was renamed Crowborough on 1 August 1880 (i.e., prior to the opening on 1 September 1880 of the Heathfield line, with a station closer to Rotherfield than that on the Uckfield line, and named accordingly). Crowborough station was again renamed on 1 May 1897, becoming Crowborough and Jarvis Brook; the latter was (and still is) a small place on the Up side of the line on to Uckfield, south of Crowborough & Jarvis Brook station.

Sheffield Park and Newick & Chailey were each provided with a goods yard in the 1890s, whilst the Kemp Town branch was doubled between Kemp Town Junction (where the branch left the Brighton–Lewes line) and Lewes Road, the first station on the branch itself.[11] This short widening, which was put in to facilitate traffic working, was brought into use on 22 July 1895.[12] A new station had been opened at the east end of London Road viaduct at Brighton, on the line to Lewes, on 1 October 1877; it was 57 chains from Brighton and was 16 chains before reaching Kemp Town Junction. It was named London Road. Further east, a new station was erected at Willingdon, on the Eastbourne side of Lockbridge Drove Crossing and 2 miles north of Eastbourne. It was opened on 1 January 1888, and was 44 chains south of Willingdon Junction where the Willingdon Loop ran towards Stone Cross Junction (see Chapter II). Eastbourne station was enlarged in 1886, with signalling similar to that already in use at London Bridge and Brighton.

Authority was given under Section 5 of 61 & 62 Vic. cap. 111 of 25 July 1898, for the Newhaven–Seaford line to be doubled. The new road was laid on the north side and hence became the Down line, the existing single road becoming the Up line. An extension of time until 25 July 1905 was granted by 3 Edw. 7 cap. 120 of 21 July 1903. This doubling was brought into use on 24 July 1904.

Various additional private sidings were connected to the Ballast Hole line at Eastbourne.[13]

Additional intermediate signal boxes were erected in 1899 to facilitate train working: Spatham Lane, on the Up side about $1\frac{1}{2}$ miles west of Plumpton and between there and Keymer Crossing; and Ripe, also on the Up side about $2\frac{1}{2}$ miles east of Glynde on the way to Berwick. Both were at level crossings and both were brought into use on Monday 12 June 1899.[14,15]

The 1867 Agreement with the S E Rly (referred to near the start of this chapter, and in more detail in Volume II, Chapter IX), was to run for 10 years and was approved by Parliament in 1870. It inaugurated a standard of improved relations between the Brighton and the South Eastern companies. Hence it was regularly reviewed, and, through extensions of its validity, was still very much in force when the period covered by the present chapter ended in 1899. It had in fact, by that time become so much an established fact that, in a period when expansion of the two companies in areas of mutual interest, had virtually ceased, it continued to be reviewed and updated in the 20th century, as noted in Chapter VII.

Mention must next be made of two schemes for nominally independent lines to connect Brighton with Eastbourne along the coast, as an alternative to the LBSC Rly route from Brighton to Lewes, from which one line went to Newhaven and Seaford and the other went to Hastings with a spur from Polegate to Eastbourne. Communication between Eastbourne and Newhaven/Seaford was thus by a very roundabout route via Lewes. Eastbourne lies to the east of Beachy Head, the highest cliff on the South Coast, to the west of which there are further high cliffs and deep valleys almost as far as Seaford. The immediate coastal area between Seaford and Newhaven is flat, but there are further cliffs to the west of that town which gradually peter out on the approach to Brighton. It was, of course, to avoid this difficult ground as well as to serve Lewes, that the Brighton company's system of lines was established. Two separate schemes were floated to build railways giving more direct communications in this area than those existing: one of these was the Eastbourne, Seaford & Newhaven; the other was the Brighton, Rottingdean & Newhaven Direct. Each received its Act on 25 June 1886, under 49 & 50 Vic. cap. 72 and 49 & 50 Vic. cap. 100 respectively.

The Eastbourne, Seaford & Newhaven intended to construct a line turning left out of the LBSC Rly's main line north from Eastbourne, the new line to run through East Dean, Friston, and West Dean to Seaford. The junction north of Eastbourne was to be 58 chains from that station, and the new line was intended to join the Brighton company's Seaford line in the parish of Blatchington, some 12 chains west of Seaford station. The new line was to be 9 miles 58¾ chains long and would involve heavy gradients between the junction at Eastbourne and East Dean. The Act allowed 5 years for completion of the works.

The Brighton, Rottingdean & Newhaven Direct was to start from Kemp Town station and was to curve right, along the coastal area. It was to cross the River Ouse by an opening bridge at Newhaven, this giving a clear opening of at least 50 ft. when operated and providing a clear headway of at least 12 ft. when closed to river traffic. A total length of 8 miles 45½ chains was involved, to the east end of the Newhaven Direct where it was to join the Brighton company's Newhaven–Seaford line. Between Newhaven and Seaford, the Newhaven Direct company's route was to make use of the Brighton company's line.

Under 50 & 51 Vic. cap. 192 of 23 August 1887, the Rottingdean company's route was altered at the Kemp Town end, whilst in 1889 an extension of time until 1893 was granted to that company. When this extension was running out, a further extension was granted to 1895, but before then the Rottingdean company obtained an abandonment Act under 57 & 58 Vic. cap. 144 of 3 July 1894.

The Eastbourne, Seaford & Newhaven got an extension of time in 1889, for a further 3 years and also alterations to its route, but eventually the Powers lapsed.

One other local company in East Sussex must be mentioned. This, the Bexhill & Rotherfield Railway, received its Act under 62 & 63 Vic. cap. 251 dated 9 August 1899. Two years previously the Crowhurst, Sidley & Bexhill company, which had an arrangement with the SE Rly, had received an Act to build a line to Bexhill off the South Eastern's Tunbridge Wells and Hastings line at Crowhurst north-west of St. Leonards (not to be confused with the Crowhurst between Oxted and Lingfield, and referred to earlier in this chapter). Hence the LBSC Rly was no doubt in the background of the Bexhill & Rotherfield company.

Bexhill, at about the turn of the century, had started to try to increase its popularity with visitors, and early permitted mixed bathing. Competition generally was then considered right and proper; and a direct route to and from London, under L B S C Rly auspices, was no doubt considered as a foil to the Crowhurst, Sidley & Bexhill line with its S E Rly support.

The Bexhill & Rotherfield intended to build a line from the L B S C Rly's Hastings line west of Bexhill, to south of Eridge, to provide direct communication between London, Croydon, Oxted, Groombridge/Tunbridge Wells, and Bexhill. In all probability the L B S C Rly would have been asked to open the Withyham spur to give direct running between the Oxted lines and Eridge and so to and from the new Bexhill line. At the north end, the junction with the new line was to be some 25 chains north of Redgate Mill Junction and about 1 mile south of Eridge. At the south end, it was to be about 1 mile 50 chains west of Bexhill. The authorized length of the line was 20 miles 55 chains. In the event, the Crowhurst, Sidley & Bexhill line was opened under S E Rly auspices in 1902, but the Bexhill & Rotherfield never came to fruition.

Finally, mention must be made of an 1882 proposal for a London & Eastbourne Railway. This was to start from the London Chatham & Dover line in the Beckenham area, and proceed in a fairly direct course south-south-east to reach Eastbourne. Heavy engineering works, with much tunnelling, would have been involved over a length of 58 miles 27 chains of new line, and gradients would have been severe. The proposals did not succeed.

NOTES

1. L B S C Rly Notice No. 51, dated 28 July 1882, announcing the forthcoming opening of the line, stated 'The Junction is immediately South of the Station', but this was undoubtedly referring to the place where the two routes divided or came together. The junction, from the operating point of view, was then north of the station.

2. L B S C Rly Notice No. 51 gave details of all operating features on the Lewes & East Grinstead line, including particulars of platforms at stations; and it referred only to the two island platforms at Horsted Keynes.

3. Goff, Martyn, *Victorian and Edwardian Survey*, Batsford, 1972, legend to photograph 61.

4. Only in recent years has use been made of the titles Littlebrown Tunnel or Little Brown's Tunnel.

5. L BSC Rly Table of Distances, November 1881, 36.
6. The popular press referred to the Sheffield Park line as 'The Bluebell Line' when efforts were made in 1955 to prevent the line from being closed, and this entirely unofficial name was adopted by the preservation group which was established to continue to run trains on the northern part of the Sheffield Park line after British Railways had finally closed it. The official L BSC Rly name was always the Sheffield Park line once that title had been given to it.
7. L BSC Rly Notice No. 80, dated 28 February 1889.
8. L BSC Rly Notice No. 82, dated May 1889. The absence of a specific date of issue in this Notice, suggests to the Author that the works concerned may have been programmed to take place in the month of May; and that relatively last-minute delays had caused the opening to be deferred until 17 June—the proof being finally returned for printing and distribution to take place, with the operative date (17 June) inserted but with the issuing date of the Notice itself left unfinished (the Notice in fact might not actually have been distributed until 13 June—at this period it was common for a Notice to be issued only on the Thursday before the operative Sunday or Monday).
9. Statements of considerable interest concerning Lewes were included in an article published in 1937: Catchpole, L. T. 'Traffic Centres and Their Work—No. 5 Lewes': *Southern Railway Magazine*, 1937, 342. There are, however, various errors (dates and otherwise) in that article, and the present Author has been unable to substantiate certain other statements made by the Writer of that article. Hence the present Author commends that article for its general data, but not as a source of historical information.
10. L BSC Rly Notice No. 23, dated 3 January. Train Staff and Ticket working was introduced at the same time between Uckfield and Rotherfield, Rotherfield and Eridge, and Eridge and Groombridge, but no crossing facilities were provided at Eridge.
11. Lewes Road station was opened on 1 September 1873.
12. L BSC Rly Notice No. 101, dated 16 July 1895.
13. Nash, S. C. 'The Ballast Line'—A Sussex Industrial Branch. *Railway Observer* (Railway Correspondence and Travel Society), February 1972, 74. *Note* Article continued in March and May 1972 issues, pp. 118 and 169 respectively.
14. L BSC Rly Notice No. 115, dated 8 June, was issued in connection with Spatham Lane, where the signal box was placed on the east (or Lewes) side of the level crossing.
15. L BSC Rly Notice No. 116, dated 8 June, was issued in connection with Ripe, where the signal box was placed on the east (or Polegate) side of the level crossing.

CHAPTER FOUR

The System completed in the West (1868-1899)

BEFORE THE financial crisis which finally occurred in the LBSC Rly in 1867 (Volume II, Chapter XIV), developments west of the main line to Brighton had been such that many of the company's lines in that area had either already been opened or were well forward. Attention must now be given to certain further lines and other developments which finally brought about the completion of the company's system in West Sussex and Hampshire.

First in importance were works at Portsmouth in connection with traffic to and from the Isle of Wight, and associated matters on the Island itself. Because of its topography and its nearness to Newport (the principal town on the Isle of Wight), Cowes had long established itself as the main point of entry to the Island, and the first railway on the Island had in fact been opened between Cowes and Newport on 16 June 1862. Many years earlier, however, places such as Sandown, Shanklin, and Ventnor had begun to grow in popularity as resorts, and before the opening of the joint LBSC Rly/LSW Rly line into Portsmouth in 1847 the Portsmouth Harbour Pier Company had obtained authority to construct a pier for vessels to and from the Island, where, at Ryde (the nearest town to Portsmouth) a pier had been built as early as 1814. Hence when train services to and from Portsmouth were started on 14 June 1847, it became possible for holidaymakers to reach the most popular parts of the Island by a much more direct route than hitherto.

The introduction of a LSW Rly service to and from Portsmouth over the 'Direct' line in January 1859 (Volume II, Chapter V) was followed by the completion of the LBSC Rly's new main line to the (south) west on 1 May 1867 (Volume II,

Chapter VI), with a further shortening (only really effective for Victoria traffic) on 1 October 1868 (Volume II, Chapter XI). In the meantime the Isle of Wight Railway had been opened from Ryde to Shanklin on 23 August 1864, and onwards to Ventnor on 10 September 1866.[1] However, there was need of considerable improvement, both at Portsmouth and at Ryde, where in each case the station was about a mile from the respective pier.

It was recorded in Volume I that early proposals for horse-operated railways to Portsmouth had not come about, for two basic reasons: lack of public support, and Defence. By the late 1830s Defence opposition was no longer a major deterrent, but the authorities concerned were still not enthusiastic about the building of a railway on to Portsea Island. Hence, as already explained in Volume I, the line, when built, finished well away from the seafront and dockyard areas. With the passage of time and changes in International matters, a further mellowing of the Defence view gradually took place, and somewhere about 1860 the Dockyard was rail-connected by means of a line from the terminus, taken on the level across what is now Commercial Road. A further development occurred in May 1865 when a non-railway owned horse-operated tramway was laid from the station to Clarence Pier, Southsea, that pier being used by a steamer service, to and from Ryde.

This tramway, which was standard gauge and which was physically connected to the LBSC Rly/LSW Rly joint line at the terminal station, was obviously an improvement on previous facilities, but passengers still had to change from train to tram and vice versa at Portsmouth station. It was therefore finally decided that the best solution to the problem would be to extend the joint railway to the old town and pier. After protracted negotiations, and insistence by the Armed Services that certain requirements must be met, authority was granted to the LSW Rly and the LBSC Rly to construct such a line under 36 & 37 Vic. Session 1873 of 7 July 1873. The official title for the authority was 'The Joint Portsmouth Railway Extension Act, 1873', and the railway was officially called 'The Joint Line'. The LSW Rly seems to have been the leader of the two companies in their efforts to bring about improvements at Portsmouth, and the various instructions relating to the Joint Line Extension normally showed the South Western first. This was perhaps because the financial agreement had ultimately been based on the LSW Rly receiving two-thirds of the receipts from the Portsmouth traffic, the remaining one-third going to the LBSC Rly.

The Act authorized the construction of two railways: No. 1 from just north of Blackfriars Road crossing, to a terminus about 5 chains south of the Common Hard, the length being 1 mile 6 chains; and No. 2 from Railway No. 1 at the west side of the Royal Albert Pier, and terminating at the south-west corner of Watering Island Jetty. Other important provisions were as follows:

> *Section 7:* A siding was to be laid to serve the Old Gun Wharf.
> *Section 8:* Railway No. 1 was not to be opened (except with the consent of the Lords Commissioners of the Admiralty), until Railway No. 2 had been completed to the satisfaction of the said Commissioners and of the War Department.
> *Section 15:* An opening bridge, with a clear width of 40 ft., was to be provided in Railway No. 2. This bridge was normally to stand open for vessels to pass, and when it was required to be closed for Government purposes (i.e. for railway traffic), that was to be done by the two railway companies at the expense of the Lords Commissioners of the Admiralty.
> *Section 20:* The Portsmouth Harbour Pier Company was authorized to sell (and the two railway companies were authorized to purchase) their undertaking authorized by the Portsmouth Harbour Act of 1846.
> *Section 26.* Expenses for the purchase of lands and the construction of Railways Nos. 1 and 2, were to be borne jointly and equally by the two companies.

As Railway No. 1, which was authorized and built as a double line, had to be taken over Commercial Road by means of an underbridge, it had to start at Blackfriars Road, some way before reaching the existing terminal station, in order to gain sufficient height. Even so, a gradient of 1 in 61 was needed to reach an island platform, which gave on to the bridge over Commercial Road. Through the high-level part of the station so formed, the gradient was reduced to 1 in 400, and beyond the bridge it then fell the rest of the way, mainly straight but with some short lengths of curvature (down to 8 chains radius), to the new terminus, which was built on a pier into Portsmouth Harbour. The descending gradients ranged from 1 in 245 to 1 in

627, but there was a final descent at 1 in 87 to the Harbour station which was level. For some distance after the bridge over Commercial Road, the line was on an embankment, but the last part was on arches. The pier itself was formed as a metal structure.

Railway No. 2 left Railway No. 1 just as the latter curved left into the Harbour station. Making a level crossing over the approach road to the Harbour station, Railway No. 2 curved to the right on a wrought-iron viaduct, and entered Watering Island over the swing bridge already referred to in Section 15 of the Act. The line fell at 1 in 100 towards Watering Island. Signals were provided at each end of the swing bridge, and, together with bridge-bolts, were worked from a ground frame beside the line on the south-east (or landward) side of the bridge. The wire to the signal on the far (or Watering Island) side of the swing bridge had of course to be disconnected before the bridge was swung to its normal (open) position. Because of the falling gradient towards the bridge moveable buffer stops had to be placed across the line before the bridge was swung open. Signals were of course provided where the Watering Island line joined the Up Main line immediately east of the Harbour station.

The Gun Wharf line was in the form of a siding trailing into the two southernmost roads in the Harbour station. It fell at 1 in 50 on to the wharf, and then curved sharply to the right. Hence only small locomotives were allowed on it.

Only water columns were provided at the Harbour station, and all engines had to run light to the depot on the up side near Blackfriars Road, for turning and coaling. Figure 7 shows the new line.

The first major change was the opening of an additional signal box, named Portsmouth East, situated on the up side immediately east of Somers Road overbridge. The box formed an intermediate block post between Copnor Crossing and Portsmouth Yard boxes, but was of course only some 21 chains east of the latter. This was brought into use on Sunday 27 February 1876. The extension line to Portsmouth Harbour was brought into use for train-working purposes on Sunday 20th August or Monday 21 August 1876; passenger traffic commenced on Monday 2 October.[2] The Watering Island line (in later years known as the South Railway Jetty line) was brought into use on Tuesday 15 January 1878[3]—so it must presumably

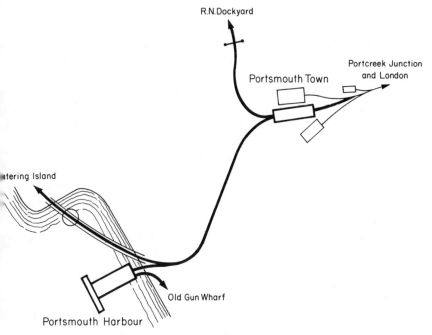

Figure 7. Portsmouth Extension as at 15 January 1878

have been completed some 17 months earlier in order to have complied with section 8 of the Act (unless special Admiralty dispensation had been given, as permitted in that section). It was worked by pilotmen. Certain alterations were authorized in 1882.

When the harbour line was opened, the original station (now with high-level through and low-level terminal sections) seems to have been renamed Portsmouth Town. Hitherto it seems to have been (plain) Portsmouth. The building of the high-level line, with its bridge across Commercial Road, enabled the previous connection into the Dockyard which crossed the street on the level, to be replaced by a trailing connection off the Up high-level line. This was led by a sharp right-hand curve down a steep incline on embankment, which then curved left to reach ground level and enter the Dockyard to pick up its former alignment. There were four level crossings on the line, over Edinburgh Road and Alfred Road, and also at Unicorn Gates and Anchor Gates. The Author has not yet traced the date when this alteration to the line into the Dockyard was made, but it was doubtless contemporary with the opening of the line to Portsmouth Harbour. Working of the connection with the Up main line from the Harbour was controlled by Portsmouth Town West box, situated in the fork of the North Dockyard line (as it was officially called) and the Up main line. A crossover between the Down and Up main lines enabled down trains to set back on to the Up road and then pull forward down the incline into the Dockyard. A train staff was employed for working the North Dockyard line, a competent man being sent from the Town station to the Edinburgh Road Gates (where the line entered the Dockyard) to receive the staff from an ingoing move, and to deliver the staff again to the driver of an outgoing move (Figure 7).

The greatly improved arrangements at Portsmouth, where vessels were able to come alongside the landing stage at the Harbour station at all states of the tide, highlighted the unsatisfactory arrangements at Ryde, where the pier built in 1814 had been extended at various times. Eventually a tramway was built from the pierhead, operated by the Pier company with horse traction and initiated on 28 August 1864 (i.e. five days after the line had been opened from Ryde station (St. John's Road, on the outskirts of the town) to Shanklin). Local efforts to improve matters mainly resulted in arguments based on vested interests, but the pier tramway was extended to St. John's Road on 1 August 1871, whilst a railway was opened on 20 December 1875 from Ryde (St. John's Road) to Newport. The extra traffic following the opening of Portsmouth Harbour station, brought matters to a head, and the joint companies (LSW Rly and LBSC Rly) finally decided that they would build a new pier at Ryde. This pier was to be long enough for vessels to use it at all states of the tide, and the joint companies also decided to construct a railway from the pierhead to Ryde (St. John's Road) to connect with the existing lines to Ventnor and Newport.

Authority was given under the South Western and Brighton Railway Companies (Isle of Wight and Ryde Pier Railway) Act, 40 & 41 Vic. cap. 107 of 23 July 1877, for the new pier to be built immediately on the east side of the existing one, and for the line along the Esplanade to be largely on the site of the existing horse tramway except over one section where, in order to cut out a sharp curve and various level crossings over streets, the railway was taken on a new, direct, course in tunnel under streets and adjacent properties.

The descent into the tunnel (which was 391 yards long), from the pier end of the line, was at 1 in 50, but the climb out of it towards St. John's Road was spread over a considerable length and the steepest pitch was at 1 in 99 for a short distance only. The pierhead and station were so laid out that the line entered a short left-hand 8-chain curve as it left the pierhead, and then ran straight for some 24 chains until it again curved left, this time at 9 chains radius. On this latter curve was situated the Esplanade station, and the line then descended to the tunnel. On the climb out of it, there were several short lengths of sharp curvature (10–12 chains radius), before the joint line made an end-on junction with the Island's own railways at Ryde St. John's Road. The Pierhead station had three roads and platforms, but the Esplanade station had only the usual two side platforms. The line was double throughout. Apart from the Esplanade station, which was partly on the landward end of the pier and partly on the Esplanade itself, the only other feature of interest was the tunnel. This started at the Esplanade end as two single-line bores, but part-way along the two were merged into an ordinary double-line bore, from which the two tracks emerged at the St. John's Road end. Esplanade station was 32 chains from Pierhead, and St. John's Road was 64 chains beyond Esplanade. The South Western and the Brighton jointly staffed the stations and maintained the line, but all trains were operated by the Isle of Wight Railway or the Ryde & Newport Railway,[4] who had running powers north of St. John's Road through to Pierhead.

The line from St. John's Road to Esplanade was opened on 5 April 1880, and from Esplanade to Pierhead on 12 July 1880 as soon as the pier itself was ready.

The joint companies' control over the route was completed in 1880 by their taking over the ships which maintained the Portsmouth–Ryde service. This was done under The South Western and Brighton Railway Companies (Steam Vessels) Act, 1879, referenced 42 & 43 Vic. Session 1879 and dated 23 May. It is worth recording in this general connection that the LSW Rly had, on their own, taken over in 1875 the pier at Stokes Bay and the line to it from Gosport, opened on 6 April 1863. Receipts from the Stokes Bay traffic were, however, pooled along with the South Western's Portsmouth traffic, so that the Brighton had their due proportion from each. The LSW Rly's approach to Portsmouth via the 'Direct' line was improved in March 1878 by the doubling of that line.

On the Island, reclamation of Brading Marshes, involving the construction of a sea wall, enabled a branch to be constructed from Brading (on the Ryde–Ventnor line of the Isle of Wight Railway) to St. Helens and Bembridge. This line, the Brading Harbour Railway, was opened on 27 May 1882, and a train-ferry service was established between St. Helens and Langston on the Hayling Island branch from Havant (Volume II). The Brading Harbour Railway's train services were worked by the Isle of Wight Railway, whilst the train-ferry was owned and worked by the Isle of Wight Marine Transit Company. The train-ferry service proved to be unsuccessful commercially, the number of vehicles exchanged between the Island and the Mainland not always being sufficient to enable costs to be met. Eventually the LBSC Rly, which had taken over the Hayling Island line in 1874 (Volume II), decided to purchase the ferry, the deal being completed on 24 November 1886. However, the train-ferry service continued to be uneconomic, and finally ceased on 31 March 1888. The quay at St. Helens was thereafter only used by small coasting vessels.

In passing it may be recorded that the Brading Harbour Railway was absorbed by the Isle of Wight Railway in 1898, while in May 1893 the LBSC Rly issued revised instructions for signals to be displayed to vessels requiring the swing bridge at Langstone (or Langton) on the Hayling Island branch to be opened for their passage. Incidentally, the LBSC Rly always used the spelling Langston, as adopted for general maps and other purposes. The spelling Langstone was, however, used locally for the bridge, thus explaining the variation used by the LBSC Rly in their 1893 Notice. The southern terminal of the Hayling Island branch, originally called South Hayling, was renamed Hayling Island on 1 June 1892. The LSW Rly's Netley line was extended to Fareham on 2 September 1889, enabling both Portsmouth and Gosport to be reached direct from the Southampton direction.

Reverting to the Portsmouth area, Southsea (situated to the south and east of the old town of Portsmouth), was proving a tourist attraction by the 1860s. With the introduction of steamer services between Clarence Pier and the Isle of Wight, proposals were made for a line into Southsea itself. The L BS C Rly and the L S W Rly gave such proposals their benevolence since the traffic would use part of the joint companies' lines to reach any line to Southsea. The opening of the street tramway to Clarence Pier in May 1865, already referred to, was a further factor in developing the popularity of Southsea.

A local company was accordingly formed, and obtained powers to construct a line to Southsea under 30 & 31 Vic. cap. 194 of 12 August 1867, entitled the Southsea Railway Act, 1867. The 'main line' was to start about 2 miles 24 chains south of Portcreek Junction, and, curving south-east, run for 1 mile 50 chains to a terminus at East Southsea. A spur 30 chains long was to form a triangle, so that traffic could work direct between East Southsea and Portsmouth, as well as between East Southsea and the Portcreek Junction direction for the Cosham/Fareham and the Havant lines. The powers were to lapse in four years if the line were not completed by that time. They lapsed.

A new Act, for a modified route, was obtained on 26 August 1880, under 43 & 44 Vic. cap. 203, entitled The Southsea Railway Act, 1880. The 'main line' (Railway No. 1) was to start some 450 yds. south of Union Bridge, carrying St. Mary's Road over the L BS C Rly and L S W Rly joint line near the end of the long near-straight from north of Green Lane Crossing, and some 30 yds. east of the joint line; and was to curve south-south-east for 1 mile $34\frac{1}{2}$ chains to a terminus at East Southsea (otherwise New Southsea). A connection from the joint line was to start some 250 yds. south of Union Bridge, and was to lead into the Southsea company's line; this connection was described as Railway No. 2 in the Act, but was shown as Railway No. 3 on the deposited plans. The Act did not cover a direct connection between Portsmouth and East Southsea.

More delays and changes of plan caused a further Act to be obtained on 2 August 1883 under 46 & 47 Vic. cap. 160, entitled The Southsea Railway Act, 1883. This authorized the following with respect to the 1880 Act:

(a) A new line, 27 chains long, to form a direct connection between Portsmouth and East Southsea, was to be constructed, similar to the spur covered by the 1867 Act;

(b) Railway No. 1 of the 1880 Act was only to be built south of the east end of the new line referred to at (a);

(c) Railway No. 2 of the 1880 Act was to be abandoned; and

(d) Further time was allowed for the completion of those parts of Railway No. 1 of the 1880 Act which were still to be built.

This 1883 Act also referred, in Section 20, to the Heads of an Agreement between the LSW Rly and the Southsea company, dated 18 November 1882 and laid down that the line to East Southsea had to conform to the following requirements:

(i) The line was to be double track, with proper signalling.

(ii) There were to be proper stations.

(iii) The line was to be laid with steel rails of a specified quality and pattern approved by the South Western company's Engineer, the rails to be double-headed and to weigh not less than 82 lb. per yard. The chairs were not to weigh less than 40 lb.

Under 46 & 47 Vic. cap. 189 dated 20 August 1883 and entitled The South Western Railway (Various Powers) Act, 1883, the LSW Rly was empowered to construct the line from the Portsmouth direction referred to at (a) above; and also to abolish Blackfriars Road crossing east of Portsmouth Town station and replace it with an overbridge for pedestrians.

The finally-authorized line was as shown in Figure 8. It will be noted that the joint companies' interests were being looked after by the LSW Rly.

The first stage in bringing the new line into use was the opening of an additional block post at Fratton East, on the down side of the joint line after the start of the right-hand curve succeeding the near-straight from Green Lanes Crossing. This was brought into use on Friday 12 June 1885.[5]

The second stage was to bring into use the line to East Southsea, with a station in the fork of the junction with the joint line. This station was called Fratton. At the same time Fratton West box was opened on the down side to control the junction with the Southsea line. The latter, Fratton station, and Fratton West box, were brought into use on 1 July 1885. The terminal station was originally called (plain) Southsea, the 'East' being added later.

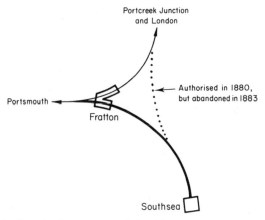

Figure 8. Southsea Railway as at 2 July 1885

The East Southsea line curved to the right more or less throughout its length, the sharpest curve being at 14 chains just after leaving the main line, and the easiest curve being at 95 chains radius. There was a falling tendency towards East Southsea after an initial short rise, but some of the line was level. There were four overbridges, and one level crossing immediately on the east (East Southsea) side of Fratton station. A double line was laid, in accordance with the Act, but there was no facing connection from the up road of the main line. Hence, while trains could run from East Southsea to Portsmouth, they could not be worked from Portsmouth to East Southsea without shunting at Fratton. There were no intermediate stations on the branch, which was 1 mile 24 chains long.

Attention must next be given to the line from Chichester to Midhurst. It was recorded in Volume II, Chapter VIII, that, after earlier proposals, an Act had been obtained by a local company, the Chichester & Midhurst Railway, to build a line from immediately west of Chichester, to Midhurst. The Act, dated 23 June 1864, was followed by another, dated 5 July 1865, for the line to be joined to the Petersfield Railway and also for it to be extended to Haslemere. The Haslemere extension was abandoned on 31 July 1868, and work on the remainder stopped later.

The LBSC Rly themselves secured powers, under 39 & 40 Vic. cap. 109 of 13 July 1876, to take over the unfinished line and complete it, but the route was extensively modified under

40 Vic. cap. 28 of 11 June 1877. This Act authorized a change at Chichester, and a major change at Midhurst. At Chichester, the route was altered so as to leave the main line onwards to Havant at Fishbourne Crossing, some ¾ mile west of Chichester, and then to curve sharply to the right through more than a right angle in order to assume, by means of a left-hand curve, the alignment proposed when the Midhurst line was to leave the main lines as soon as it left Chichester. At the Midhurst end, the original route was planned to approach from the south and to curve left to join the line from Petworth outside Midhurst station; the latter was so sited that a direct connection over Bepton Road could be made on to the Petersfield line (in lieu of the transfer siding actually in existence), whilst a right-hand curve from west of Midhurst station would enable the Haslemere extension to reach that town.

With the abandonment of the Haslemere line in 1868 (Volume II), an entirely new alignment could be planned at Midhurst which would give through running between the Petworth line and Chichester. To achieve this, the line approaching Midhurst from Chichester was to start to curve left at a more southerly position than hitherto, and was then to swing sharply right, across its previously-planned route, to run into the Petworth line some 15-20 chains east of Midhurst station. A new station was to be built immediately east of where the Chichester line was now to join the Petworth line, and the existing station by Bepton Road was to be done away with, the line to it being used only for freight (including transfers to and from the Petersfield line). Figure 9a shows the finally authorized arrangements at Midhurst and Figure 9b those at Chichester (see next paragraph).

The South Downs form an east-west barrier to communication between Chichester and other towns near the coast, and places in the Rother Valley, north of the South Downs. There is, however, a gap north of Chichester and south of Midhurst, which forms the watershed between the River Lavant running south, and a tributary to the Rother running east to Pulborough. The road from Chichester to Midhurst (now A286) had been made through this gap, and it was the obvious route for the railway. The southern end of the gap faces south-west, and hence the line from Chichester had to approach in a north-easterly direction and then to turn generally north over the watershed and then down towards Midhurst. Hence relatively heavy gradients were involved, with three tunnels. Under the 1877 Act, Fishbourne Crossing was to be the junction, but under 43 & 44 Vic. cap. 71 of 19 July 1880, the branch was run separately to Chichester, Fishbourne Crossing being widened accordingly (Figure 9b).

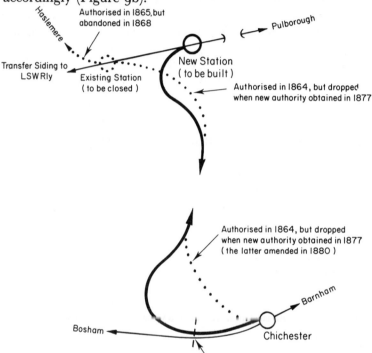

Figure 9a, b. Routes of Ends of Chichester–Midhurst Line, as Finally Authorized
  At Midhurst on 11 June 1877
  At Chichester on 19 July 1880

The curve away from alongside the West Coast line immediately west of Fishbourne Crossing was at 13/15 chains for some 20 chains, and took the line in a north-north-easterly direction for over ½ mile until a 60-chain left-hand curve just under ½ mile long brought the direction practically north and on the 1864 alignment. A 2-mile long virtual straight was succeeded by nearly ½ mile of 48-chain right-hand curve, and some 55 chains of further straight. Goodwood Park and racecourse lay to the east-south-east. The line was now near the entrance to the gap through the hills, and the next $3\frac{1}{2}$ miles were mainly curved. A reverse curve, 44 chains left/32 chains right, brought the alignment and direction round to the north-east as the line entered the gap, this curve being a mile long in all. About 30 chains of straight followed, leading into a 50/38-chain left-hand curve nearly a mile long, to be followed by $\frac{1}{2}$ mile straight. To this point, some 7 miles beyond Fishbourne Crossing, there was an almost continuous rise, a considerable amount being at 1 in 75 or 1 in 76.

The first station, Lavant, was built 3 miles 31 chains from Chichester and 2 miles 53 chains beyond Fishbourne Crossing. It was on the 2-mile long near-straight length, where the gradient was as easy as 1 in 690 (there was actually a short fall at 1 in 80 a little distance south of the station). The second station, Singleton, was 3 miles 18 chains north of Lavant; it was approached by a rise at 1 in 75, but the gradient was locally reduced to 1 in 264 through the station before resuming at 1 in 75 for a further short length, after which it again eased. The first tunnel, West Dean was 443 yds. long and was situated on the 32-chain right-hand curve leading into the gap in the South Downs. That curve ended at the northern portal of the tunnel, which was through a south-facing spur at the south-west end of the gap. The northern portal was not a great way south of Singleton station. The second tunnel, Singleton, was 744 yds. long and straight. Its southern portal was some $\frac{3}{4}$ mile north of Singleton station, and its northern portal was just past the end of the long climb from Chichester; it was through the saddle of the gap.

Immediately over the summit, there was a double reverse curve, 32 chains/40 chains/30 chains, right/left/right, over a distance of some 50 chains, but after that curvature was slight until, just over 3 miles beyond the summit, the line curved left at 30/130/50 chains radius before reversing into 10/24 chains right to join the Petworth line. This reverse curve totalled over a mile in length, the last $\frac{1}{2}$ mile (mainly 10 chains radius) forming virtually a horse-shoe bend. From the summit the line fell at broken gradients, some of it as steep as 1 in 60. The remaining intermediate station on the line, Cocking, was situated about half-way down the bank; it was 3 miles 2 chains from Singleton, and 2 miles 32 chains from the new station at Midhurst. The third tunnel on the line, Cocking, 740 yds. long and straight, was situated where two lengths of 1 in 60 fall was joined by a short level; the latter was in the middle of the tunnel. The north portal of Cocking Tunnel was about 25 chains south of Cocking station, and there was about 1 mile between Singleton and Cocking Tunnels. There were about 35 bridges, but no public level crossings.

Lavant station had a single platform on the up (to Midhurst) side, immediately north of the bridge carrying the Chichester–Midhurst road (A286) over the line. The entrance to the station was from the main road, and the station building was, unusually for a country station, a three-storey structure of which two storeys appeared above the main road. The yard was on the west (up) side, and the layout included a loop into which an engine or a non-passenger train could be turned to clear the road: two passenger trains were not allowed to cross at Lavant.

Singleton, where normal traffic would only have justified a country station, was provided with extensive facilities for dealing with Goodwood race traffic, hitherto handled at Drayton or Chichester on the West Coast line. Singleton had two island platforms, serving respectively the Up Loop and the Up Main lines, and the Down Main and the Down Loop lines. The yard was on the east (down) side, north of the platforms, whilst a locomotive turntable was provided east of the station, on a siding on the down side with an outlet on to the Down Loop line towards the south (Lavant) end.

Cocking station had a single platform on the down side, with a small yard on the down side south of the station. It was not possible to cross trains at Cocking. The new Midhurst station had two side platforms to serve a crossing loop, with two dock roads behind the up platform, accessible from the yard on the up side south of the station, which was alongside of, and to the west of, the connecting line to the LSW Rly's Petersfield line. The Brighton's station also had an engine shed north of (i.e. 'outside') the up yard.

The Chichester and Midhurst line, always single, was regarded as an extension of the Hardham Junction–Petworth–Midhurst line, traffic from Midhurst to Chichester being described as 'down' (as will have been inferred from the foregoing particulars of the stations on the line). The station-to-station distances are those given in the official Opening Notice, dated 8 July 1881, and are not necessarily in accordance with later official figures. The line was opened on Monday 11 July 1881.

Traffic was stopped for a time by a chalk fall at West Dean in December 1886.

The line went through some very attractive scenery, and had a fairly staple traffic in passengers and agricultural produce, at least when the Author first saw it about 1917. His maternal grandparents had what they called their 'country cottage' at Lavant. It was on the down side south of the station, on land owned by the Duke of Richmond and Gordon; the garden extended to the railway fence. The Author often stayed with his grandparents and saw, as a boy, the line and the working at Chichester at first hand near the end of the First World War, and for a short while afterwards.

It was recorded in Volume II (Chapters VI and VIII) that authority to reconstruct Arun (now Ford) Bridge had been given subject to the construction of a line to Littlehampton which would enable that port to be in direct communication with (New) Arundel on the Mid-Sussex Junction line; but that when the Littlehampton branch was built under 23 & 24 Vic. cap. 171 of 23 July 1860, that branch joined the West Coast line at Ford Junction in such a way that traffic both from the Mid-Sussex Junction line, and from the West Coast line from the Brighton direction, had to reverse at Ford. Authority was granted under 27 & 28 Vic. cap. 314 of 29 July 1864 for a direct connection to be built between the Mid-Sussex Junction line and the Littlehampton branch; but, as amplified in footnote reference 1 to Chapter VIII of Volume II, further authority under 29 & 30 Vic. cap. 281 of 30 July 1866 still did not lead to the construction of such a direct connection, due to Board of Trade objections to a proposed flat crossing of the Mid-Sussex Junction connection over the West Coast line. A connection round to the West Coast line in the Brighton direction, was also not constructed, although authorized by the 1866 Act.

Finally, under 39 & 40 Vic. cap. 144 of 13 July 1876 (LBSC Rly (Various Powers) Act, 1876), penalties that had been imposed for not building the 1866 connections were removed and authority was granted for two new lines, as follows:

Railway No. 1 was to curve north away from the West Coast line, from a point about ½ mile west of Lyminster Crossing (site of the original Littlehampton station), to join the Mid-Sussex Junction line some 35 chains east of Ford Junction.

Railway No. 2 was to curve left out of the Mid-Sussex
Junction line about 50 yds. west of where Railway No. 1
was to join the Mid-Sussex Junction line; and was to join
the Littlehampton branch some 35 chains on the Littlehampton side of Ford Junction.

Railways Nos. 1 and 2 were calculated to be just over 56 and just
over 22 chains long respectively (Figure 10).

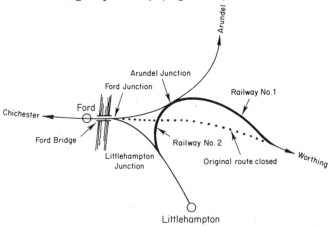

Figure. 10. Re-Routing in Littlehampton Area, as at 1 January 1887

The original West Coast line, from the start of Railway No. 1
to Ford Junction, could either be used for sidings or could be
sold. The company was to have five years to build these two
railways with a £50 per day penalty for non completion. Again
there were delays, and it was not until Monday 28 September
1885 that Railway No. 1 was brought into use, the original West
Coast line along this length being abandoned.[6] The pole-line
telegraph circuits were, however, not then removed, and
enabled the course of the former line to be traced (apart from the
continued existence of a shallow cutting with an occupation
overbridge). The junction of the west end of the new line with the
Mid-Sussex Junction line, was called Arundel Junction. The
latter must not be confused with the junction at the east end of
the river bridge (itself originally called Arun Bridge and later
renamed Ford Bridge). The junction beside the river was called
Arundel Junction when the Mid-Sussex Junction line and the
Littlehampton branch were authorized in 1860 to leave the
West Coast line at that point. The latter junction was renamed

Ford Junction when the original Arundel station on the West Coast line was itself renamed Ford, this event occurring when the new station to serve Arundel on the Mid-Sussex Junction line, was opened in 1863 (see Volume II, Chapters VI and VIII). The Arundel Junction brought into use in 1885 was, as already stated, 35 chains to the east of that originally so named. The completion of the scheme, with the opening of Railway No. 2 from Arundel Junction to Littlehampton Junction on the Littlehampton branch, took place on 1 January 1887. Railway No. 1 started with a 90-chain right-hand curve which reversed into a 30-chain left-hand one to join the Mid-Sussex Junction line. The Arundel Junction to Littlehampton Junction Spur (Railway No. 2) involved a left hand 12-chain radius curve. Gradients on both lines were relatively slight. There had been a stop-block collision at Ford on Sunday 20 February 1876, due to excessive speed and the brake being mishandled.[7] Local suggestions in March 1876 that the original Littlehampton station on the West Coast line should be reopened did not bear fruit at the time.

Some five miles north-west of Brighton, not far from the villages of Fulking and Poynings, there is a deep natural declivity in the South Downs. Sussex legend ascribed it, however, to the work of the Devil, and as Sussex peasants were afraid to use the word 'Devil' they called him 'The Poor Man' and the gorge became known as 'The Poor Man's Well'. Satan, according to legend, tried to make a huge cut through the South Downs in order that the fertile Weald to the north of the Downs would be flooded from the English Channel. He had to finish the whole job in one night as his powers disappeared with the coming of the dawn. Unfortunately for him, however, he seriously underestimated the size of the task, started to overrun his 'possession', and had to abandon the job. In later times the gorge acquired, in plain-speaking style, the title of the Devil's Dyke (dyke being a Saxon word for a wall or fence).

By about 1870 the Devil's Dyke area, a place of great natural beauty, had become popular with visitors, and local interests began to give serious thought to the construction of a railway to open up the area. Eventually, under 40 & 41 Vic. cap. 189 of 2 August 1877, the Brighton & Dyke Railway Company was authorized to build such a line; but progress was so slow that an extension of time was sought, and was granted by 44 & 45 Vic.

cap. 118 of 18 July 1881. It was expected that the line would be finished within five years of the 1881 Act, but a further year's extension had to be obtained, under 49 Vic. cap. 45 of 4 June 1886. Even this was not quite sufficient, and yet another Act, 50 & 51 Vic. cap. 168 of 8 August 1887, gave a final extension of time for completion, until 1 September 1887. The line, which was always single, was duly opened on that date (Figure 11). Although the LBSC Rly worked the line, the Brighton & Dyke company remained a separate entity.

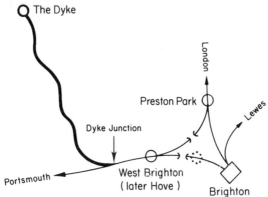

Figure 11. Dyke Branch as at 1 September 1887

It left the West Coast line at Dyke Junction, 1 mile 62 chains from Brighton, by means of a 15-chain right-hand curve about 8 chains long and ran for 3 miles 45 chains over virtually continuous reverse curves on a serpentine course to reach a terminus some way below the summit of the Downs, beyond which is the head of the Dyke. The great majority of the line rose at 1 in 40, and the curvature ranged from 36 chains down to 13 chains.

The line had no intermediate stations until near the end of its life. There were four bridges but no public or private road crossings.

The building of the Cliftonville spur, to complete a triangle between the main line as it entered Brighton, and the West Coast line, and so to enable the latter to be in direct communication with Croydon and London, is considered to be more logically a development of the main line than of the West Coast line. Hence it is dealt with in Chapter VI.

Certain other events relating to the area and period being covered by this chapter, must now have brief mention. The first of these was that relations with the LSW Rly became slightly sour in the early 1870s concerning the accommodation for freight traffic at Havant. As a result, the South Western sought powers in 1874 to build a goods yard of their own at that station, but tempers cooled and in the end nothing was done to build such a yard. About 1876 it was decided to establish a proper locomotive depot at Horsham. Authority for the purchase of the necessary land (on the down side, east of the station, nearly opposite where the line from Dorking joined the original line from Three Bridges) was obtained in 1877, and it seems that the depot was brought into use in 1878. The purchase by the LBSC Rly of Hayling Bridge and Causeway was authorized by 41 Vic. cap. 74 of 17 June 1878 (the company's Various Powers Act, 1878). The railway to South Hayling had been leased to the Brighton under 37 & 38 Vic. cap. 54 of 30 June 1874.

Worthing station was resited immediately west of the existing station, in 1870. Portslade station was resited east of the level crossing in 1881, after an initial rebuilding in 1857. A new station, West Worthing, was opened on 4 November 1889 about ¾ mile west of Worthing. The Steyning line was doubled during 1877-79. The first crossing loop on the Cranleigh line was provided about 1880 at Cranleigh station; the latter was given a second platform on the Down (to Guildford) side, to serve the new loop. By 1882 there were also loops and second platforms at Baynards and Bramley; the official designation was now the Guildford Line.

One other matter must also be recorded. It will be recalled from Volume II, Chapter XIII, that powers were obtained in 1866 for a double-line loop at Shoreham, to enable traffic to run direct between the West Coast line in the Worthing direction, and the Steyning line; and that these powers were abandoned in 1870. A new plan, this time for an Up loop only (i.e., facing off the West Coast line to Brighton, and trailing into the Up Steyning line) was prepared and was authorized by 45 & 46 Vic. cap. 93 of 3 July 1882 (the company's Various Powers Act of 1882). This suffered the same fate as its predecessor, being abandoned under section 6 of 48 & 49 Vic. cap. 67 of 16 July 1885 (the LBSC Rly's (Various Powers) Act, 1885).

Part of Betchworth tunnel fell in on 27 July 1887, and had to have extensive repairs before being reopened on 1 March 1888.[8]

It must also be recorded that the Hundred of Manhood &

Selsey Tramways Company was incorporated on 29 April 1896 to build what was, in effect, a light railway from Chichester to Selsey. The company apparently had no legal authority to run their line, but this did not deter them from opening it on 27 August 1897. Legal authority was forthcoming in 1924. The line had its own station at Chichester, south of the Brighton company's station, with which there was a siding connection.

Horsham station was partly rebuilt, and was resignalled, in 1875. Three signal boxes were involved: Horsham Junction (on the Down side near the junction where the Dorking line joined the earlier line from Three Bridges); Horsham Shunting (near the junction end of the island platform between the Down Main and the Down Loop lines; this later ceased to be a block post); and Horsham South (on the Up side at the country end of the Up platform; it was renamed Horsham West by 1882).

Additional signal boxes were built to facilitate traffic-working, as follows:

SIGNAL BOX	BETWEEN	DATE
Bedhampton Mill	Havant West and Farlington Junction boxes	1876
Lodge Farm Crossing	Dorking and Holmwood boxes	1887
Peasmarsh Junction	Bramley & Wonersh and Peasmarsh Junction (LSW Rly) boxes. The new LBSC Rly Peasmarsh Junction box was placed where the single line from Bramley became a double line prior to joining the LSW Rly at the latter company's Peasmarsh Junction Box	1882
Mickleham Crossing	Leatherhead station and Boxhill boxes	1891
Bedhampton Mill Intermediate	Bedhampton Mill and Farlington Junction boxes	Probably late 1890s
Ashtead Woods*	Ashtead and Leatherhead Junction boxes	1898
Beeding	Bramber and Old Shoreham Bridge boxes	1898
Epsom Common*	Epsom West and Ashtead boxes	1899
Northwood	Ockley and Warnham boxes	1899
Cray Lane	Billingshurst and Pulborough boxes, at level crossing	1899[9]

*Built by LSW Rly during one of that company's periods of responsibility for maintaining the joint LBSC Rly/LSW Rly Epsom- Leatherhead line.

Ford bridge was strengthened in the 1890s. Plate 7 shows Bramley & Wonersh station in 1965, and Plate 8 shows Slinfold signal box (formerly Slinfold North) in the same year. A view of Lake Lane Crossing, west of Yapton, in 1901, appears as Plate 9.

Attention must next be given to certain changes to stations other than those already referred to earlier in this chapter:

| | | DATE | |
STATION	POSITION	OPENED	CLOSED
	WEST COAST LINE		
Cliftonville*	Between Hove and Portslade	1 Oct. 1865	—
Hove	West of Brighton but east of new station at Cliftonville (see above)	—	1 March 1880†
Kingston	East of Shoreham	—	1 April 1879†
	PULBOROUGH-HARDHAM JCT-PETWORTH-MIDHURST LINE		
Fittleworth	Between Hardham Jct and Petworth	2 Sept. 1889	—
Selham	Between Petworth and Midhurst	1 July 1872	—

*Renamed West Brighton on 1 July 1879. Again renamed Hove & West Brighton on 1 October 1894. Became Hove on 1 July 1895.
†Closed to passengers, but remained open for freight.

Although most of the small companies which had been formed in LBSC Rly territory in the 1850s and 1860s had ceased to exist when the lines concerned had been acquired by the Brighton (see Volume II), a number were still in existence in 1866. Authority to dissolve the small companies concerned had been granted to the LBSC Rly under 29 & 30 Vic. cap. 281 of 30 July of that year, but one of those listed in Section 52 of that Act (namely, the Bognor Railway Company) did not finally cease to exist as a separate entity until 1870, when the LBSC Rly took it over.

Mention must next be made of four proposed lines.

In 1896 the Light Railways Act had been passed, under which many of the then Board of Trade requirements for railways could be waived under certain circumstances. Under that Act, plans were deposited in 1896 for a light railway to run between

Ockley (the next station south of Holmwood, on the Dorking-Horsham line) and Selham (west of Petworth, on the line from Hardham Junction to Midhurst). Connections were to be made at Cranleigh with the LBSC Rly's Guildford line. Nothing materialized, but shortly afterwards a scheme was launched to build an 'ordinary' railway from near Holmwood direct to Cranleigh; plans for this latter line were deposited in 1898/99, but the line was never built.

Interest was renewed in 1898 in means of improving communications between Worthing and Horsham (and hence, of course, with London). Those behind the scheme considered that the line should start on the north-west side of the Up platform at West Worthing station, and should then turn towards the north and pass through Findon Village[10]—in other words, the line should follow a route similar to that proposed for the southern part of the London & Worthing Direct Railway of the 1860s (see Volume II, p. 249). This 1898 proposal for a line through Findon gap never materialized. The LBSC Rly's own schemes for west curves at Shoreham, connecting the West Coast line with the Steyning line, have been reviewed earlier in this chapter.

Finally, attempts were also made in 1898 to launch a further scheme for a direct line between Chichester and Bognor.[11] Proposals for such a line had been made as early as 1845, and lines to Bognor had been authorized in 1853 and 1855 (in each case to be built by local companies), but nothing had been done (see Volume II, p. 140). Moreover, when, under an 1861 Act, action was eventually started to build a railway to Bognor, that line would not provide direct connection between Chichester and Bognor. Hence new proposals for such a direct line were put forward in 1861, but again nothing materialized (see Volume II, pp. 143-143). The 1898 proposals, like their predecessors, failed to mature.

One other event of great importance must be recorded here. For some time the Brighton had felt that there should be an equal division of receipts with the South Western, for the Portsmouth traffic to and from London. Eventually the case went to arbitration, and the LBSC Rly won: the award of Mr. Thomas Houghton, made on 18 April 1895, was that on and from 1 January 1895 the LBSC Rly and the LSW Rly were to share the receipts equally. This decision was made binding on the two companies by their Agreement concerning the Joint Portsmouth line, dated 7 February 1896.

NOTES

1. Offical opening ceremony on Saturday 8 September.
2. On page 46 of the LBSC Rly Appendix for October 1882, is a statement referring to the Watering Island line signals at the junction with the Up Main line at the Harbour station. This statement says that the signals concerned were described 'on Diagram, page 3 of Joint Notice, dated 17 August 1876, when the Portsmouth Harbour Line and Station were opened'.

The Author does not have, nor has he seen, a copy of the Notice concerned, but 17 August 1876 was a Thursday, and evidence from many other contemporary notices in the Author's Library makes it clear that such notices were often dated only two or three days before the work concerned was brought into use. Hence the likely date of 'opening' of the harbour line seems to be Sunday 20 August 1876 (or possibly Monday 21 August). In actual fact, it seems that that date was when train working commenced, as distinct from the line being brought into use for passenger traffic.

There was an inspection by Colonel (as he then was) Hutchinson, on behalf of the Board of Trade, on Tuesday 29 August,[a] but he obviously required changes or improvements because he carried out another inspection on Friday 29 September,[b] after which he sanctioned the opening to passenger traffic—this event taking place on Monday 2 October 1876.

[a] *Railway Times*, XXXIX (2 September 1876), 801.
[b] *Railway News*, XXVI (7 October 1876), 452.

3. LBSC Rly Appendix for October 1882, page 46.
4. The Ryde & Newport trains did not actually start running until October 1880. The Ryde & Newport Railway was amalgamated with others in 1887 to form the Isle of Wight Central Railway.
5. South Western Railway and London Brighton & South Coast Railway Instruction No. 271, 1885.
6. LBSC Rly Notice No. 65, dated 23 September 1885.
7. *Railway World*, XVII (1956), 220.
8. Lopes, G. The Reparation of Betchworth Tunnel, Dorking. *Excerpt* Minutes of Proceedings Inst. C.E., 1889.
9. LBSC Rly Notice No. 117, dated 8 June 1899. Box brought into use on Monday 19 June 1899.
10. *Brighton Gazette & Sussex Telegraph*, 7 July 1898.
11. *Ibid.*, 24 September 1898.

CHAPTER FIVE

Developments in the London area (1870-1899)

DURING THE period 1870–1899 a considerable number of important developments occurred, apart from those already covered in Chapters III and IV. Some of these developments were concerned solely with the main line to Brighton, both at the London end and farther out. Others were concerned with the London area only, and were not associated with the line to Brighton. In order to enable the overall picture to be appreciated in the best way, the Author has thought it desirable to divide the account of these developments into two chapters, one dealing with works and events at the London end, and the other with the main line south of the London area. The natural point of division is South Croydon. Not only was it, for virtually the whole of the period 1870–1899, the terminus of local services from London, but from 10 March 1884 it was the point where Oxted line traffic left or joined the main line (see Chapter III). Hence the present chapter deals with matters as far out from London as South Croydon, and also Epsom and Epsom Downs, whilst Chapter VI covers works to the south of South Croydon, associated with the main line to Brighton.

The various developments which must be recorded in the present chapter, fall into two main groups: changes affecting complete lines, including extensions and widenings; and works at individual places, including new and rebuilt stations and a number of intermediate sidings. In addition, certain general matters require notice. Attention will first be given to matters affecting complete lines.

The opening in 1868 of the line to Central Croydon from New Croydon (the local-line side of East Croydon) was recorded in Volume II, where it was explained that the attitude of the

Croydon Council was strongly in support of the line, possibly even to the extent of encouraging the L B S C Rly to build it. The results, however, did not live up to expectations and the service was withdrawn on Friday 1 December 1871. The actual line, and the station at Central Croydon, remained, however, and may well have been used as sidings as no work of major importance appeared to have been needed when, after a gap of 15 years, a second (and equally unsuccessful) attempt was made to run an economically justifiable service to Central Croydon (see later in this chapter).

Attention must now be given to various developments in the New Cross area. The first of these was the opening of the Up Side connection to the East London Railway (Railway No. 3 of 28 Vic. cap. 51 of 26 May 1865—see Volume II, Chapter XII). This connection ran from the Up Local and Up Main lines at New Cross to the East London Railway at Deptford Road Junction, as a single line. It crossed over the Brighton company's Old Kent Road Junction—New Cross Lift Bridge line which gave access to the Deptford Wharf branch, and then ran on the east side of the double-track East London Railway connection from Old Kent Road Junction to Deptford Road Junction. The Up Side connection, which enabled through running to take place off both Up roads south of New Cross on to the East London Railway, was 74 chains long. It was opened on Sunday 2 April 1876.[1] The East London's platform at New Cross was by then known as New Cross (Low Level), the Brighton company's station being New Cross (High Level). The East London Railway was itself extended from Wapping to Shoreditch to join the Great Eastern Railway, and so enabled through running to take place between Liverpool Street (G E Rly) and New Cross and stations to the south, on Monday 10 April 1876.[2] The train service between Liverpool Street and Old Kent Road was extended from the latter to Peckham Rye on 1 August 1877.

The connection from Old Kent Road to the Down side at New Cross, authorized in 1865 and probably brought into use about January 1871 (see Volume II, Chapter XII), had a short life, because it must have been closed before April 1876.[3] Thereafter, the connection from New Cross Up Side to Old Kent Road Junction was worked both ways.

The firm of Saxby & Farmer normally supplied signal frames and signals to the L B S C Rly, but were not involved in block instruments (except for Hodgson's pattern, referred to in Chapter III), telegraph apparatus, block bells, repeaters, etc. Also, it seems doubtful how much of the mechanical maintenance was done by Saxby & Farmer. The LBSC Rly established shops, for signal work and wagon repair, on the north side of Cold Blow Lane and on the west side of the main line north of New Cross, on land already owned by the Brighton company. Across this land was a viaduct on a descending grade, taking Wharf Road Up Side from the level of the main line at New Cross, down to ground level just before that Road was joined by the spur (opened on 15 May 1869) from Old Kent Road Junction. Wharf Road Up Side then passed under the LBSC Rly's main lines and thence over New Cross Lift Bridge and on to Deptford Wharf. Workshops were built in the arches of the viaduct, and also in the form of buildings clear of those arches, whilst sidings were also laid, both between the viaduct and the main lines on their embankment, and to the west of the Wharf Road Up Side viaduct. Some of these sidings connected with Wharf Road Up Side and others with the Old Kent Road spur, the connections being in each case trailing for trains going towards Deptford Wharf. This work seems to have been done by about 1877, but no records have yet been discovered by the Author; as all the land involved was already in Brighton ownership, no Act seems to have been needed. By 1879 traffic from Deptford Wharf had expanded sufficiently to require additional sidings to be laid for holding supplies of empty wagons. The most convenient site at which land could be obtained was north-east of the existing Field Sidings on the Up side at New Cross, the latter sidings being on made ground some 18-20 ft. above the general level of the land (see Volume II). Hence a further trailing connection was laid in the Old Kent Road spur just before the latter itself joined Wharf Road Up Side. This additional trailing connection led back southwards, crossing Cold Blow Lane on the level and then passing under the East London Up Side connection and the New Cross–Old Kent Road Junction spur in order to reach sidings at ground level to the north-east of the Field Sidings. As extra land had to be taken, and Cold Blow Lane had to be crossed on the level, Parliamentary Authority was needed, and was granted in the 1879 Session. These sidings seem to have been brought into use in 1880; they were named Ballarat Sidings, after contemporary events in Australia, but were virtually invisible from the main line. Later, the local names 'Sandhole' and 'Greasehole' were applied to two sidings off the Ballarat group. A siding for coal traffic was provided west of the line to Ballarat Sidings, and south of Cold Blow Crossing. As the land had hitherto been agricultural, some wit applied the name Rhubarb to it.

It was also decided to provide an improved terminal station for East London traffic at New Cross, where the existing facilities were, as already noted, known as New Cross Low Level. Parliamentary action was taken in the 1879 Session, and the improvements seem to have been carried out fairly quickly.

The South Eastern Railway took over the maintenance of the East London Railway on 1 July 1885, on behalf of the East London Joint Committee. The latter had been formed in 1882 to represent the LBSC Rly, the SE Rly, the LCD Rly, the Metropolitan Railway, and the Metropolitan District Railway. The Great Eastern Railway joined in 1885.

Later, a direct connection was made from the New Cross end down to Cold Blow, to enable the Shops there to be served more effectively. This line, on a steep falling gradient down to Cold Blow, was some 350 yards long, and a covered ground frame was erected at Cold Blow to regulate the working and to control the level crossing. It was brought into use on 1 October 1884, and in effect provided an additional Up side connection from New Cross down to the Deptford Wharf branch although it was not a running road (Plate 10). The layout at Bricklayers Arms Junction in 1894 is shown in Figure 12.

Reference was made in Chapter III to the Woodside and South Croydon Railway. Although this line was joint LBSC Rly/SE Rly, the moves to build it came from the SE Rly in order that that company could reach the Oxted line from the South Eastern's Mid-Kent line. It started immediately south of Woodside station on the South Eastern's line to Addiscombe Road (nowadays known as Addiscombe), and ran for some 2 miles 30 chains to join the Croydon, Oxted and East Grinstead line 30 chains after the latter left the Brighton main line at South Croydon. It was authorized under 43 & 44 Vic. cap. 150 of 6 August 1880, and a deviation at the south (or Croydon) end was allowed under 45 & 46 Vic. cap. 93 of 3 July 1882. The powers for this deviation were annulled by Sections 5, 6 and 7 of 51 Vic. cap. 17 of 16 May 1888.

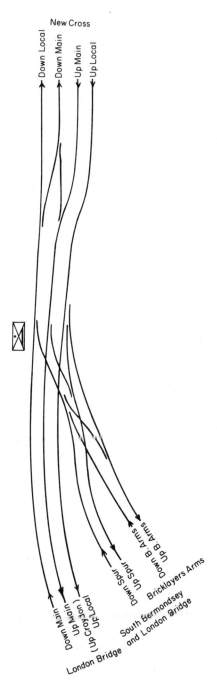

Figure 12. Bricklayers Arms Junction: 1894

Layout shown in diagrammatic form only, with London to the left, to facilitate quick assimilation of essential features. The actual Signal Box Diagram (which does not seem to have survived) would have shown the layout the other way round—see relative position of level frame in signal box, then on the Down side

The Woodside and South Croydon line (Figure 13) turned left out of the SE Rly's line to Addiscombe Road, by a 33-chain radius left-hand curve some 30 chains long, and then ran nearly straight for about $1\frac{3}{4}$ miles until it entered another 33-chain left-hand curve some 20 chains long to bring it into the Croydon, Oxted and East Grinstead line. There was a virtually continuous rise from the junction south of Woodside, for some $1\frac{3}{4}$ miles, part of it as steep as 1 in 70, much of it at 1 in 116, and other lengths at 1 in 100, 1 in 125, and 1 in 158. Coombe Lane, the only intermediate station, was situated 1 mile 48 chains south of Woodside and almost at the summit of the bank, after which the line fell at 1 in 173 to join the line to Oxted. There were three tunnels extremely close together on the ascent from Woodside, named Woodside, Park Hill, and Coombe Lane respectively, and having lengths, in order, of 164 yds., 121 yds., and 157 yds. In addition there were about eight over or under bridges. The line was opened on 10 August 1885, a station also being then opened in the fork of the junction with the Oxted line and named Selsdon Road (now Selsdon). Maintenance of the Woodside and South Croydon line was done by the SE Rly, as already explained in Chapter III.

The general expansion of freight traffic, particularly that coming off the West London Extension line at Clapham Junction and that from Deptford Wharf, as well as considerable volumes from Battersea Wharf and from Willow Walk, necessitated adequate marshalling facilities from which trains could leave for all parts of the LBSC Rly system. South of Norwood Junction land was therefore acquired on which several sets of sidings were laid, their outlet being mainly at Windmill Bridge Junction at the south end; traffic for destinations, reached via Norwood Fork had to be propelled to Norwood Junction and then worked to destination from there, over the flyover. Some part of the Down side yard seems to have been in use by the 1870s, and extensions were planned in 1882, but similar facilities for up traffic were not authorized until later. Earlier, about 1881, two up loops had been laid between Windmill Bridge Junction and Norwood Fork, for freight traffic; and a third was put in some 20 years later. The Brighton's staff record for abstemiousness was good, but long waits in these loops far from any possibility of obtaining refreshments, led to their becoming known as the Teetotal sidings.

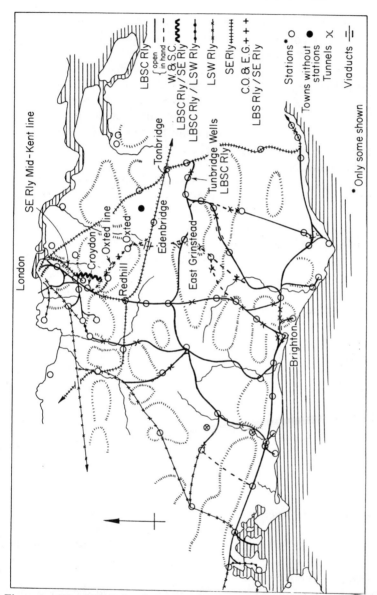

Figure 13. Woodside & South Croydon Railway (Joint LBSC Rly/SE Rly) as Authorized on 6 August 1880

Showing line in relation to the SE Rly's Mid-Kent line and to the Croydon, Oxted & East Grinstead line (Joint LBSC Rly/SE Rly as far as connection to SE Rly west of Edenbridge, and LBSC Rly south to East Grinstead)

The Peckham Rye–Mitcham Junction–Sutton line had been opened in 1868 as recorded in Volume II. In the vicinity of Streatham this line, running north-north-east to south-south-west, crossed over the Balham–Windmill Bridge Junction line opened in 1862 (Volume II), running north-west to south-east. A double-line spur in the south-west angle between the two lines had been brought into use simultaneously with the Peckham Rye-Mitcham Junction-Sutton line, and enabled through running to take place in each direction between Balham and Mitcham Junction.

The corresponding spur in the north-east angle, to enable through running to take place between Streatham on the Peckham Rye-Mitcham Junction-Sutton line, and Streatham Common on the Balham–Windmill Bridge Junction line, although authorized as Railway No. 4 with the other spur and the Peckham Rye-Mitcham Junction Sutton line in 1863 (Volume II), had however not been completed when the remaining new lines in the area were opened on 1 October 1868. It turned left out of the Peckham Rye–Mitcham Junction–Sutton line a short way south of Streatham station, where the line to Mitcham Junction was itself on a 60-chain radius left-hand curve, and, having assumed a direction nearly parallel to the Mitcham Junction line (but of course on the east side of the latter), curved left at 65-chains radius until the curvature sharpened to about 20 chains to take the spur into the Balham–Windmill Bridge Junction line immediately west of Streatham Common station. The line fell sharply throughout its length of about 760 yards, the gradients being at 1 in 256 to clear the Junction at Streatham and then at 1 in 79, 1 in 94 and 1 in 75. There was a footpath, Potter's Lane, along the north-east side of the Balham–Windmill Bridge Junction line, and authority was granted under Section 8 of 47 & 48 Vic. cap. 97 of 3 July 1884, for this to be altered: a footbridge was provided over the new spur just before it joined the Balham–Windmill Bridge Junction line. The Streatham Common spur was opened on Friday 1 January 1886.[4]

While dealing with the various junctions in the Streatham area, attention must be drawn to the fact that, in the LBSC Rly Table of Distances of 1881, the designations of certain junctions differed from those normally used and officially given in the LBSC Rly Appendix for 1882 and subsequent issues. The designations shown in the Table of Distances,[5] were probably linked with Parliamentary matters, and used by the Secretary's office in the calculation of rates and fares. To avoid any possible misconception in this history the various designations must be made clear as follows:

NORMAL DESIGNATION	TABLE OF DISTANCES DESIGNATION
Streatham Junction North	Greyhound Lane Junction North
Streatham Junction South	Streatham Junction South
Streatham Junction (south of Streatham station, on Tulse Hill–Mitcham Junction line)	Streatham Junction North
Streatham Common Junction (north-west of Streatham Common station, on Balham–Windmill Bridge Junction line)	Greyhound Lane Junction South

Incidentally, the Table of Distances also showed a junction where the West Croydon–Wimbledon single line curved away from the West Croydon–Sutton–Epsom line. There was never any physical junction at that situation.

The 1877 proposal to eliminate the sharp curves, and consequent slow running, through Mitcham Junction on the Peckham Rye–Sutton line, by taking a direct line from Beehive Bridge north of Mitcham Junction to North Farm crossing south of Mitcham Junction, was referred to in Volume II. It would have crossed over the West Croydon–Wimbledon line to the east of Mitcham Junction station.

The growing importance of Sutton and the good traffic at the station, raised the interests of competition, and earlier ideas led to a firm proposal for a line from Worcester Park on the LSW Rly to Sutton in 1882, with a terminus in the north-west corner of the Cheam Road/High Street Crossroads. The line was not built. Another proposal, for a line from near Raynes Park, was made in 1888.

After the coming of the railway, Croydon gradually lost its 'market town' character and became increasingly a residential area with growing business influences. Apart from markets and the fair, there were two racecourses, one for flat racing and the other for steeplechases: the former was north-west of the town and to the south-west of the Windmill Bridge Junction–Balham line (being, in fact, south of Streatham Common station in the area known as Pollards Hill); the steeplechase course, after having had various earlier sites, was in 1866 established at Stroud Green, about a mile east of Norwood Fork and hence about ½ mile east of the SE Rly's line to Addiscombe Road station. The Stroud Green course attracted so much traffic that in 1871 the SE Rly built Woodside station on their Addiscombe Road line in order to cater for race traffic as well as to serve the district lying south-east of the LBSC Rly's Norwood Junction station. However, the apparently inevitable rowdiness at last caused the course to be shut down after the meeting on 25 and 26 November 1890; a new course then being built at Gatwick, between Horley and Three Bridges on the main line to Brighton (see Chapter VI).

The importance of Croydon markets and the annual fair also declined, and the closing of the fair after 1867 has already been noted in Volume II. At the same time businesses grew up and commercial activity steadily increased. As the population of Croydon continued to grow (it was 55,652 in 1871, and 78,953 in 1881), there was another move by the Croydon Council to provide a passenger-train service to Central Croydon. In consequence that station was refurbished, and a service restarted on 1 June 1886. Initially, several of the trains ran via Crystal Palace to and from Willesden Junction, this service being provided by the LNW Rly; whilst from 1887 there was also a GE Rly service via the East London line to and from Liverpool Street. No alterations seem to have been made to the layout or facilities at Central Croydon, which apparently remained as originally opened in 1868 (Volume II, Chapter XIII). It has been stated that, on reopening, the name of the station was changed from Central Croydon to Croydon Central.[6] Poster and photographic evidence does not support this.[7,8]

The new service did not produce much traffic, the poor results being possibly associated with the starting of tram services into the town in October 1879. By 1889 it was clear that the line was unlikely ever to be economic, and the LBSC Rly therefore sought powers to close the branch. Such powers were granted in Section 36 of 53 & 54 Vic. Session 1890, dated 4 August 1890, which stated that there was no longer any obligation to maintain or use as a railway the Croydon Central line;[9] but that the company might retain and use for sidings or other purposes of their undertaking, so much of the said railway and station site, and any lands required for the purpose thereof, as was not sold to the Croydon Corporation. Under this authority the train service was again (and, this time, finally) withdrawn on and after 1 September 1890. The site of the terminal station and the land to the west of Park Lane were then sold to the Croydon Corporation, who erected a replacement town hall and public gardens on the site of the station; sidings east of Park Lane were retained for traffic purposes and were also used by the Engineer. They became known as the Fairfield Yard. The population of Croydon reached 102,795 in 1901.

Next to be considered must be the West End line to and from Victoria. From the opening in 1862 of the Balham Hill line between Balham and Windmill Bridge Junction (north of Croydon), there were two distinct traffic flows to and from the London end, as far out as Balham—that over the original West End line via Streatham (Hill), and that over the Balham Hill line via Windmill Bridge Junction. As a result of the opening of the West London Extension Railway in 1863, another flow (running via the W L E Rly Branch No. 1) entered or left the first two at Falcon Road Junction (Clapham Junction). South of Clapham Junction, this flow was merged in one or other of the first two flows.

When the lines via Mitcham Junction and Sutton, and from Streatham Junction South via Tooting to Wimbledon, were opened in 1868, with a spur between the Balham Hill line and the new lines, a third flow along the West End line was established in the form of trains running to and from the Streatham Junction South direction. This third flow was also, of course, made up of a portion to and from the WLE Rly, although the bulk was to and from Victoria/Battersea.

Hence between Clapham Junction and Balham there were three flows in the outward direction (to Streatham (Hill), to Streatham Common, and to Streatham Junction South); whilst there were two inward flows, the greater to Battersea or Victoria and the lesser leaving at Clapham Junction and running on to the WLE Rly. The inward traffic had been eased by the provision of a second up road from Balham, probably brought into use on 2 March 1863 (Volume II, Chapter XIII), and down-side widening works between Clapham Junction and Balham (the most heavily worked section) were authorized by Section 9 of 42 Vic. cap. 31 dated 23 May 1879.

Due to the very small space between the existing Down line and the property of the Royal Masonic School for Girls just south of Clapham Junction, where the Down line was on the site of the 1862/63 widening, it was decided to start the new works immediately south of the school. That is to say, the second down line was to start a short way beyond where the connection from the W L E Rly joined the existing Down line, so that there would still be 100–150 yards of single down road forming a bottleneck between the entry of the W L E Rly traffic flow and the start of the widening.

The deposited plans show that Boutflower overbridge, immediately south of the school, was to be widened to take one extra track. No widening was necessary at Battersea Rise overbridge as there was space for the second down road to pass under the east span of that bridge, which had had an additional span added on the west side in 1862/63 (see Volume II, Chapter XIII). The next important bridge, carrying Bellevue Road over the line immediately north of Wandsworth Common station, was to be widened to take two extra roads, perhaps because a down loop was envisaged at that station (or approaching it) in addition to the second down line itself. Boundaries Road underbridge, which came next, was to be widened for one extra road only, but the succeeding one, Balham High Road underbridge, was to be widened to take three extra roads—possibly to make provision for two down loops as well as the additional down road, or for part of a new platform.

In the event the powers lapsed before the road was laid, but action could not be put off indefinitely and hence new powers were obtained under Section 5 of 53 & 54 Vic. Session 1890, dated 4 August 1890, as part of a larger scheme to widen the line to four roads from Poupart's Junction to Balham and then on to Streatham Junction North, with consequential alterations as far as Streatham Junction South. The object of starting the second down road at Poupart's Junction was to make provision for freight traffic off the low-level line from Battersea via Long-hedge Junction. The widening was to be on the down side throughout from Poupart's Junction to Balham, and hence involved rebuilding part of Clapham Junction station as well as finding a solution to the problem of getting a fourth line past the Royal Masonic School for Girls.

The line at this point is in a cutting some 25–30 ft. deep, the cutting taking not only the LBSC Rly but also the LSW Rly to the west of the Brighton's lines. The widening works necessitated a new brick retaining wall being built on the down side, far enough from the existing Down line that there was space for the additional down road; but that wall could not be carried up to the top of the cutting because if so it would encroach upon school property. To avoid taking any land away from the school at surface level, the wall, strengthened with closely-spaced buttresses, was only taken a few feet above structure-gauge height for the new track—a height at which its top was well below the general level of the school grounds. Cantilevers were built into the wall near the top of, and on the vertical centre line of, each buttress, on which oversailing courses of bricks were carried. Arches were formed between successive buttresses and thus parallel to the line of the railway, each arch being sprung from the top of the oversailed brickwork. By this means, a series of arches was formed, each arch being over the space between successive buttresses. Seen in frontal elevation, each arch was therefore fully formed, but only went back a short distance before reaching the solid brickwork of the retaining wall itself. On the tops of these arches a continuous longitudinal foundation was formed, well below the general level of the school ground but, in plan, partly over the site of the new down line. A parapet wall was then built on this foundation, so as to form the edge of the school grounds at their full existing extent.

The provisions of a schedule attached to the Act authorizing the work to be done, included the following:

Clause 6: The retaining wall had to be maintained for ever by the railway company.

Clause 9: Fencing and trellis work had to be erected on top of the retaining wall, and maintained for ever, by the railway company.

The alterations at Clapham Junction consisted, in essence, of taking the Up West London Extension Railway line (i.e. from the WLE Rly) outside (i.e. to the east of) the platform previously serving that line, and sluing the Down WLE Rly (i.e. to the WLE Rly) line to serve the west face of that platform. In this connection it must be appreciated that the WLE Rly line from Kensington southwards across the River Thames was 'Up', so that trains arriving at Clapham Junction from the WLE Rly were 'Up'. Hence when an up WLE Rly train continued beyond Clapham Junction in the Balham direction, it was redesignated a down train. The alterations at Clapham Junction therefore involved rebuilding the existing up WLE Rly platform and making it into an island between the two WLE Rly lines. The site of the former down WLE Rly line (i.e. that towards Kensington), was now available for the second down LBSC Rly road. Figures 14 and 15 show the basic layouts before and after the alterations. Details, including non-running connections, have been omitted for clarity.

At Wandsworth Common, the station was rebuilt with two side platforms and a centre island, but at Balham the new down line was taken behind the existing down platform (which was fenced off from it) and an extra down platform was erected outside (i.e. to the north-east of) the new down road. The layout at Balham before the works were started is shown in Figure 16.

Beyond Balham, on the way to Windmill Bridge Junction, two new roads were constructed, one normally on each side of the existing pair. That on the down side was entirely new, but that on the up side was on the site of an existing siding until the stops of that siding were reached. Before dealing with this length, however, it is important to explain how the four roads were to be worked when the widening was complete. From Poupart's Junction to Balham, the working was to be Down Local, Down Main, Up Local, and Up Main: that is to say, the up lines were to remain as before, the existing Down line was to become the Down Main, and the new down line was to become the Down Local.

Coming now to the widening beyond Balham, the new Down line was to run beside the Down Main as far as Streatham Junction North (where the existing spur turned right to Streatham Junction South, for Mitcham Junction or Tooting Junction), and was then to curve left, climb, and form a flyover over the existing two roads on to Windmill Bridge Junction; from the top of the flyover the new line would trail into the Down line from Tulse Hill and Streatham. That is to say, the new Down line became the Down Sutton and Portsmouth at Balham. Similarly, the Up spur from Streatham Junction South was led into the new Up line at Streatham Junction North, the

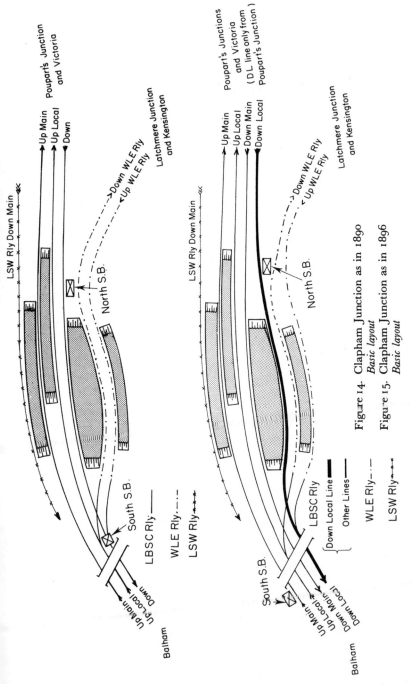

Figure 14. Clapham Junction as in 1890
Basic layout

Figure 15. Clapham Junction as in 1896
Basic layout

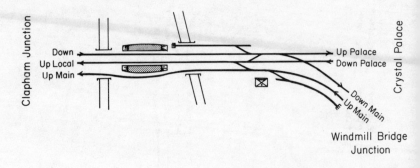

Figure 16. Balham as in 1890
Note continued use of old designations (Up/Down) on Crystal Palace line

new line (the Up Portsmouth and Sutton) running into the Up Main at Balham Junction, south-east of Balham station and where the line from Windmill Bridge Junction joined the original line from the Crystal Palace direction and Streatham Hill. Connections between the various roads at Balham Junction enabled maximum use to be made of the new facilities. The basic layouts at Streatham Junction North and Streatham Junction South, after the alterations, are shown in Figure 17.

The works involved new signal boxes at Poupart's Junction, Clapham Junction North and South, and Balham Junction; the new road was brought into use from Poupart's Junction to Clapham Junction North on 9 June 1895,[10] and was extended on to Balham shortly afterwards. In the absence so far of positive information, the Author is of the opinion that completion on to Streatham Junctions North and South occurred about 1897. The original line into Victoria, from Poupart's Junction to Battersea Pier Junction via Stewarts Lane, had become 'freight only' by 1882. It may have been so made when, or soon after, the High-level lines between Poupart's Junction and York Road Junction (later Battersea Park) were opened in 1867.

As recorded in Volume II, Chapter XIII, the Down and Up local lines between Norwood Fork Junction and Windmill Bridge Junction, made a junction with the Norwood Fork-West Croydon line at Gloucester Road Junction. In 1895 the facing and trailing leads at the latter were taken out and new leads

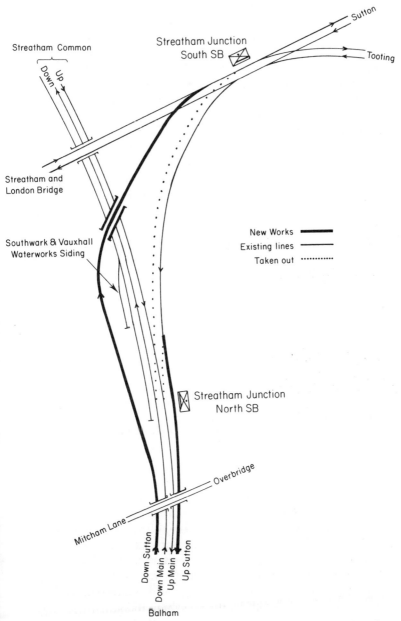

Figure 17. Streatham Junction North and Streatham Junction South as in
1899
Basic layout

were put in at Norwood Fork Junction, with interlaced or gauntletted roads as far as the site of Gloucester Road Junction. This work, which included the abolition of Gloucester Road Junction box, was carried out on Sunday 17 March 1895.[11] The Brighton company, in the Notice concerned, used the old Parliamentary term 'duplicate rails' to describe the interlaced or gauntletted section.

Major works at Victoria and immediately south thereof must now be described. Away from Victoria there was one road, which extended to Poupart's Junction where, from 1895 (as just recorded) the second down road started. On the up side, the two roads extended as far as Grosvenor Road box, at the north end of the bridge over the Thames. From Grosvenor Road to Victoria there was only one up road, that and the down road forming, in fact, the original pair of 1860; on most of the length of Grosvenor Bank they occupied the positions of the present Central Division Local or Slow lines. Carriage sidings, of limited capacity, existed on the Up side at the approach to Victoria, but there was virtually no room for worthwhile expansion on the up (or west) side due to the proximity of the Grosvenor Canal, whose original basin had been utilized for the site of the Victoria stations. To the east was the London Chatham & Dover Railway's approach to Victoria.

Although London Bridge was the main terminus, and the headquarters of the LBSC Rly, Victoria had been growing in importance for non-business traffic since the middle 1860s; and this was, of course, a major factor in the widening works dealt with earlier in this chapter as well as in the improved approaches to Victoria detailed in Volume II, Chapter X. Local improvements at Victoria were authorized under the LBSC Rly (Various Powers) Act, 1890, referenced 53 & 54 Vic. Session 1890, dated 4 August; the powers allowed land to be acquired for the rearrangement of the carriage sidings, and in Sections 21 & 22 for 82 yds. of roofing over the approach lines, south of Elizabeth Bridge, which had been required under the 1858 and 1863 Acts (Volume II, Chapters VII and X), to be removed; the corresponding roofing over the LCD Rly could also be removed unless that company objected. As the Chatham did not object, the two operations were carried out together. Perhaps the tone of the surrounding property had already fallen (as was common adjacent to railways), since soot and smuts, at least, would still no doubt have been thrown by hard-working locomotives getting some speed into their trains before starting the climb up Grosvenor Bank. The works involved were probably completed by about 1892-93. Earlier, probably about 1880, alterations had taken place in the relative positions of certain roads and the wide platform on Grosvenor Bridge, this platform henceforth being between the Up local and the Down road.

Although actual widening works between Victoria and Poupart's Junction, and between Streatham Junction North and Windmill Bridge Junction, were authorized in 1898-1899, this work properly belongs to the twentieth century, and hence will be dealt with in a subsequent chapter.

As already recorded (Volume II) Deptford Dockyard was closed in 1869 and most of it was converted into a Foreign Cattle Market. In 1897 it was decided that that market should be rail-connected, and as this could only readily be done by laying what was in effect a street tramway for some distance, an Act had to be obtained for the purpose: 61 & 62 Vic. cap. 51 of 1 July 1898, entitled the Foreign Cattle Market Deptford Act, 1898. Section 6 of this Act authorized the construction of the railway; Section 7 allowed a connection to be made with H.M. Victualling Yard adjacent to the market; and Section 14 authorized the line to be worked by animal power as agreed by the local authorities, or by mechanical power provided that it was not steam or electric. Section 14 was no doubt included in the Act to safeguard the interests of other road users, but one wonders what forms of mechanical power were available in 1898 other than steam or electric traction. Internal combustion engines running on some form of liquid fuel, had hardly reached the stage where they could be considered to be really practicable in a locomotive, whilst rope-haulage would undoubtedly have been difficult along a highway. Perhaps there was some thought of a return to a form of atmospheric working! The Author has not yet found the date when the line was brought into use but it was probably about 1900, no doubt using horses. Steam working was instituted later. The Cattle Market became, in later years, the Army Reserve Depot.

In the 1880s Tadworth, on the North Downs to the south-wards of Epsom, was growing in popularity as a high-class residential area. Hence railway communication began to be a subject for discussion among private parties. Among the proposals considered in 1891 was one for a line off the Epsom Downs branch, to run southwards and so to enter Tadworth from the north, and then to continue into the upper end of the Chipstead Valley (whose lower end was beside the LBSC Rly's main line to Brighton). LBSC Rly interest was minimal, even when an Act was obtained in 1892 for such a line through Tadworth. Separate parties proposed that Tadworth should be reached by a branch, starting from the LBSC Rly main line and running up the Chipstead Valley to connect with that from the Epsom Downs branch. As the line off the Epsom Downs branch was never built, whereas a line from the LBSC Rly main line to the Tadworth area was later constructed, further details of the overall scheme are best considered when developments in connection with the LBSC Rly main line to Brighton are reviewed in the next chapter.

A siding had been laid in on the down side at South Croydon in the early 1880s, in connection with the building of the Croydon, Oxted, and Groombridge line (Chapter III). Later, a Down Relief line was laid southwards from East Croydon (where it started from the Down Main Loop line) to join the siding at South Croydon and so convert the latter into a running road. Relatively heavy work was involved in widening the cutting, extending bridges, and building retaining walls. At South Croydon the Down Relief line was led direct into the Down 'Oxted' line, and a connection across to the Down Main line was also provided. The Author has not yet found the date when this line was brought into use, but it seems to have been during 1896.[12] A Down Goods line from Norwood Fork to Windmill Bridge Junction, and a Down Relief line onwards to East Croydon North, where it ran into the Down Main Loop, was opened on 4 July 1897.[13] Five running roads were thenceforth available from Windmill Bridge Junction to South Croydon.

Coming now to works at individual places within the London area, the most important developments were the building of three entirely new stations—Brockley in 1871, Norbury in 1878, and Honor Oak Park in 1886. Brockley was built to serve a large area to the south of New Cross on the Main line, which was about to be traversed in a west to east direction by a LCD Rly line from Nunhead (on the Chatham's Crystal Palace line) to Blackheath Hill in the direction of Greenwich. This Chatham line would pass over the Brighton's main line, and the newcomer might be expected to be a serious competitor of the Brighton if the Chatham built a station in the area: the latter company would be in a position to offer services direct to the City and to Victoria. The L B S C Rly station at Brockley was placed where the new LCD Rly line would cross over the Brighton's line. It was provided with side platforms for the Up Local and Down Local respectively, but had no freight facilities. It was opened on 6 March 1871, and was 64 chains south of New Cross on a gradient of 1 in 100 falling towards the latter. The line curved left towards New Cross at 126 chains radius. The LCD Rly line was opened in September 1871, and that company's station in 1872.

Norbury was built between Streatham Common and Thornton Heath stations, on the Balham–Windmill Bridge Junction line. Until about 1865, the district, south-east of Streatham, was very rural and there were hardly any houses, but gradually a good-class area grew up and it was considered that it was economically worthwhile to build a station there. The site selected was immediately on the Croydon side of the London Road, itself a continuation south-eastwards of Streatham High Road. The railway was on an embankment, an underbridge having been provided for London Road when the line was built. The ordinary two side platforms were provided, but no freight facilities. The station was 68 chains on the Croydon side of Streatham Common, on an 87-chain radius curve which was left-hand for trains proceeding towards Streatham Common and London, and on a rising gradient, for such trains, of 1 in 264 (which changed to a fall at 1 in 126 towards Balham). It was 10 chains on the London side of Norbury Crossing, and 1 mile 17 chains separated it from Thornton Heath, the next station towards Croydon. It was opened on 1 January 1878.[14]

The relatively long gap between Brockley and Forest Hill was filled by the erection of a station called Honor Oak Park, intended to serve a growing residential area. The station was placed in the deep cutting along this length, being situated immediately on the north (or London) side of the road called Honor Oak Park. The main buildings were, in fact, on the overbridge carrying that road. The station had two side platforms, serving the Up Local and Down Local respectively, but no provision was (or could be, without great expense) made for freight traffic. It was 1 mile 3 chains south of Brockley, on a gradient of 1 in 100 falling towards the latter, and was opened on 1 April 1886.

Apart from the opening of the above three entirely new stations, two others were rebuilt in positions near to, but distinct from, their original positions—namely, Forest Hill and Tooting Junction. The former was renewed some 5 chains nearer to London Bridge than the original (1839) station, mainly to provide adequate space for handling the ever-growing milk traffic on the up side. Sufficient land could be obtained north of the foot subway that had maintained the pedestrian access from one side of the railway to the other when the original level crossing had been abolished in 1844 (see Volume I); and hence the renewed station buildings and two side platforms serving the Up and Down Local lines were constructed north of that subway whereas the original station was south of the subway. However, the centre island platform (originally that provided for down London & Croydon trains, with the outer face later used by atmospheric trains—see Volume I) had already been extended northwards (see Volume II, Chapter XIII), and this extension was abolished in the rebuilding works. Hence the renewed station had a most unusual appearance by having the centre island platform south of the two side platforms. Originally, it was intended that there should be a loop off the Up Local line, with an island platform between the Up Local and the Up Loop and a single-sided platform (with station buildings) outside the Up Loop. Although this loop was never constructed, the Up-side buildings were erected in the planned position, resulting in the exceptionally wide centre part of the Up Local platform which remained until the station was again reconstructed within the last few years. The station was resited under authority obtained in the 1880 Session of Parliament, and the work was completed by 1884. The remains of the original Up platform of the London & Croydon Railway's Dartmouth Arms station, as now existing, are shown in Plate 11.

Tooting Junction station, hitherto in the fork of the junction between the Upper Loop to Wimbledon (i.e. via Haydons Road[15]) and the Lower Loop (i.e. via Merton Abbey), was renewed east of the junction, some 15 chains east of the original station of 1868. The reasons for this alteration appear to have been to reduce working expenses by having only two platforms instead of four; and the expectation of increased traffic since the main buildings were on Mitcham Road overbridge, so that public access to the station was improved. The freight facilities were not altered. The new station was brought into use on 12 August 1894.

A view of Old Kent Road Junction, looking north towards London Bridge (to left in distance) and showing the original and the replacement signal boxes (the latter in the background), appears as Plate 12. The Author has not yet found any record of the date of this photograph, but it would seem to have been taken in the 1890s.

Works were carried out at a number of other places, of which the following merit attention:

Crystal Palace: station buildings altered, 1874/75.

Crystal Palace Bank: new signal box between Sydenham and Crystal Palace, on Down side of line, 1878.

Clapham Junction: sidings added to the north of the West London Extension Railway, east of the station, and were known as Pig Hill Sidings. They were brought into use about 1879.

Note: In an 1879 Deposit, the Up Local line is shown as running into the Up Main immediately on the Poupart's Junction side of Clapham Junction station. Some temporary alterations (e.g work at Pig Hill or Latchmere Road underbridge) which needed possession of the Up Local on the Poupart's Junction side of Clapham Junction, must have been in hand when the survey was made for the plan to be deposited.

Epsom (Joint station): facing crossover between Up and Down lines at west end of station, laid on Sunday 26 April 1885.[16] It was installed to facilitate the working of return L S W Rly race trains to Waterloo, and was probably one of the earliest instances of the use of such a crossover at an intermediate station.

Mitcham–Mitcham Junction: line doubled about 1879.

Windmill Bridge Junction–East Croydon: Windmill Bridge over main line, provided with additional span on Down (east) side to take Down Relief line, 1882 (but line not laid until 1897).

Knight's Hill: LNW Rly coal depot constructed on Down side north of Knight's Hill Tunnel, about 1891.

Peckham Rye: Joint LNW Rly/M Rly coal depot constructed on Up (north) side, east of station, and between the South London lines and the separate viaduct carrying the lines used by the LCD Rly. Depot was at street level, a hoist being used to lower and lift wagons from and to the level of the viaduct, on which the companies' sidings were placed and which were connected with the LBSC Rly's South London line. Depot and hoist brought into use on 24 March 1891.

Streatham Common: siding provided on Down side west of station, and on Balham side of Peckham Rye–Mitcham Junction–Sutton line overbridge, to serve pumping station of the Southwark & Vauxhall Water Works, 1892.

East Croydon: station rebuilt, with Down Loop, Down Main, Up Main, Up Loop, Down Local, and Up Local lines; three island platforms as follows: one between the Down Loop and the Down Main, one between the Up Main and the Up Loop, and one between the Down Local and the Up Local. Work done in 1894/95.

Norbury: Norbury Crossing abolished under section 17 of the LBSC Rly Act of 1896 (59 & 60 Vic. cap. 128) dated 20 July 1896. Footbridge built to replace crossing.

Deptford Wharf: extension of sidings, etc. 1899. There had been an earlier scheme in 1896, for a branch line to serve the South Dock (which was done at a later date).

On the Bricklayers Arms branch, extension of SE Rly facilities necessitated the cutting off of Hyson Road on the north (Down side) of the line, and the blocking up of the underbridge concerned (referred to in Volume I).

On the Epsom Downs branch, California station was renamed Belmont[17] on 1 October 1875, and a yard was added on the down side beyond the Brighton (or California) overbridge about 1880. At Banstead, a yard was added on the Down side west of the station, about 1880; and an intermediate siding, to serve the Kensington and Chelsea District Schools[18] and named Crockett's Siding, was constructed on the Down side some 400 yds. on the Epsom Downs side of the station, also about 1880. Crockett's Siding was worked by means of an Annett's key from

Banstead signal box. Finally, between Epsom Downs and Banstead on the Up side, another intermediate siding was put in to serve North Looe Farm, and was named Gadesden's Siding. It was about 58 chains on the Banstead side of Epsom Downs, and was worked by an Annett's key from Epsom Downs signal box. It was brought into use on 1 January 1886.[19] Later this siding became known as the Kensington and Chelsea District Schools Siding (i.e. the same authority as was served by Crockett's Siding, which itself later became known as the Residential Schools Siding). Banstead station was renamed Banstead & Burgh Heath on 1 June 1898. At Epsom Downs, a new signal box was brought into use on 27 May 1879.

A new signal box was built at the Cheam (or west) end of Sutton in 1899. It was originally called Sutton Main Line box, but was renamed Sutton West on 5 January 1900.

Attention must now be given to important matters concerning the approach to London Bridge. Under the 1847-1850 SE Rly widening to six roads, and resulting rearrangement of working between Corbett's Lane Junction and London Bridge (Volume II, Chapter I), the fifth road from the north side (i.e. the Up Main line) was shared between the Brighton and the South Eastern companies, and the sixth from the north (i.e. the Up Croydon line) was used for Croydon (i.e. local) traffic off the Brighton company's system. In other words, the Brighton might be said to have the use of $1\frac{1}{2}$ roads whereas the South Eastern had only $\frac{1}{2}$ road. The Down Main line was of course shared, whereas the three roads nearest to the north (or river) side of the viaduct were used by SE Rly traffic via North Kent East Junction only, and so were of no concern in the handling of traffic via Bricklayers Arms Junction. All six roads on the viaduct were owned by the SE Rly. The foregoing position was not materially altered by the opening of the South Eastern extensions into Charing Cross in 1864 and Cannon Street in 1866, in that most South Eastern trains then continued beyond London Bridge to serve Charing Cross and Cannon Street, but still used the same roads south of London Bridge.

The further widening of the viaduct on the south side in 1866, which was done by the LBSC Rly to make provision for three more roads exclusively for that company's use in connection with the Brighton's South London line service (Volume II, Chapter X), had no immediate effect on the volume of traffic running via Bricklayers Arms Junction and Corbett's Lane Junction, but some easement to the latter traffic flow did occur on and after 1 October 1868 when the Peckham Rye and Sutton line was opened (Volume II, Chapter XI), since some of the longer-distance LBSC Rly traffic to and from London Bridge was then sent that way rather than via West Croydon as hitherto (see Volume II, Figure 35).

Completion of the South Eastern's new main line to Tonbridge via Chislehurst in 1868 reduced the number of SE Rly trains running via Bricklayers Arms Junction and Corbett's Lane Junction, whilst the opening in 1871 of the LBSC Rly's South Bermondsey Spur between Bricklayers Arms Junction and South Bermondsey (Volume II, Chapter XII), enabled the Brighton to reduce somewhat their traffic via Corbett's Lane Junction. The South London side at London Bridge station, opened in 1866 (Volume II, Chapter X) had been designed to handle the LBSC Rly traffic that would, from late 1868, necessarily have to be dealt with on the three South London lines inwards from Peckham Rye; hence it had limited capacity, only, to deal with a large additional traffic flow via the South Bermondsey Spur. Easement of the congestion on the three roads was, moreover, soon nullified by increases in train services that had perforce to be so routed.

The layout of the Brighton's 'main line' part of London Bridge station, was improved in 1878, longer platforms being provided which it was intended could each be used to take two reasonable-length trains. To regulate the working, new signalling was introduced, involving the construction of new signal boxes. A view of London Bridge North Signal Box soon after it was brought into use in 1878, is included as Plate 13. This box contained 280 levers in two 140-lever frames, and was fitted with gridiron locking. It was not a block post, but operated switches and signals in the 'main-line' part of the LBSC Rly station, as well as slots on relevant SE Rly signals governing incoming moves. The adjacent SE Rly box similarly slotted LBSC Rly signals for outward moves, as well as being the block post controlling all LBSC Rly traffic from and to the 'main' lines. The Brighton company also had a South Box, containing 98 levers similarly interlocked, which controlled the 'South London' part of the LBSC Rly station, and approach lines, and hence was a full block post.

The Author has no space in this account to deal in any way with these interesting and important changes, but what must be appreciated is that any hold-up to a Brighton company's train on the Up Main line completely stopped all up South Eastern traffic via Bricklayers Arms Junction and Corbett's Lane Junction, including trains to Charing Cross and Cannon Street as well as those terminating at London Bridge. Any delay to a Brighton company's train on the Up Local (Up Croydon) line, however, only affected following trains of that company.

The South Eastern had by this time begun to feel, perhaps not unreasonably, that as sole owners of the three lines from and to the Croydon direction (as well as, of course, the three lines on the north side of the Croydon lines), they should not be at a disadvantage as compared with the LBSC Rly—as already explained, the latter company had, in effect, the use of $1\frac{1}{2}$ up roads in comparison with the South Eastern's use of $\frac{1}{2}$ road, this position having come into existence in 1850 (since when the Up Local (Up Croydon) line had been used only by the Brighton company). By 1878 the SE Rly had reached the conclusion that the LBSC Rly did *not* have a legal right to the sole use of the Up Local line—the Brighton's position appeared to the South Eastern as being somewhat akin to the old argument that possession was nine points of the law.

Hence the SE Rly decided to make a slightly more equable arrangement than hitherto, by taking sole possession of the Up Main line for the last $\frac{1}{2}$ mile or so into London Bridge. This the South Eastern did in 1878 by laying in a connection from the Up Main to the Up Local (Up Croydon) at that point (London Bridge No. 4 Signal Box), and normally turning all Up Main LBSC Rly traffic over it. In other words, from No. 4 Box into London Bridge, all incoming LBSC Rly traffic via Corbett's Lane Junction was run on the Up Local (Up Croydon) line only. Since the Brighton would almost certainly give preference to main-line trains (this being common policy among railway companies), that company would have made appropriate paths for such trains on the Up Local line, if necessary, to the detriment of the Brighton's own local services on that line.[20] The South Eastern's gain was therefore the Brighton's loss.

The South Eastern's difficulties in handling incoming empty trains to form outgoing services, were also increasing. The main carriage sidings were situated at Rotherhithe Road, on the

Surrey Canal Junction side of North Kent West Junction, and were so arranged that empty trains for stations away from London could pull out of the sidings and run direct to destination. Stock for the formation of every down train from Charing Cross, Cannon Street, or London Bridge, however, had to be pulled out from the sidings and then run round (or a fresh engine provided) at Surrey Canal Junction, this operation completely stopping all down North Kent and Greenwich trains while it was being performed, as well as delaying up North Kent trains. Hence, the S E Rly put forward a scheme in 1881 for a connection between the Up road of the Surrey Canal Junction–North Kent West Junction line, and the Up Local (Up Croydon) line towards London Bridge; this connection was to pass under the three 'Croydon' lines on the Bricklayers Arms Junction side of Corbett's Lane Junction.[21,22] The South Eastern felt that, in the evenings, there would be a reduced number of incoming L B S C Rly passenger trains, and that the latter company's up empty trains to form outgoing services could run via the South Bermondsey Spur and the Up South London lines. This South Eastern scheme was dropped, but that company still sought means of facilitating the working into London Bridge.

The 1878 Up Main to Up Local connection at London Bridge No. 4 Signal Box, only enabled the S E Rly to have sole use of the Up Main line, and limited the L B S C Rly to the sole use of the Up Local line, between that box and London Bridge station. It did nothing to give equal facilities to the two companies on the approach side of that box. Hence the S E Rly decided to provide for this by making the Up Local accessible to their trains as far out as possible, so that both the Up Main and the Up Local would be available to the trains of both companies. Having satisfied themselves that the Brighton company did not have any legal right to be sole user of the Up Local (Up Croydon) line on the viaduct, the South Eastern then installed, apparently late in 1883, a connection from the Up Main to the Up Local a short distance on the London Bridge side of Corbett's Lane Junction. A new signal box was needed, and, under the title of Up Croydon Line Junction, was brought into use on Sunday 30 March 1884. The delay in bringing the box into commission was apparently caused by work being in abeyance during the Court of Chancery's consideration of an application by the L B S C Rly for an interlocutory injunction to restrain the SE Rly from carrying out the work. The Brighton company's application was dismissed, on the ground that there was nothing to show that exclusive user of the Up Local line had been granted to the Brighton company, although that company had admittedly been in undisturbed possession for more than 30 years.[23,24]

In 1888 the South Eastern put forward a revised version of their 1881 scheme for a burrowing connection between the Surrey Canal Junction–North Kent West Junction line and the Up Croydon line, coupled with a proposal to build a station on the Croydon lines near the point where the burrowing connection would come in. This station would have been opposite to the Brighton company's South Bermondsey station on the South London line, and not a great way from the SE Rly's own Commercial Docks station (closed for many years) on their Greenwich/North Kent line. This 1888 scheme was strongly opposed by the LBSC Rly, and was dropped.[25]

Occasional earth slips took place between New Cross and Honor Oak Park, during the period covered by this chapter, but the Author has not found any record of major slips such as that which took place in November 1841 and which was noted on page 165 of Volume I. Provided that the cutting sides were not disturbed, they stood fairly well. A potential source of trouble in connection with railway works at London Bridge, namely the closeness of the line to St. Thomas' Hospital, was eliminated in 1871 when the hospital was removed to a riverside site near the eastern end of Westminster Bridge.

York Road station was renamed Battersea Park & York Road on 1 January 1877, and Battersea Park on 1 June 1885. The goods yard at Haydens Lane, situated behind the Up platform, is thought to have been built in the 1870s. That station was renamed Haydons Road on 1 October 1889.

Authority was granted, under section 5 of the LBSC Rly Various Powers Act of 1896 (59 & 60 Vic. cap. 128 of 20 July), for the West Croydon–Wimbledon line to be widened over the length between West Croydon and Waddon Marsh Crossing. The extra road was, of course, to be to the west and north of the existing single line. The work was not, however, carried out during the lifetime of the LBSC Rly.

Sykes lock-and-block equipment began to be installed in certain signal boxes from about 1880. The interior of East

Croydon South signal box, as it was in 1955 shortly before abolition, is shown in Plate 14.

Only two London-area accidents, both associated with the same underbridge, need be noted in this account. Cast iron had been used for bridges long before steam operation on railways became standard practice, and many underbridges had been designed on the basis of cast-iron girders which were in general durable and cheap. It was one of these bridges that was concerned in the two accidents to be reviewed here.

The bridge over Portland Road, a short way north of Norwood Junction station, had originally been built about 1838 by the London & Croydon Railway, with spans of 20 ft., and was south of the then station of Jolly Sailor. The station, later renamed Norwood Junction, was reconstructed some little way south of the bridge in 1859, the bridge having then been rebuilt to include spans of 26 ft. 9 in. It carried seven tracks, each supported by a girder on each side (i.e. fourteen girders in all). One track, a siding, had been shortened about 1872 and no longer extended from the station direction over the bridge. Exit from that siding was by three-throw switches leading into running lines on either side of the siding. That portion of the siding which had previously extended over the bridge, and had since been shortened, was that which formed the centre of the three-throw, and hence acted as a safety siding only. For this reason it had not been provided with either buffer stops or wheel stops. On 10 December 1876 a shunting engine coupled to some freight stock in the siding, was awaiting a signal to pull out on to one of the running roads; the three-throw turnout was provided with ground disc signals, but the driver mistakenly accepted a hand signal, meant for another engine, as authority to start with his shunt move, and before he realized his error his engine had gone along the safety siding too far for him to stop it before it ran off the end of the track and then dropped on to the empty span of the bridge. Both girders of the span concerned broke, possibly under the impact of the front wheels of the engine dropping on to the span, and the engine then fell into the street below. The driver received a fractured arm but there were no other casualties. Fortunately there was no one in the thoroughfare below the bridge when the span collapsed. Calculations showed that the girders were not strong enough even to carry the weight of the locomotive involved (D class 0-4-2T No. 228, with maximum axle loading of 15.1 tons and a total weight of 39.55 tons on a wheelbase of 14 ft. 6 in.).

The Inspecting Officer's recommendations were that stronger girders should be fitted instead of those then in the bridge, or alternatively that lighter shunting engines should be used. The latter was hardly a practicable suggestion, as main-line engines had to cross other spans of the bridge, all of which were, as already intimated, of similar construction. However, the Brighton company did not reconstruct this bridge, and there was a second accident involving it on 1 May 1891.

In the second case, one of the girders of the span carrying the Up Main line failed as a train from Brighton was crossing it at some 40 m.p.h., derailing the engine and the entire train. One passenger had his ankle dislocated, and there were a large number shaken (and probably frightened). The train crew were also shaken. The locomotive was B class 0-4-2 tender engine No. 175, and the twelve vehicles included Pullman car 'Jupiter'. The girder which failed had a large flaw in it which was invisible externally, but in any case (as was shown by the 1876 failure of two identical girders) it was of inadequate design strength for the locomotives then in service.

The Inspecting Officer severely castigated the LBSC Rly for their failure to substitute stronger girders for those in the bridge, after the Board of Trade's recommendations to that effect as a result of the 1876 collapse.

Shortly before the 1891 collapse, it had been arranged between the Corporation of Croydon and the LBSC Rly that the street beneath the bridge should be widened so that, with footpaths, there would be a width of 42 ft., which of course meant the construction of an entirely new bridge. During the interval between the Accident Report having been received, and the bridge reconstruction, each existing span was halved by the provision of a central timber upright under the bottom flange of each girder.

Cast-iron girders in underbridges had been gradually replaced as the bridges were reconstructed for one reason or another, and the Board of Trade had prohibited their use (except in arch form) in new lines of railway since August 1883. Mr. F. D. Banister, the LBSC Rly Chief Engineer, informed the Inspecting Officer after the collapse that there were then (i.e. in May 1891) only five cast-iron girder underbridges on the main line between London and Brighton, and the Inspecting Officer included in his Report the blunt words '... I trust that in view of this very serious accident no unnecessary time will be lost in replacing cast-iron girders ... by wrought-iron girders, both upon the main line, as well as upon other parts of the system, and this more especially where the existing girders have not the margin of safety consistent with the use of the heavy engines now employed upon the line.'

This Report was sent to the LBSC Rly Secretary on 16 June 1891, but before even the Inspecting Officer's Report had been compiled the Brighton directorate had asked Sir John Fowler to report to them on the state of the underbridges throughout the LBSC Rly. Fowler's report dated 17 June 1891 showed that there were in all 181 cast-iron underbridges on LBSC Rly lines; Fowler stated that he understood that 80 or 81 of them were to be reconstructed in the shortest time reasonably possible, and in any case within the next two to three years. Fowler concluded his report by stating that the results of his investigation did not indicate any unusual weakness in the Brighton bridges, which were neither better nor worse in that respect than those on similar lines of railway at home or abroad.

The LBSC Rly's reply to the Board of Trade's letter of 16 June was sent on 17 June, and was accompanied by a copy of Sir John Fowler's report. The company's letter was of course signed by Allen Sarle, the Secretary, who not only expressed the frank regrets of the Brighton's directors, at the 1891 accident, but stated that they had acted at the time of the 1876 accident in accordance with the opinions of their professional advisers.

The 1891 accident had very far-reaching consequences, since all railways undertook reviews of their cast-iron underbridges, and extensive works of reconstruction were undertaken.

NOTES

1. LBSC Rly Notice dated 30 March 1876.
2. LBSC Rly Notice dated 6 April 1876. Services to and from Liverpool Street are believed to have started on 11 April.
3. Had the New Cross Down Spur from Old Kent Road Junction still been in use by 2 April 1876, particulars of the signalling at the New Cross end would naturally have been included in the LBSC Rly Notice dated 30 March 1876 and referred to in Note 1 above.

4. LBSC Rly Notice No. 66, undated.
5. Table of Distances between Stations, Junctions, etc., on LBSC Rly, November 1881, 13-14 and 15-16.
6. Clark, R. H. *A Southern Region Chronology and Record, 1803-1965*, Oakwood Press, 1964, 69 and 71.
7. An LBSC Rly poster was issued in August 1890, announcing the closure of Central Croydon station on and from Monday 1 September 1890. This poster was photographically reproduced in an article by Treby, E. H., entitled 'The Central Croydon Branch' (*Railway World*, 35 (1974), 108).
8. A photograph stated to have been taken about 1890, and showing a tree bearing full foliage (thereby suggesting that the picture was taken before the Autumn), included a clear view of the station nameboard and makes it obvious that at the time of the photograph the name was Central Croydon. As an empty cab is waiting outside the station, the photograph could hardly have been taken before the station was reopened in 1886. *See Croydon: the Story of a Hundred Years*, The Croydon Natural History & Scientific Society, 1970, 20.
9. The difference between the Parliamentary description of the line (Croydon Central) and the name of the station itself (Central Croydon), will be noted (see Notes 6-8 above).
10. LBSC Rly Notice No. 100, dated June 1895.
11. LBSC Rly Notice No. 99, dated March 1895.
12. Private notes to the Author from his old friend the late Mr. J. Pelham Maitland, written about 1950 but relating to the period 1895-1906. All those statements contained in these notes which the Author has since been able to verify from official references have proved fully correct, and the Author therefore considers that the remaining as yet unverified statements are equally reliable.

In what was obviously a contributed article in a newspaper, written about the widening works south of South Croydon and the new line avoiding Redhill (see Chapter VI), it was stated that 'The first section of the doubled line was opened for passenger traffic on Tuesday 28 July [1896]'. As stated in Chapter VI, the widening south of South Croydon and the new line on to Earlswood were not opened until 5 November 1899; and hence the 1896 statement and date of partial opening must have referred to some event which appeared to an observer with inadequate knowledge, to be part of the developments south of South Croydon. In the absence so far of any evidence as to when the Down Relief line from East Croydon to South Croydon was brought into use, the Author is inclined to the opinion that this might well have been the event reported as having occurred on 28 July 1896.
13. LBSC Rly Notice No. 111, dated July 1897.

14. A contemporary statement regarding the train services from Norbury at the opening, was worded in an unfortunate manner. It reads 'Mr. J. P. Knight [then General Manager] has arranged to provide an excellent train service to Victoria Station on the one hand, and London Bridge and Liverpool Street Stations via Tulse Hill and North Dulwich, on the other'. *The Engineer*, XLV (4 January 1878), 3.

Since the Streatham Common spur was not opened until 1 January 1886 (see earlier in this chapter and Note 4 above), services from Norbury to London Bridge must have run via Selhurst and Norwood Junction; the direct route to London Bridge would then have been via New Cross (from which station there was an East London line service to Liverpool Street). Any service via Selhurst to Norwood Junction, and thence via Crystal Palace and Tulse Hill to London Bridge, with East London line connections, at Peckham Rye (to which the Liverpool Street and Old Kent Road service had been extended on 1 August 1877), would have been very round-about and could hardly be called 'excellent'.

15. Hayden's Lane until 1 October 1889.
16. L S W Rly and L B S C Rly Instruction No. 186, dated 23 April 1885.
17. The Author has seen it suggested that the name Belmont was proposed by the wife of the then station master.
18. The whole estate was, after the Second World War, named Beechholme.
19. Last page of L B S C Rly Notice No. 66, undated.
20. Badly distorted and factually incorrect statements of these events, not even presented in their correct order or context, were given in Dendy Marshall, C.F., *A History of the South Railway*, The Southern Railway Company, 1936, 316-317. Also 2nd Edition, revised by Kidner, R. W., Ian Allen, 1963, Vol. I, 232-233.
21. Also wrongly presented in Dendy Marshall, *Ibid.* 317, and 2nd Edition, *Ibid.* 232.
22. Only the bare facts are presented, of course correctly, by Banister, F. D. (Engineer of the London Brighton & South Coast Railway), in an Official Report entitled 'Historical Notes' and relating to relations with the London & Greenwich and South Eastern Railways, 1888, 14.
23. Banister, F. D. *Ibid.*, 16.
24. Badly distorted and factually incorrect statements of these events, not even presented in their correct order or context, were given in Dendy Marshall, *Ibid.*, 317; and 2nd Edition, *Ibid.*, 232-233.
25. Banister, F. D., *Ibid.*, 16.

CHAPTER SIX

Development of the Main Line from South Croydon to Brighton (1870-1899)

THE OPENING of the Mid-Sussex Junction line in 1863 and the Leatherhead–Dorking–Horsham line in 1867 (Volume II) had enabled trains between London and Croydon, on the one hand, and Ford and places west of that station, on the other hand, to be routed via Horsham. The benefit of the shortened distance of running via Horsham instead of via Brighton, was of course accompanied by two other important advantages: not only was reversal at Brighton avoided, but occupancy of the Brighton main line and of the West Coast line between Brighton and Ford was reduced. These benefits were obviously not gained by traffic to and from places on the West Coast line east of Ford, all trains to and from which had still to run via Brighton if they did not in any case start from, or terminate, there.

With the development of Hove as a residential district immediately west of Brighton, and the build-up of traffic to the west of Hove as far as Shoreham; and with the steadily growing importance of Worthing as a centre, it was decided that whenever through trains could be operated between the London direction and the West Coast line east of Ford, they should not have to run into Brighton and out again. It was therefore decided in 1874 that a loop should be built, connecting the London and West Coast lines to the north-west of Brighton terminus, and authority was given under 38 & 39 Vic. cap. 96 of 29 June 1875.

The new line started about 1 mile 20 chains before reaching Brighton from the London direction, where the main line to Brighton was on a 100-chain radius left-hand curve on a falling gradient of 1 in 264. The junction was, in fact, immediately south of Preston station. Short lengths of right-hand and left-hand curvature took the new line out of the existing main line, and brought it parallel to, and on the west side of, the latter, beside which it ran for about ¼ mile until it curved right at 14 chains radius to enter a tunnel under the high ground behind the north-west part of Brighton. On leaving the main line, the fall eased from 1 in 264 to 1 in 314 for a few chains, but then steepened to 1 in 137 and 1 in 93 as the line entered the tunnel. The latter was straight and 536 yds. long, and the falling gradient eased slightly from 1 in 93 to 1 in 100 immediately inside the entrance. The junction with the main line was made on a high embankment which had therefore to be widened, and the new line as well as the main line ran on embankment until the new line curved right towards the tunnel, which it entered after passing through a very short cutting.

On leaving the tunnel, the line continued straight for a few chains in a deep cutting, where the falling gradient eased from 1 in 100 immediately beyond the tunnel, to 1 in 139. Then followed a 15-chain right-hand curve some 25 chains long to bring the new line parallel to, and on the north side of, the West Coast line, into which the former ran just under 1¼ miles from its commencement at Brighton and immediately east of Cliftonville station. Around the 15-chain radius curve the line fell at 1 in 90. There were four overbridges south of the tunnel, but no underbridges on the new line, which was 1 mile 34 chains long and was designated the Cliftonville Spur.

Preston station, immediately north of the junction in the main line, was rebuilt to provide two island platforms, one for down trains and the other for up trains. The Down and Up main lines ran between the two platforms, and there was an ordinary double-line junction on to the new line just south of the platforms. A Down Loop line ran along the outer (east) face of the down platform, and an Up Loop line ran along the outer (west) face of the up platform. South of Preston, an additional down line, then officially designated the Second Down line, was provided to Brighton, and connections both ways were provided between the two down lines so that trains on either the Down Main or the Down Loop in Preston station, could run forward to Brighton on either the Second Down line or the Down Main line, or could run on to the Cliftonville Spur. On the Up side, there was a facing lead in the Up Spur leading into the Up Loop, so that trains off the Spur could run either onto the Up

Main or the Up Loop, but Up Main line trains from Brighton could only use the Up Main through Preston station. The Up Loop had an exit on to the Up Main at the north end of the station, and was parallelled on the west with a run-round siding; the Up Loop was signalled for starting trains back down the Spur. Signal boxes were provided at both ends of the rebuilt station, in each case on the Up side.

Cliftonville station was rebuilt so as to give an island platform on the Up (to Brighton) side. The inner face served the Up Main line, and the outer face served a Down Loop line. A left-hand junction immediately east of the station led to the Spur line, as already stated, and Up trains had to use the Up Main line on entering the station from the Shoreham (west) direction, whether they were to go forward to Brighton or to Preston. Trains from Preston, however, could either reach the Down Main through Cliftonville station, or (by continuing straight instead of curving left into the Down Main) enter the Down Loop. At the west end, trains on the Down Loop could cross the Up Main to join the Down Main. Outside (i.e. to the north of) the Down Loop was an Up Siding for freight trains, entered by a facing lead in the Up Main line west of the station, and so arranged that Up freight trains could run into the Up Siding while a train was leaving the Down Loop for the Down Main. The Up Siding gave access to the Up Yard to the north and north-west of the station, and could be left at the east end both on to the Up Main (to Brighton) and the Up Spur (to Preston). Signal Boxes were provided at both ends of the rebuilt station, in each case on the Up (north) side.

The works were brought into use in three stages, as under:

Rebuilt station at Preston, with new junction.... Sunday 25 May 1879[1]
   layout, and new signal boxes and signalling
   (Spur line itself not yet in use)

Rebuilt station at Cliftonville, with new .... Sunday 22 June 1879[2]
   junction layout, and new signal boxes and
   signalling (Spur line itself not yet in use)

Cliftonville Spur line .... Tuesday 1 July 1879[3]

Preston station was renamed Preston Park when the Spur was opened.

Attention must next be given to Keymer Junction, where the line to Lewes left the main line to Brighton by a 14-chain radius left-hand curve. The line to Lewes (the 'Keymer line') carried virtually all the traffic between the London end of the company's system, and Newhaven, Eastbourne, and Hastings. It was the rule on all railways that facing points had to be taken cautiously, even after facing point locks had been fitted, so that the severe speed restriction due to the sharp curve for Down trains on to the Keymer line, was less of a hindrance to working than might at first sight appear to have been the case. The real difficulty arose in working Up traffic off the Keymer line, as the low speed of such trains was not only liable to cause delays to the faster-moving traffic flow from Brighton, but in addition of course Up Keymer line trains completely stopped down traffic to Brighton.

It was therefore planned that the Up Keymer line should be carried over the Down and Up Brighton lines, and then swung right on a descending gradient to join the Up Brighton line. The line up to the flyover was to start over ½ mile on the Lewes side of the junction and to curve left, so that the actual flyover bridge would be some considerable way south of the existing flat junction. The line from the flyover bridge was to join the Up Brighton line well northwards of where the existing Up Keymer line joined it, as by this means the existing occupation bridge immediately north of the junction would not have to be altered. The new alignment of the Up Keymer line well to the south of the existing alignment, enabled a considerably easier curve to be planned for the new Down Keymer line, which would rejoin its existing alignment close to the point where the new Up Keymer line left its existing alignment.

Authority was granted under section 4 of 42 Vic. cap. 31 dated 23 May 1879, the powers forming part of the LBSC Rly (Various Powers) Act, 1879. The new Up Keymer connection was to be 58.30 chains long and the new Down Keymer connection 52.40 chains long.

Modifications to the Up Keymer connection were authorized under the LBSC Rly (Various Powers) Act, 1882, 45 & 46 Vic. cap. 93 dated 3 July, but eventually it was decided that the expenditure would not be justifiable and the scheme was abandoned under section 6 of the Various Powers Act of 1885 (48 & 49 Vic. cap. 67, dated 16 July). Consequential alterations to stations in the area are dealt with later in this chapter.

This was not the end of the matter, however, because an entirely new scheme was prepared 14 years later, in 1899, in the light of extensive plans for the main line itself. As such plans were themselves part of a larger scheme taken in hand in the early 1900s, it is considered best to review the 1899 Keymer scheme in a later chapter in association with other works. In the meantime, therefore, the basic layout of a double-track left-hand junction continued at Keymer Junction throughout the period covered by this chapter.

By the late 1870s, Brighton station itself was becoming in need of modernization to cater for the steadily increasing passenger traffic. The work involved extensive track and signal alterations, as well as platform extensions and a new, longer and higher, roof over the platforms. Outside, a large porte cochere was erected so that passengers joining or leaving street vehicles could do so protected from the weather. In recent years certain preservationists and architects have taken the line that the porte cochere, of iron and glass, spoiled the appearance of Mocatta's fine station building. On the other hand, however, tens of thousands of passengers must have been grateful for the protection that the structure provided, and it seems likely that the expenditure was only incurred because of complaints about the lack of shelter before the porte cochere was erected. Architectural blemish or no, the covered cab yard must undoubtedly have helped business, and was therefore no doubt welcomed by the Brighton's shareholders. The work of rebuilding the station seems to have been completed about 1883. The old and new signal boxes at Lovers Walk are shown in Plate 15.

The station's lack of accommodation for dealing with the ever-increasing numbers of trains, could not be met by adding more platforms as the site precluded lateral expansion. Hence a scheme was evolved for lengthening several of the platforms sufficiently to enable two medium-length trains to be dealt with on the same platform face, one train being at the inner or stop-block end of the platform line concerned and the other train being handled alongside the outward end of the platform. To indicate to the driver of an incoming train whether the platform line that he was about to enter was clear to the stop blocks or was partly occupied by another train, Messrs. Saxby & Farmer made use of the signalling principle that they had introduced successfully at London Bridge under similar circumstances. Briefly, each platform line in the station was provided with an arrival signal post which carried both a stop arm and a distant arm. When the line concerned was clear to the stop blocks, both the stop and the distant arms were pulled 'off'. If however a train (or even a single vehicle or engine) were at the stop-block (inner) end of the platform line concerned, only the stop arm would be pulled 'off', the distant arm being left 'on' as an indication to the driver of the incoming train that part of the platform line was already occupied and hence that he had to enter the station with extreme caution.

It had long been the rule of all railway companies that trains had to enter stations very slowly since only hand brakes were available in many instances. Even when continuous brakes became a requirement on passenger trains, railway companies retained that rule for a long period; drivers had still to bring their trains into stations on hand brakes only, leaving the continuous brake for emergency use.

Brief mention was made in Chapter V of a proposed line to Tadworth from a junction with the Epsom Downs branch, and of an independent proposal that Tadworth should be reached by means of a line up the Chipstead Valley, from a junction on the main line to Brighton. A more detailed review was left to the present chapter.

As explained in Volume II (pp. 216-217), the Epsom Downs branch from Sutton ran roughly south until it curved right to run almost west toward its terminus at Epsom Downs. The latter station was, in fact, at a lower level than where the line changed direction some way from Banstead Village, but what was much more important was that both Banstead and Epsom Downs stations were on the north slopes of the Downs, some 120-130 feet below that area of the Downs on which the Epsom racecourse was situated. South of the high ground, there are fairly flat areas extending as a tableland for some way until the steep southern escarpment of the Downs is reached. The Chipstead Valley (having left the deep dry valley south of Croydon which was utilized for the main line to Brighton) runs south-west and west into this tableland, and provides a sheltered area in which there were a number of gentlemen's country seats. The Chipstead Valley was without any railway, so that, as the crow flies, the nearest station was at Banstead on the LBSC Rly's Epsom Downs branch. It should be remembered that as long ago as the 1860s, the London Chatham & Dover Railway had schemes for the area; that company had been first in the field for a line to Epsom Downs (Volume II, pp. 204-205), and it had also proposed a line up the Chipstead Valley (Volume II, p. 249).

By 1891 local interests, headed by Mr. Cosmo Bonsor, who was a director of the Bank of England and who lived in Kingswood Warren, had decided that it would be advantageous if a railway were built to serve the upper end of the Chipstead Valley, and that the best route would be from the Banstead area, on the Epsom Downs line, thence curving left and climbing steeply, to cross under the high ground in a tunnel to reach the Tadworth area. An Act was obtained in 1892 for such a line, under 55 & 56 Vic. cap. 145, under the title of the Epsom Downs Extension Railway Act, but difficulties of various kinds arose, including the vital one that insufficient capital could be raised. The LBSC Rly was not interested in this venture, except to keep abreast of events.

Separate interests then planned a railway up the Chipstead Valley from a junction with the LBSC Rly main line at Purley (as Caterham Junction station had by then been renamed—see later), and an Act for this was obtained in 1893. This was to connect with the Epsom Downs Extension Railway, so making a through link between Purley and Sutton. Cosmo Bonsor was also behind this scheme, which was entitled the Chipstead Valley Railway Company.

Meanwhile, support for the Epsom Downs Extension Railway appeared to suggest that the capital could ultimately be raised and hence, under 60 Vic. cap. 92 of 3 June 1897, a further two years were granted before the powers expired.

The Chipstead Valley company was more fortunate in that by this time Cosmo Bonsor had become Deputy Chairman of the South Eastern Railway (he had joined that company's board in 1894). Hence the South Eastern took over the Chipstead Valley company and the line was built as a SE Rly branch, which started from Purley and extended to Tattenham Corner beyond Tadworth. At Purley, the line commenced at a junction with the Caterham line, south of the station on the down side, and curved right on a falling gradient to pass under the LBSC Rly main line. After doing so, it curved left on a rising gradient to run parallel to, and on the west (or up) side of, the Brighton main line for over a mile until it curved away to the right to enter the Chipstead Valley. Details are outside the scope of this account since it was a S E Rly line, but it must be recorded that the line was opened from Purley to Kingswood on 2 November 1897 and, after extension to Tadworth, completed to Tattenham Corner on 4 June 1901. Originally planned as a single line, it was later doubled in stages. It may also be noted here that the S E Rly line from Purley to Caterham was doubled in 1899. The 1848 and 1854 Agreements between the L BS C Rly and the S E Rly did not prevent any such line as the Chipstead Valley from being promoted or built, as the district concerned, being to the north of the S E Rly's Redhill–Guildford line, was outside the area covered by those Agreements (for details, see Volume II (Chapter II and associated Figure 2)). A new double-line junction at the north end of Purley station giving direct running to and from the Caterham line, had been brought into use on 31 October 1897.[4] It gave similar facilities to and from the Chipstead Valley line when the latter was opened.

Walton-on-the-Hill would not be served directly either by the Chipstead Valley line or by the Epsom Downs Extension Railway. A rumour was reported in 1896[5] to the effect that there was some suggestion that a line should be built between Walton-on-the-Hill and Wimbledon, but details of any such proposal have not been discovered by the Author. Tadworth station was intended to serve Walton-on-the-Hill, although a fair way from the latter.

The arrangements under which the South Eastern Railway became the owner of the line from Coulsdon to Redhill, where their line turned east towards Tunbridge, Ashford, Folkestone, and Dover, were recorded in Volume I, and it was explained in Volume II (Chapter II) that under the 1848 Agreement between the L BS C Rly and the S E Rly, tolls were abolished between the two companies where they had hitherto been payable (i.e. north of Norwood Junction). In 1849 the S E Rly had opened their line westward from Redhill through Dorking to Shalford Junction, and thence from Ash Junction to Reading.

Separate arrangements had been made between the two companies for payment by the L BS C Rly to the S E Rly for the actual use by the Brighton company of the line between Coulsdon and Redhill, depending on the amount of traffic sent over the line. An Agreement dated 1 February 1869 was applicable for 10 years and was based on a gross L BS C Rly traffic to the value of £2,500,000; under it the L BS C Rly paid the SE Rly about £14,000 per year. On expiry in 1879, this Agreement was renewed for a further 10 years, but during this second period relations between the two companies became unhappy due to the South Eastern finding that they were unable to improve their own train services because there were so many LBSC Rly trains. LBSC Rly trains were not allowed to call at Merstham, then the only intermediate station on the SE Rly-owned line.

Eventually the SE Rly appears to have tried to force the Brighton's hand by claiming a share in the latter's local traffic between London and Croydon, and in suggesting arbitration by the Attorney-General, Lord Justice Lopes. The Attorney-General, however, when he knew what would be put to him as a result of a study of the provisions of the LBSC Rly/SE Rly Agreement of 10 July 1848, declined to act on the matter. Thereupon Samuel Laing, the Brighton's Chairman, advised his shareholders at his company's half-yearly meeting on 26 January 1887, not to agree to go to arbitration on what he (Laing) considered, in the light of Lopes' informal views, was a case which the Brighton company would undoubtedly be held to be in the right.[6] The strained relationship with the South Eastern gradually became known as the 'Southern Lines Controversy', and eventually the two companies accepted the necessity for reference to an independent assessor. Hence the General Manager of the Great Northern Railway, Henry Oakley (afterwards Sir Henry) was asked to make an award. This he did in July 1889, raising the LBSC Rly's payment to the SE Rly to about £20,000 per year. The Brighton company obtained Parliamentary approval to this new Agreement in the 1890 session.

This did not, however, really settle the matter, because the SE Rly continued to complain that the heavy LBSC Rly traffic did not allow them (the SE Rly) to work their own traffic properly. Redhill, in fact, became a source of difficulty for both companies. The Author does not attach much weight to well-worn stories that the SE Rly deliberately obstructed LBSC Rly traffic by giving preference to their own (South Eastern) trains; certain SE Rly trains were no doubt hooked to precede certain LBSC Rly trains, and late running elsewhere might well have caused reactions at Redhill. As however the SE Rly owned the line for some 6 miles north of Redhill, late running of trains would have been a nuisance regardless of which company's trains were involved. Surely the basic difficulty was that inherent in the layout, as all up Tonbridge (SE Rly) traffic, and all down Reading line (SE Rly) traffic, had to cross LBSC Rly main line traffic.

Eventually the LBSC Rly took the bull by the horns and decided that the best (if not the only) solution to what seemed likely to be a never-ending difficulty, was to build a line of their own from Coulsdon to south of Redhill. By this means the LBSC Rly would not have to run over any part of the SE Rly south of Coulsdon, and they would have their own metals throughout from Corbetts Lane Junction—as, of course, would have been the case from the start if Parliament, in its wisdom, had not made it clear that separate SE Rly and London & Brighton Rly routes south of Norwood should be avoided (see Volume I, Chapter II).

At the same time the Brighton company decided to extend their local lines southward from their existing termination at South Croydon, as far as Coulsdon—where, in addition to terminal facilities, the Local lines could join the new 'avoiding' lines onwards to beyond Redhill.

At Redhill it was impracticable for the new 'avoiding' line to be taken to the west of the existing station, as such a route would have gone through the main part of the town (or, if further west, through Reigate); hence a route to the east had to be found. North of Coulsdon, however, the new Local lines would be to the west of the existing main lines. To meet these two desiderata meant crossing over (or under) the existing SE Rly main line at some intermediate point; and at Redhill it meant crossing over (or under) the Tonbridge line. Taking into consideration the gradients and curvature of the existing SE Rly lines, it was decided to start the new line some way to the north of Coulsdon station on the SE Rly (opened on 1 October 1889) with apparently some slight realignment, and to run to the west of the existing SE Rly line on a steeper rising gradient than the latter for some $1\frac{1}{2}$ miles. In that distance the line would gain sufficient height relative to the existing SE Rly line that it could be taken over the latter and then continued southwards on the east side of the existing line and roughly parallel to it. By a falling gradient the new line would eventually reach the same level as the existing line, and, continuing to fall, would pass under the

Redhill-Tonbridge line and rejoin the main LBSC Rly line itself nearly ½ mile to the south.

Extension of the Local lines southward from South Croydon was, by comparison, a much easier task, as the lines concerned were alongside the existing ones (Figure 18).

Authority for both works was given by 57 & 58 Vic. cap. 104 dated 20 July 1894, the lengths quoted in that Act being 3 miles 57.15 chains for the extension of the local lines and 6 miles 48 chains for the new 'avoiding' lines. There were no South Eastern objections to the new 'avoiding' line—after all, the SE Rly stood to benefit by it—but there were to be no intermediate stations. The Brighton company's capital was authorized to be increased by £360,000 in shares and £120,000 in loans.

Engineering works on the widening south of South Croydon were relatively light. Most of the existing (main) line was on embankment, and this therefore had to be widened and bridges extended as necessary. The chalk required for the embankments came from that taken out in the construction of the new line south of Coulsdon. Plate 16 shows the start of the widening works, south of South Croydon.

The level crossing at Stoat's Nest was abolished as part of the work. Under section 11(5) of the LBSC Rly Act of 1894, which authorized the widening works (i.e. 57 & 58 Vic. cap. 104, dated 20 July), the crossing was to be replaced by an overbridge. This permission was amended by section 11 of 59 & 60 Vic. cap. 128, dated 20 July 1896 (the LBSC Act of that year), and an underbridge had to be provided instead of an overbridge. The change was a result of the proximity of the modified Chipstead Valley line.

By contrast, engineering works on the new 'avoiding' line were very heavy. For virtually its whole length of over 6½ miles, the new line was either in cutting or tunnel, or was on embankment. After leaving the existing line at Coulsdon, the line had to cross over the main road to Brighton (now A23) twice some ¼ mile apart, as the public road curved first left and then right whilst the new railway ran virtually straight; lattice girder bridges at large skews were needed. Moreover, as, between the bridges, the line had to be taken across part of the grounds of Cane Hill Asylum (now Cane Hill Hospital) in a cutting, section 7(3) of the Act required that the line had to be temporarily fenced before and during construction. Later, the cutting,

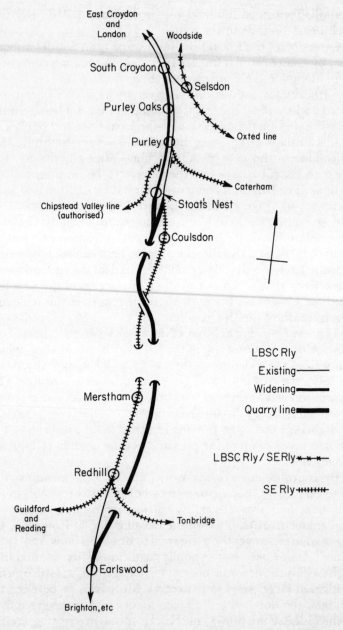

Figure 18. Quarry Line and South Croydon–Stoat's Nest Widening, as Authorized on 20 July 1894

which had been constructed with brick side walls, was roofed over and the ground replaced on top. As a result, the structure was known officially as the Cane Hill Covered Way, although to the public at large it was a tunnel. It extended for virtually the whole distance between the two skew underbridges already mentioned, so that it presented the rare (for the UK) feature of, at each end, a 'tunnel' leading straight on to an underbridge. The southern end of Mickleham Tunnel, leading straight on to a bridge over the River Mole, was another example (see Volume II, p. 107). The covered way was 411⅔ yds. long.[6,7,8]

The first ¾ mile beyond the skew bridge over the Brighton road, south of the Covered Way, was close to the west side of the existing line. Along this section the new line involved a steeper ascent than the existing one, and it therefore rose steadily above the latter as seen in notional side elevation. Hence the formation of the new line was somewhat akin to a 'bench' along much of this section, as the west (or up) side of the SE Rly cutting had to be largely removed in order that the cutting for the new line could be made. A diagrammatic cross-section of a typical part of this work is shown in Figure 19 (p. 123). The latter is intended to depict the general form of construction only, as seen looking to the south, and the Author wishes to stress that it is not to any scale. At the end of this ¾ mile 'half-cutting', the new railway curved right at 140 chains radius, that curve reversing into a 50-chain left-hand curve to takm the line over the SE Rly by a girder bridge at a considerable skew; this reverse curve was in normal chalk cutting. Along part of the length between the second skew bridge over the Brighton road just south of the Covered Way, and the bridge over the SE Rly, the new line occupied the general site of the Croydon, Merstham & Godstone Railway (see Volume I), although it was at a lower level than the old horse railway.

South of the bridge over the SE Rly line, the new line entered a chalk cutting some 50 chains long, before reaching the new Merstham Tunnel. The sides of this cutting were up to 100 feet deep in places, but the works—although close to the original very deep cutting—were sufficiently far to the east of the latter that the construction of the new cutting did not involve any removal of chalk from the top of the east (or down) side of the original cutting. The formation level of the new cutting was of the order of 25 ft. above that of the old line, at the commencement of the new tunnel, which was roughly parallel to the existing Merstham Tunnel.

As originally planned, the new tunnel (originally also called Merstham) was to be some 1743 yds. long, but under section 5 of 59 & 60 Vic. cap. 128 of 20 July 1896 (the LBSC Rly Act, 1896), the tunnel was to be extended at the north end by about 220 yds., and at the south end by about 160 yds. As built, it was recorded as 2113⅓ yds. long;[9,10] it was straight except for a short length of right-hand 80-chain radius curve at the south end. The first few chains included the final rise from Stoat's Nest, but the major part of the tunnel was on a falling gradient of 1 in 206 towards the south so that the tunnel drainage was in that direction.

Beyond the tunnel there was a relatively short cutting and then the line was more or less continuously on embankment for about 1¾ miles until it reached the other tunnel, which was necessary to carry the new railway under the eminence known as Red Hill, where the new line passed to the east of Redhill station. At each end of this tunnel there were short lengths of covered way, that at the south end being under the SE Rly's Tonbridge line and sidings. The tunnel and associated covered ways were straight, the total length being 648⅓ yds.[11,12]

Some 16 bridges were needed other than those already mentioned, whilst one additional underbridge had to be built to the north of old (closed in 1856) Stoat's Nest station in order that the level crossing immediately south of that station (Volume I, pp. 125 and 166) could be closed under section 11(5) of the 1894 Act as amended by section 11 of the 1896 Act. This new bridge had, of course, to be wide enough to carry the extended Local lines as well as the existing Main lines.

There is no need for a description to be given here of the alignment and gradients of the extended local lines, since these were, in essence, the same as those already given for the adjacent main lines (Volume I, Chapter VII). The new 'avoiding' line started by a tangent from the existing main lines which were slightly realigned just before the latter became SE Rly property. At the point of junction, the existing lines were on a very short left-hand curve, which was put in to facilitate laying the junction and which was later recorded as of 60 chains radius; the existing lines were rising at 1 in 263.[13] The point of junction was known as Stoat's Nest, although well to the south of the existing (but long closed) station of that name. A rise at 1 in 100, along which the extended local lines joined the new line, led up to the Covered Way, which itself was on a rising gradient of 1 in 125; and, after a short length of easier but broken gradients the climb settled down to 1 in 165. This gradient was maintained to the summit, a few chains inside the long tunnel. The fall now started, and continued practically to the end of the new line. Initially it was at 1 in 206 to the south end of the tunnel, but then eased to 1 in 230 for some ¾ mile. After there, it steepened to 1 in 200 to the end of the covered approach to Red Hill Tunnel, and steepened further to 1 in 163 through practically the whole length of that tunnel and its two covered extensions. At the south end, there was a slight local summit formed by a rise at 1 in 254 and a succeeding fall at 1 in 180, as the line crossed an underbridge.

All curvature was easy, mostly of 80 chains radius or more, but there was a 50-chain left-hand curve some 15 chains long to bring the line across the SE Rly from the west side on which it approached the skew bridge involved; and the line joined the existing line just north of Earlswood by means of a 40-chain left-hand curve some 20 chains long. The official distance from South Croydon station to Earlswood station was 10 miles 27.83 chains.[14]

Two new stations were built, and South Croydon and Purley (as Caterham Junction had become in 1888) were extended. The new stations were Purley Oaks, just over 1 mile 13 chains south of South Croydon, and about 74½ chains north of Purley; and Stoat's Nest, just over 1 mile 37 chains south of Purley. Purley Oaks had platforms for the local lines only. Stoat's Nest was sited just before (i.e. north of) the point where the extended local lines joined the new 'avoiding' lines; it had a side platform for the Down local; an island platform serving the Up local and a bay road; and another side platform outside a second bay road. The two bay roads were separated by a middle road, and all three were extended into a fan of carriage sidings, with adjacent goods sidings south of the station. At South Croydon, the two existing terminal platforms on the Local side of the station, were used for local traffic to and from the south. It would appear that the main line part of the station was added before the widening was done, but the Author has not yet been able to confirm this.

The works for the extension of the Local lines did not present any particular difficulties to the contractors, Messrs. Joseph Firbank, although a considerable quantity of chalk was needed for widening the existing embankments.

Construction of the new 'avoiding' line was, however, much more difficult in view of the fact that not only was there a very large quantity of chalk to be moved from north of the new Merstham Tunnel, but a considerable amount of it was needed for embankments south of the tunnel. Hence the contractors for the new line, Messrs. Oliver & Son, no doubt had to work with Messrs. Firbank to ensure that there was adequate chalk for the widening works to be done by Firbank, but no more.

The construction of the original line from Croydon to Merstham involved the excavation of a long and very deep cutting in chalk on the northern approach to Merstham Tunnel (see Volume I). Only some of that chalk was needed to construct the various embankments between Croydon and Coulsdon, to supplement material excavated from cuttings along that length. The very large surplus from the great cutting was mostly dumped on a site close to the west of the line, south of Coulsdon. The spoil-banks so created about 1838–1840 were thus on the route to be followed by the new 'avoiding' line, and hence they had to be cleared away and the ground levelled as part of the works undertaken by Joseph Firbank; not only was the new Stoat's Nest station on the extended Local lines to be immediately north of this site, but the sidings south of that station were to be on a site that was then hollow. Additionally, chalk would be required for the widened embankments northwards to South Croydon. When the hollow had been filled and levelled, a quantity of the old chalk was still surplus after allowance had been made for whatever was needed for the widened embankments; this surplus was got rid of by filling worked-out gravel pits in the area.

The Author has been unable to find any proper engineering description of the works as a whole, which were started in 1896. What was clearly a contributed article on the whole of the widening works and the new line, from South Croydon to Earlswood, was published in a local Surrey newspaper on Friday, 11 September 1896,[15] as a reprint from a London daily paper 'of Tuesday last'. Whilst ostensibly the original publication (which the Author has not seen) would therefore have been on

Tuesday 8 September, the Author has on more than one occasion found that the use of the word 'last' in the sense that it was employed in the local newspaper, implied that the event referred to had occurred in the week previous to that of publication (i.e., in this instance, on Tuesday 1 September 1896). The Author has only personally seen the article as it appeared in the local newspaper.

Whilst the article concerned does not contain any data not otherwise known to the Author, it does include one statement for which he is unable to account—namely, 'The first section of the doubled line was opened for passenger traffic on Tuesday 28 July'. According to the copy of the official Opening Notice[16] in the Author's library, the new lines between South Croydon, Stoat's Nest and Earlswood were brought into use throughout on the same date (namely, 5 November 1899); there is no suggestion of there having been any earlier opening, particularly for passenger traffic, as the Opening Notice concerned states clearly that the new stations (e.g. Purley Oaks) were opened on the same date. It should also be noted that the new 'avoiding' line between Stoat's Nest and Earlswood was in fact only used for freight traffic on and from 5 November 1899, the three intermediate signal boxes then being installed (i.e. Star Lane, Quarry, and Worsted Green respectively, from north to south) not being ready for use.

Hence, in the absence of any confirmatory official data and having regard to what was clearly stated in the Opening Notice for 5 November 1899, the Author feels that the statement in the newspaper article referred to above, to the effect that there was a partial opening for passenger traffic on 28 July 1896, must be suspect. The statement may have referred to the opening of the Down Relief line from East Croydon to South Croydon (see Note 11 to Chapter V), and if so was, of course, an irrelevancy as regards the new works south of South Croydon.

A replacement box was provided at South Croydon Junction, south of the previous box and in the fork of the junction with the Oxted lines. Two entirely new boxes, together with a shunting box, were erected at Stoat's Nest, where the existing cabin became the North box.

Although, as stated above, the Author has been unable to find any adequate engineering account of the complete works, he considers it likely that an early start was made at the south end of the long tunnel in order to form an access road to the sites of the working shafts for that tunnel and of the very deep and long cutting to the north of it. As already stated, there was a lengthy embankment south of the long tunnel, and hence most of the fill for this must have come from the cutting north of that tunnel. As the southerly face of the North Downs is, in general, steep, the direct transference of excavated material over the hill, even with access roads, must have entailed considerable difficulties. To the Author's mind it might well have been easier if some of it had been transferred over the existing S E Rly until the tunnel was sufficiently advanced for the contractors to use it themselves; the contractors would in any case have used locomotives on temporary tracks along the length of the new line. It was naturally far easier to make the new cutting than the original one nearby, as by the 1890s mechanical plant was in regular use by contractors on all large jobs (e.g. dams, harbour works, etc., as well as railways). Steam-driven excavators and shovels made the carrying out of such works a very different proposition to the enormous amount of manual labour, with assistance by horses, that was the normal means of carrying out large contracts in the days when the main line to Brighton was being built, and for a considerable period afterwards.

It was stated that the cost of the new Merstham Tunnel was about £85,000,[17] and that the costs of the new line from Stoat's Nest to Earlswood, together with those of the widening between South Croydon and Stoat's Nest, were about £350,000.[17]

It appears that not all the chalk excavated north of the new tunnel, was required south of it, and that there was a surplus which had to be disposed of before the line was finished. The Author was told more than 40 years ago, by more than one elderly person, that chalk trains were run from the Coulsdon area towards London, returning empty, in the 1890s; but the only use for such chalk then, in the London area of the L B S C Rly, would apparently have been to widen short embankments between Streatham Common and Norbury, and in the vicinity of Selhurst. Just before this Volume went to the publishers, the Author received information[18] that, according to two elderly retired railwaymen, who had both since died but who had, in their youth, seen such chalk trains, the material was destined for the Crystal Palace. The Author is unable to suggest for what purpose the chalk was required at the Palace. Disposal to the

South Eastern Railway, for use on the Chipstead Valley line, might be thought to be a more likely way of getting rid of the surplus, but such arrangements would not have necessitated trains going towards the Crystal Palace, or otherwise into London.

The Author has since heard, on more than one occasion, a story of an alleged incident concerning a connection passage between the two Merstham Tunnels. Since rail level in the new tunnel is some 25 ft. higher than that in the original one, whilst the two tunnels are quite close together, a connection passage would have had a steep inclination. Moreover, the value of any

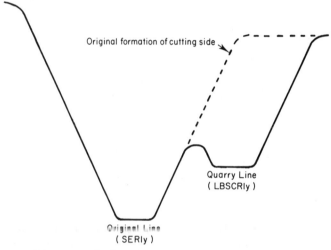

Original formation of cutting side

Quarry Line
(LBSCRly)

Original Line
(SERly)

Figure 19. Diagrammatic Cross-Section of Old and New Cuttings South of Coulsdon/Stoat's End Area, Looking South (see p. 117)   *Not to scale*

such passage must be questioned, especially as the two tunnels were in the ownership of separate railway companies. Nevertheless, the Author asked for records to be investigated. He was advised that there was no indication of such a passage, and hence that the alleged incident could not have taken place.

The extension of the local lines from South Croydon to Stoat's Nest, and the new line from there to Earlswood, were both brought into use on Sunday 5 November 1899,[14] together with the new stations at Purley Oaks and Stoat's Nest. When opened, the new 'avoiding' line was at first used for freight only, and was officially called the Through line, but it was not long before it became known as the Quarry line,[19] and later that became the official designation. Passenger trains started working over the new line on 1 April 1900.

Attention must now be drawn to the growth of Brighton itself; by 1861, 20 years after the town was connected to London by railway, the population of Brighton was 87,000; and by 1881 it had risen to 110,000. An outline of schemes and proposals put forward even before the Brighton main line was authorized, are given in Volume I. A recrudescence of proposals during the 1860s, with either London Chatham & Dover Railway or South Eastern Railway support (in one case as a joint scheme by those companies), was dealt with in Volume II, Chapter IX. The financial crisis following the collapse in 1866 of Messrs. Overend, Gurney & Co., acted as a damper, and no further serious moves to bring about competition to Brighton were made until the 1870s.

The first of the new schemes to be noticed here was the Metropolitan & Brighton Railway, which proposed to operate from Moorgate Street in the City of London, over the 'Widened Lines' and across the River Thames to Blackfriars, thence either via the joint SE Rly/LCD Rly connection to Metropolitan Junction, and down the South Eastern to New Beckenham; or via the LCD Rly to the Kent House area. Thus far no new construction would be needed. From the Beckenham area, there was to be a new line on a route generally similar to the various schemes outlined in Volume II, Chapter IX, as far as Horsted Keynes (south of East Grinstead); but from there an entirely new route was planned, going south-south-west to the vicinity of Lindfield and then south-west to the Hurstpierpoint area, after which Brighton would be reached via the Newtimber gap. From Hurstpierpoint to Brighton the route would have been similar to proposals of the 1830s. The route of the Metropolitan & Brighton would have crossed that of the LBSC Rly between Haywards Heath and Keymer Junction. The Engineer for this 1875 scheme was Edward Wilson. The South Eastern's Chairman was also the Chairman of the Metropolitan Railway, and was no doubt concerned with the proposed line.

Another scheme was launched in Brighton by a gentleman named Verrall in 1883, under the title of the Brighton Direct Railway (later revived as the London, Reigate & Brighton Railway). This was to start from two places in the London area; one line was to commence at Kensington (now Olympia) on the

1 KINGSCOTE
Road underbridge, with East
Grinstead-Horsted Keynes Line
on high embankment, carried
over Road B.2110. Photographed
about 1960   (Author)

2 OXTED VIADUCT
As completed in 1884
         (National Railway Museum)

3 EAST GRINSTEAD

Retaining wall for Dr. Whyte's garden, as completed in 1884. Looking north towards St. Margaret's Junction   (National Railway Museum)

4 EDENBRIDGE TUNNEL

North (on left) and south sections of tunnel, on either side of bridge under South Eastern Railway. View looking east along S E Rly, towards Edenbridge

(Lens of Sutton)

5 MARK BEECH TUNNEL
South entrance, on 27 February 1977 (Author)

6 LEWES
Looking north-east towards the original (1846) Friars Walk station, from site of
north-east end of second (1857) station, on 11 September 1976 (Author)

7 BRAMLEY & WONERSH STATION
Looking north towards Peasmarsh Junction and Guildford, on 15 May 1965
(Author)

8 SLINFOLD BOX
Originally the North box. Looking south-east on 15 May 1965 (Author)

9 LAKE LANE CROSSING
Looking east towards Yapton in January 1901. Down Royal train conveying
H.R.H. The Prince of Wales   (Author's Collection)

10 NEW CROSS (Now New Cross Gate)
Showing, in middle distance, Incline from East London Up Junction to Cold
Blow. Millers' Sidings on main-line level on left, Up Side connection down to
East London line on embankment on right, and roads to Ballarat Sidings in centre
in distance, as in 1963   (G. H. Platt)

11 FOREST HILL
Remains of Up platform of London & Croydon Railway's Dartmouth Arms
station of 1839, beside Up Local (now Up Slow) line south of Forest Hill station
on 15 April 1971 (Author)

12 OLD KENT ROAD JUNCTION
Looking north towards London Bridge (roads curving to left of far signal box).
Showing original and replacement (in distance) signal boxes, probably in the 1890s
(National Railway Museum)

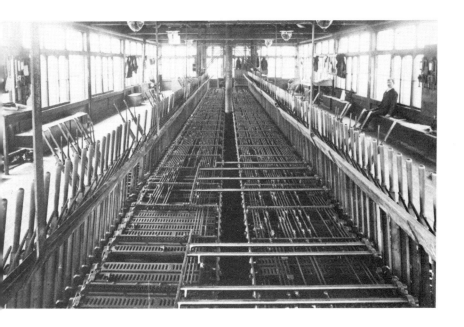

13 LONDON BRIDGE NORTH BOX
Looking north soon after installation in 1878, and showing gridiron interlocking.
This 280-lever box was not a block post; it regulated the working of the "main
line" part of the L B S C Rly station, under the control of an adjacent S E Rly block
post   (National Railway Museum)

14 EAST CROYDON SOUTH BOX
Photographed on 1 May 1955   (Author)

15 LOVERS WALK BOXES
Original signal box of about 1862, showing replacement box slightly nearer to
Brighton, on left. Photographed about 1880   (Lens of Sutton)

16 SOUTH CROYDON
Looking south from south of station, showing (on right) extension of Local lines
to Stoat's Nest in hand. Oxted lines on left. Up Royal train conveying H.R.H.
The Prince of Wales. Photographed in summer of 1899
(National Railway Museum)

17 HIGH LEVEL LINES BRIDGES BETWEEN BATTERSEA PARK AND
POUPART'S JUNCTION (TO RIGHT), OVER LOW-LEVEL AND
ex-L C D Rly LINES
Bridge for Fourth-road Widening (c. 1905), with overhead stiffeners to main
girders, nearest camera; original (1867) bridge behind. Looking north-east from
Longhedge Junction box on 27 September 1952 (Author)

18 FOUR SPAN BRIDGE
Bridge carries High Level lines between Battersea Park and Poupart's Junction,
over Ludgate lines (centre) and West London Extension Railway lines (on right).
Looking south on 4 May 1973 (Author)

19 POUPART'S JUNCTION BOX

Photographed during Railway Strike on 18–19 August 1911. Note that nameboard shows the spelling as "Pouparts'" (National Railway Museum)

20 SELHURST

Local lines shortly before completion on 6 July 1903. Looking towards Thornton Heath in early summer of that year (Lens of Sutton)

21 CHEAM
Looking east towards Sutton about 1906 (Lens of Sutton)

22 BANDON HALT
Looking towards Waddon, probably soon after opening on 11 June 1906, with up motor train (locomotive at rear) (Lens of Sutton)

23 ELECTRIC MOTOR COACH
South London Line services   (Lens of Sutton)

24 ELECTRIFICATION
Supports for overhead conductors, west of Denmark Hill, about winter 1908/
1909. Looking west towards East Brixton   (Author's collection)

25 ELECTRIFICATION
Trial train at Peckham Rye, crossing from Up Local to Down Road, about
summer 1909   (Lens of Sutton)

26 ELECTRIFICATION
Special cantilever supports between Poupart's Junction and Clapham Junction,
designed for possible fifth road through uprights of structures. Electric train on Up
Local line, and L S W Rly on far right. Photographed about the summer of 1911
                                                    (National Railway Museum)

27 ELECTRIFICATION
Clapham Junction – Balham sec
with Main as well as Local lines
electrically equipped. Victoria t
Gatwick (via Quarry Line) race
special on Down Main line abou
1912
Note use of L B S C Rly Royal
stock behind front brake van
(Lens of S

28 Mr. H.W.B. EASTLAND
Station Master, West Croydon,
1911-1924. Photographed abou
(Miss Joan Ea

29 ELECTRIFICATION
Old part of West Croydon station, showing limited headroom for supporting
conductors. Photographed about the spring of 1925

(National Railway Museum)

30 ELECTRIFICATION
Arrival of inaugural electric train at Carshalton Beeches, en route for Sutton, on
31 March 1925. Station still under reconstruction from former Beeches Halt, and
officially opened, with public electric services, on 1 April 1925   (Lens of Sutton)

31 SOUTH CROYDON
Brighton to Battersea Yard (via R...
freight train on Up Main line, ben...
"Overhead" electrical equipment...
Photographed about the summer ...
1925   (Lens of S...

32 LITTLEHAMPTON
Photograph taken c.1930
                        (Lens of S...

West London Extension Railway, and to run via Wimbledon, Merton, and Morden to join the second line west of Sutton. The second line was to have its own City terminus in Queen Victoria Street, more or less on the site occupied by the present Blackfriars station of British Railways. By running powers over the London Chatham & Dover Railway it was to reach West Dulwich and then run west of the Crystal Palace area south-west to Sutton. From the junction of the two lines, the route was to lie south-west near Epsom College, and then to go through the North Downs towards Walton-on-the-Hill before turning east-south-east to Buckland, west of Reigate. From there the route was to be through Charlwood and Poynings, then west of the Devil's Dyke to enter Brighton from the west to a station near the Pavilion. A branch was to lead to Portslade. The engineers were Messrs. Brunlees and McKerrow; the initial scheme seems to have been engineered by Mr. Aitken.

Dissatisfaction with the existing LBSC Rly service to Brighton, caused a suggestion to be made in 1896 that a new line should be built from the SE Rly at Merstham, to Brighton.[20] The route proposed was to the west of the LBSC Rly main line, passing through, or near, Charlwood, Colgate, and Plummers Plain. It would then go between Bolney and Cowfold, and would reach Brighton via Newtimber. It was thought that no tunnelling would be needed. Such a route was not altogether unlike that surveyed by Fulton for Rennie in 1829-30.[21]

If the South Eastern had evinced any support for such a proposal, such action would have been contrary to one of the provisions of the 1848 Agreement with the LBSC Rly.[22] This scheme, like large numbers of others put forward over the years, for lines in competition with existing ones in various parts of the United Kingdom, did not come to anything.

By the end of the nineteenth century, the practicability of a future for electric railway traction had been established, and hence schemes for new lines to Brighton arose, the first in 1899. As, however, these schemes, and their repercussions, were almost entirely associated with the twentieth century, they will be dealt with in a subsequent chapter.

When the Post Office was founded, it was essentially for the purpose of dealing with letters. With the coming of railways, the latter soon began to be used wherever practicable for the long-distance transport of mail, Royal Mail road coaches being progressively withdrawn as railway facilities became available. Parcels continued to be dealt with by carriers, and the railways soon obtained a large share of this business: they provided their own collection and delivery services for those who needed door-to-door facilities for parcels as well as for other goods.

In 1883 the Post Office decided that parcels traffic should be handled by Royal Mail, as well as letters, of course using railway facilities for long distances but the Post Office doing delivery from their own offices at the end of the railway journey. Railway charges for actually carrying the parcels seem to have suggested to the Post Office that it could save money if it handled the whole business itself, so in 1887 horse-drawn Royal Mail road coaches reappeared on routes from which they had vanished some 40–45 years before, and were used for the conveyance of Parcel Mails.

The first service was between London and Brighton, two return trips being made each 24 hours. Shortly afterwards similar services were started between London and several places within about 70 miles of the capital; those services to towns in or near LBSC Rly territory were to Tunbridge Wells and to Guildford. Horse-drawn Royal Mail coaches for the carriage of Parcel Mails continued into Edwardian times, the Brighton route, at any rate, being still so operated at least until late 1904.[23] The Author has not found any figures showing the extent to which the LBSC Rly's revenue from parcels traffic fell off as a result of the diversion of some business from rail to road.

Horley station was rebuilt about 1883 with side platform loops and centre through roads.

Certain new stations were built on the main line to Brighton, and others were renamed, during the period covered by this chapter. In chronological order, the first change was at Keymer Junction.

A line direct to Lewes had been opened in 1847 (Volume I, Chapter XIII), the junction with the main line to Brighton being some ½ mile north of Burgess Hill station on the main line. The actual village of Keymer lies to the south of the parish and is east of Hassocks. To enable passengers from the areas of St. John's Common and Burgess Hill, to reach Lewes without having to travel either via Haywards Heath or via Brighton, trains on the Keymer line called at Keymer Crossing, immediately on the Lewes side of Keymer Junction; and as recorded in

Volume II (Appendix to Chapter XIII, and amplified in Note 9 to that chapter), station facilities were provided at the crossing from late 1854.

As already stated earlier in the present chapter, authority was given, under the LBSC Rly (Various Powers) Act, 1879, for the construction of a new Up Keymer line in the vicinity of the junction, involving a flyover across the two Brighton main lines; and for a re-aligned Down Keymer line with an easier left-hand curve from its junction off the Down Main line. Modifications to the alignment of the Up Keymer line, authorized in 1882 (see earlier in this chapter) did not affect the overall principles of the scheme, which was such that the existing Keymer Junction station would not be served by the rearranged layout. Hence Keymer Junction station was closed on 1 November 1883. This withdrawal of facilities for direct travel to and from the Lewes direction was the cause of local resentment although those facilities were hardly likely to have been heavily utilized.

Hence when the Brighton sought permission to abandon their authorized rearrangement at Keymer Junction, authority was given to them subject to a proviso that a new station was to be provided north of the junction. Section 9 of 48 & 49 Vic. cap. 67, dated 16 July 1885, stated that

> In lieu of Keymer Junction Station which has been closed by the Company, the Company shall on or before 1 July 1886 make and for ever after maintain and work a passenger station on their main line between London and Brighton on the south side of Leylands Road (formerly called Lye Lane) in the parish of Keymer.

Not less than three trains each way each weekday, and not less than two trains each way on Sundays, were to call at the station for Hastings line traffic. The company was liable to a penalty of £20 for each default.

Construction of the new station involved widening the embankment on which it was partly formed.

The new station does not seem to have been opened until 1 August 1886 (i.e., one month later than stipulated by the 1885 Act); it was given the revived name of Keymer Junction. It had side platforms only, and no freight facilities. The signal box was at the south end of the up platform. October 1886 was very wet and the widened embankment slipped, causing a length of the up platform to collapse, taking with it the waiting room. The station was renamed Wivelsfield on 1 July 1896;[24] as already explained, the village of Keymer lies well south of the area which was, however, within the parish of that name. The village of Wivelsfield lies north-east of the station.

Caterham Junction station was renamed Purley on 1 October 1888. The new name was derived from that of the Pirelea family, who once owned the district; one descendant was Reginald de Pirle (1332), and a later one was John de Purle.[25] The opening by the South Eastern Railway on 1 October 1889 of a new station at Coulsdon, 1 mile 66 chains south of Purley and only a few chains south of the start of that company's ownership of their section of the main line onwards to Redhill, has been briefly mentioned earlier in this chapter.

Between South Croydon and Purley certain alterations took place which must now be recorded. As already stated in Volume II, p. 303, Selsdon signal box had been erected between South Croydon and Purley (then Caterham Junction), about 1865. This box was abolished on 29 January 1882 and was replaced by Purley Intermediate, some 1000 yds. farther south. Finally, Purley Intermediate was itself closed on 23 July 1899, and was replaced by Purley Oaks, about 300 yds. to the south again. Purley Oaks station was, as already recorded earlier in this chapter, opened on 5 November 1899, with platforms on the Local lines only; the new station was a few chains north of Purley Oaks box, itself on the down side of the line.

The last important change which needs recording in this chapter was the building of a new station south of Horley to cater for the racecourse that had been established on the up side of the line after Croydon steeplechase had been closed in November 1890. The new station was just under a mile south of Horley, and 2 miles 54 chains north of Three Bridges. On the Down side, there were an island platform between the existing Down Main line and a new loop line. On the Up side, there were an island platform between the existing Up Main line and a new loop line; and outside the Up Loop a second up loop served by a single-sided up platform with direct footpath connections to the racecourse. Sidings for holding race trains for return workings, were also provided. The new station, named Gatwick, was then used only for race traffic. It was completed in September 1891, there being signal boxes at each end of the station, both on the Down side. The boxes were brought into use on 1 October 1891.[26] An Up Relief line was opened from Gatwick to Horley in October 1892.

A local proposal was made in 1896 that a station should be provided to serve Salfords, between Earlswood and Horley,[27] but the LBSC Rly did not respond. See, however, Chapter XI for a First World War development on this matter.

Widening at Earlswood and Three Bridges had been proposed in 1890.

One other matter needs to be noted, in connection with Redhill station which had been rebuilt by the SE Rly in 1858 (Volume II, Chapter XIII, Appendix). In that rebuilding, the loop roads were protected by extensions to the platform roofs, carried on rows of cast-iron columns between the through roads and the loops; this practice was at one time common on many railways, and the LBSC Rly itself had various examples. It was satisfactory provided that adequate space for the columns was left between the through road and the loop next to it, but at Redhill this was apparently not the case. As locomotive boilers were increased in size and, as a result, had to be more highly pitched, footplate crews could no longer see over them, and hence had perforce to put their heads outside weather-boards and cabs in order to get a reasonable view ahead. Accidents resulted at places such as Redhill where clearances were limited, and led to a warning being included on page 10 of the LBSC Rly 1882 Appendix. The roofing over the loops was later removed, the rows of columns being of course abolished at the same time.

At Three Bridges, facing leads in the Down Main line, on to the Horsham and East Grinstead lines, had been put in by 1890. Down and up bays at the London end of Haywards Heath were put in in 1883.

Mention need only be made of one other proposal for a new line associated with the main line to Brighton, during the period covered by this chapter. In 1874 plans were deposited for the South Caterham Railway, to run from Purley to Caterham. The existing line from Purley (then Caterham Junction) to Caterham was by that date South Eastern Railway property, so that any review of the proposals would be outside the scope of the present account.

To show typical signalling arrangements of the 1870s, the Author has selected Burgess Hill as being representative of a small intermediate station on the main line. The original from which Figure 20 has been prepared, is dated 1 May 1874.

Only one accident on the main line to Brighton need be referred to in this account. This occurred at Wivelsfield on 23 December 1899. An up boat train from Newhaven had been stopped by signal at Wivelsfield in dense fog, and was just starting again under a clear signal when it was run into by an up train from Brighton. Whilst this was, in essence, a simple case of a run-by in dense fog, there were a number of features which contributed to this error.

(a) In the first place, Wivelsfield's up distant and up home were in the form of controls on Keymer Junction's up distant and up home levers, both from Burgess Hill and from Keymer Crossing on the Lewes line; Wivelsfield's only independent up signal was his starter, beyond the London end of the up platform.

Hence Wivelsfield could have a train which he had not accepted, coming up to what amounted to his Up Home (because it also functioned as Keymer Junction's Up Home), while he (Wivelsfield) still had one at his Up Starter (although the two signals were 895 yds. apart).

No doubt this had actually occurred from time to time over the years, but no trouble had been caused as the second train had always stopped at the Up Home.

(b) In the second place, Keymer Junction's Up Main distant, although situated at the London end of Burgess Hill station, was not placed under Burgess Hill's Up Starter but was on a separate post directly opposite to that starter and so on the down side of the line. In other words, in thick weather a driver might find it virtually impossible to see both signals simultaneously. Keymer Junction's Up Main Distant signal was a high one to give visibility above the overbridge at the north end of Burgess Hill station, the arm and lamp being 65 and 61 ft. above rail level respectively, but a co-acting arm and lamp were provided 18 ft. and 14 ft. respectively above rail level. Keymer Junction's Up Main Home signal was 58 ft. above rail level, with the lamp 54 ft. high. There were no co-acters to the Up Main

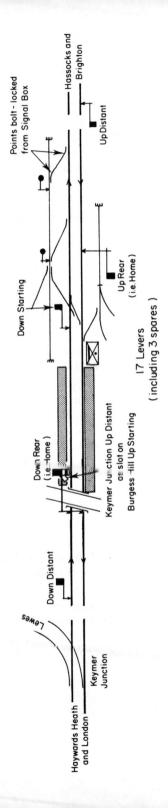

Figure 20. Burgess Hill: Signalling to be installed in 1874
Taken from Messrs. Saxby & Farmer's plan dated 1 May 1874. Note square-ended semaphore Distant signals

Home. The Home was 700 yds. beyond the Distant, and 142 yds. short of the box.

(c) In the third place, Keymer Junction box was built very high, and hence the signalman could not quickly reach ground level to lay detonators in an emergency, or even to comply with Rule 68A.[28] This was a serious disadvantage of high boxes, as noted in Volume II, pp. 287-288. The Junction box was 315 yds. from Wivelsfield box, whose Up Starter was 438 yds. beyond that box.

(d) In the fourth place, due to a combination of circumstances, fogmen were not on duty at a number of important points, including Keymer Junction's Up Main Distant.

In the ordinary way, the 1745 Brighton to Victoria preceded, from Keymer Junction, the 1735 Newhaven-Victoria and London Bridge, but the former was some seven minutes late in starting on this particular evening and dropped time on the road due to slow running in foggy conditions, although not checked by signals. The Newhaven train, in contrast, ran well, and hence was allowed by Keymer Junction, quite properly, to precede that from Brighton; but it (the Newhaven train) was itself stopped at Wivelsfield's starter, waiting 'line clear' (i.e. in modern parlance, train out of section) from Folly Hill box (the next one towards London) behind the 1720 Lewes up. The driver of the 1745 Brighton up admitted missing Keymer Junction's Up Main Distant (also acting as Wivelsfield's Up Distant) and the Junction box's Up Main Home (also acting as Wivelsfield's Up Home), but undoubtedly took a chance that the road ahead was clear for him as it had been from Brighton, and that the Newhaven train would also be late and hence would, as usual, follow him.

The Inspecting Officer was not impressed with the signalling arrangements and recommended that these be changed. He also considered that Keymer Junction Up Main Home signal should have a co-acting arm and lamp. Further, he considered that better arrangements were needed to ensure that fogmen were more easily obtainable than most unfortunately was the case prior to the collision. The accident resulted in six deaths, whilst 20 were injured.

NOTES

1. LBSC Rly Notice No. 32, dated 23 May 1879.
2. LBSC Rly Notice No. 34, dated 20 June 1879.
3. The date is correctly given in Dendy Marshall, C.F. *A History of the Southern Railway*, The Southern Railway Company, 1936, 308, but is wrongly shown as 1 July 1889 in the 2nd Edition of that work, revised by Kidner, R. W. (Ian Allan, 1963, Vol. I, 226).
4. LBSC Rly Notice No. 112, dated October 1897.
5. *The Surrey Mirror*, 14 February 1896, 5.
6. *The Railway News*, XLVII (Supplement to 29 January 1887), 190.
7. Taken from LBSC Rly Notice No. 121, dated 31 October 1899.
8. The Southern Railway's official length was 417 yds.
9. Taken from LBSC Rly Notice No. 121, dated 31 October 1899.
10. The LBSC Rly's later official length, and the Southern Railway's official length, was 2,113 yds.
11. Taken from LBSC Rly Notice No. 121, dated 31 October 1899.
12. The LBSC Rly's later official length was given as 502 yds., and thus represented the length of the actual tunnel portion.

   The Southern Railway's official length was 649 yds., this again regarding the two lengths of covered way as part of the whole.
13. Official figure (see Volume I, p. 117). A gradient of 1 in 264 (i.e. 20 ft. to the mile) was intended.
14. LBSC Rly Notice No. 121, dated 31 October 1899. The new junction south of Stoat's Nest was actually put in on 24 September of that year.
15. *The Surrey Mirror*, 11 September 1896, 2.
16. LBSC Rly Notice No. 121, dated 31 October 1899.
17. *Tuesday Mirror and Reigate Borough Advertiser*, 10 April 1900, 4.
18. Private communication from Mr. J. T. Charman to the Author, enclosing copies of relevant pages of a letter to Mr. Charman from Mr. W. G. Tharby (well known for his knowledge of the Surrey Iron Railway and the Croydon, Merstham & Godstone Railway, and referenced as such by the Author in Volume I, pp. 24-25). Mr. Tharby died in the summer of 1977.
19. Because at the south end of the new Merstham Tunnel, it ran immediately to the west of the quarry that had been the southern end of the Croydon, Merstham & Godstone Railway (see Volume I).

   The quarry was connected by rail to the South Eastern Railway a short distance north of Merstham station, the siding (forming a connection with the Down line approaching Merstham) going up an incline and then curving to the north east to enter the quarry. The new LBSC Rly line had to be taken under this siding, the bridge carrying the siding being very close to the south portal of the new Merstham Tunnel.

20. *The Surrey Mirror*, 10 January 1896, 3.
21. Volume I, 66.
22. Volume II, chapter II.
23. *The Times*. 1 April 1959. Article by A Correspondent, on Royal Mail coach services, written to commemorate the final ending, on 31 March 1909, of Royal Mail horse-drawn coaches, and giving personal records of such coach services between 1904 and 1909.
24. The date was given as 1 July 1897 in *Southern Railway Magazine*, 1935, 270. This date may have been a misprint.
25. Goff, Martyn, *Victorian and Edwardian Surrey from old Photographs*, Batsford, 1972, legend to Fig. 119.
26. LBSC Rly Notice No. 86, dated September 1891.
27 *The Surrey Mirror*, 7 August 1896, 8.
28. Rule 68A of the LBSC Rly Rule Book dated 1 January 1886 required the signalman himself at an intermediate box to undertake fogging duties for his own home signals, if practicable, in the absence of fogmen.

CHAPTER SEVEN

The Final Period of Growth (1899-1912)

W ITH THE opening of the Through line between Stoat's Nest and Earlswood on 5 November 1899, and the commencement of passenger traffic over it on 1 April 1900 (Chapter VI), the LBSC Rly system was completed except for the opening of the Withyham Spur (Ashurst Junction–Eridge Junction—(then so designated)). That spur had been constructed by 1888 but not brought into use (see Chapter III). However, there were two very important developments in the years up to 1912 which, had progress not been subsequently interrupted by the First World War, would have brought about immense changes. These are reviewed, with other less major but still important events, in the present chapter and the next.

From the relatively early days of railways, management had had a difficult task. On the one hand were the shareholders, who put up the money for building the line; and on the other hand there were those who used the railways, either for personal travel or for the transport of freight of various types, and who therefore provided the revenue. The shareholders wanted bigger and better dividends; the users wanted cheaper and better services. As long as a railway company had a monopoly within a particular area, and economic conditions were reasonable, it would generally be able to establish, in the end, a workable compromise between the demands of the two factions. It was, of course, the realization by one railway that such problems were not peculiar to itself, that led to agreements between a number of companies not to complicate matters by adding the effect of competition to an already difficult situation (see Volume II, Chapter II, in particular). The LBSC Rly had such territorial agreements with the neighbouring South Eastern and South Western companies, and in addition had financial agreements with them concerning the sharing of revenue from certain towns or areas, as already referred to earlier in this account.

In a commercial world, however, it was the customer on whose support the success of an enterprise depended; and the customer was quick to withdraw that support in favour of a competitor if he (the customer) were not satisfied. Moreover, if there were no competitor, the customer would always actively support any moves to bring one into being—he would not indefinitely accept a 'take it or leave it' attitude.

The slow recovery of the Brighton company after near bankruptcy in 1867 meant that for some time its shareholders did not get returns as good as those from many other companies; and to get even poor returns, for a time necessitated a reduction in the level of services as well as other economies (see Volume II, Chapter XIV). Hence the shareholders were gloomy, whilst the customers, already not over-impressed by the services offered by the Brighton in comparison with those offered by other companies, became increasingly disillusioned and hence ready to support competitive lines. Attention was paid in Chapter VI to moves to build entirely new lines from London to Brighton in 1875 and 1883, and mention was made of the emergence of electric traction as a future potential competitor to the steam locomotive.

In the late 1890s the Brighton began to shake off its lethargy and to make plans for offering greatly improved services, in an awakening to the realization that it was not a 'popular' line with many of its customers, most of whom used it from necessity rather than from choice; and that if it did not act quickly, its future might not be rosy. The forthcoming completion of the Brighton's new line from Coulsdon to Earlswood, avoiding the necessity of always having to use the South Eastern's metals between Coulsdon and Redhill (see Chapter VI), pointed the way.

The forthcoming extension of the local lines from South Croydon to Stoat's Nest (near Coulsdon) would give four roads throughout from Bricklayers Arms Junction to Earlswood. If the existing four roads between Balham and Streatham Junction North were re-arranged for normal four-track working, and if two new roads were laid from Streatham Junction North to Windmill Bridge Junction with a suitable layout at the latter, then there would be effective quadrupling between Poupart's Junction and Windmill Bridge Junction, and hence also on to Earlswood. Moreover, if the line between Victoria and Poupart's Junction were also widened to four roads, there would be four roads throughout from Victoria to Earlswood. Further, by making use of the South Bermondsey spur in conjunction with an altered layout at Bricklayers Arms Junction, it would also be possible to provide four roads for LBSC Rly traffic throughout from London Bridge to Earlswood.

Such considerations highlighted the possibilities of quadrupling south of Earlswood; but in such an event there would be a bottleneck south of where the quadrupling stopped. Hence thought was given to widening to four roads the whole way to Brighton.

All these schemes were developed in detail, and plans were deposited from 1897 onwards. Authorities for the works north of Balcombe Tunnel were obtained during 1898 and 1899, as follows:

Victoria Station enlargement.....	62 & 63 Vic. cap. 205 (LBSC Rly Various Powers Act, 1899) 1 August 1899
*Victoria-Battersea Pier Jct. *Battersea Pier Jct.-Poupart's Jct. Streatham Jct. Nth.-Windmill Bridge Jct.	61 & 62 Vic. cap. 111 (LBSC Rly Act, 1898) 25 July 1898
Streatham Jct. Nth.-Streatham Jct. Sth. (Main and Local Spurs)	60 & 63 Vic. cap. 205 (LBSC Rly Various Powers Act, 1899) 1 August 1899
Earlswood-Balcombe Tunnel .... (north end)	62 & 63 Vic. cap. 205 (LBSC Rly Various Powers Act, 1899) 1 August 1899

*Extension of time for completion to 25 July 1905, granted by 3 Edw. 7 cap. 120, dated 21 July 1903.

Southward from the north end of Balcombe Tunnel, matters did not proceed so fast, and it was not until 1903 (as will be recorded later in this chapter) that authority was granted for the widening of the section onwards to Keymer Junction. In the meantime, an entirely different factor was beginning to assume great importance: the possibilities of electric traction, put forward in 1899 as the means of working an independent competitive line between London and Brighton.

Although nothing came of the 1899 contender, it set the scene for the future, and in September 1901 a scheme was launched by the London & Brighton Electric Railway company which aroused considerable interest. The route was to be virtually straight, from a terminus at Lupus Street, Pimlico, just east of the London Chatham & Dover's line into Victoria station, to a terminus at Furze Hill at the back of Brunswick Square in Brighton. The Brighton terminus was to be some 75 ft. above ground level, and would be reached by hydraulic lifts. The engineers were Messrs. F. H. Cheesewright and John Brunlees. Among the promoters' plans were a non-stop journey time of 32 minutes with a line speed of 90 m.p.h., and return fares of 5 shillings (25p) first class and 3 shillings (15p) third class (corresponding to present-day second class).

The Brighton's London area suburban services were also experiencing a marked falling-off of traffic, which it was thought was due, at least in part, to competition by tramcars and omnibuses. The need to find some way of stopping this decline, and if possible of winning back at least some of the lost traffic, was naturally reinforced by the threat of competition to the main-line traffic. The Brighton board therefore looked into the possibilities of adopting electric traction for their own line, more particularly for suburban traffic, and in consequence Charles L. Morgan, who had succeeded F. D. Banister as Chief Engineer in 1896, visited Italy in 1901 to study the relative merits of the two methods of railway electrification already in use in that country—namely the alternating-current three-phase 'overhead' system, and the direct-current third-rail system. Morgan's report to the Brighton board in January 1902 was chiefly concerned with listing the disadvantages for L B S C Rly purposes of the third-rail system as he saw it in operation in Italy.

Shortly after this, the London & Brighton Electric Railway's Bill was thrown out of the Commons on failure to comply with Standing Orders, and later in 1902 another attempt to get authority for an electric railway to Brighton, also failed.

Matters within the Brighton's board were, however, kept alive by the advocacy of one of the directors, Major Cardew. Cardew drew up a memorandum in which he said

The real advantage of electric traction to the public is to be found in the much improved service which can be given, the trains being more frequent and run on a regular time schedule, instead of at irregular intervals, and the mean speed of stopping trains being considerably increased, without increase in maximum speed.

These advantages diminish as the length of line is increased, especially in respect of express trains, but on our system the distances are such that no doubt considerable advantages can be secured from electrification.

This carried weight, and, in conjunction with the outside pressures that have already been mentioned, made the Brighton's directors decide to seek powers to work trains electrically. The board appreciated that efforts would have to be made even to retain existing traffic, let alone increase it. The necessary authority was granted under section 38 of 3 Edw. 7 cap. 120 (the LBSC Rly Act, 1903) dated 21 July 1903. Other companies faced with similar problems also sought, and obtained, powers for the use of electric traction.

While this authority was being obtained, the Brighton planned a publicity run to Brighton and back, and this took place on Sunday 26 July 1903 (i.e., five days after the company had been empowered to use electric traction). With B4 class 4-4-0 No. 70 and a train reported to have consisted of three Pullman cars and two brakes, a time of 48 minutes 41 seconds from start to stop was achieved for the trip from Victoria to Brighton, and 50 minutes 21 seconds for the up journey. Hence the company was in the position that it had shown what it could do by steam (but obviously under very carefully planned conditions), and at the same time was forward-looking in having powers to use electric traction.

The two major developments already referred to—namely, what might be called the great awakening and the decision to quadruple the most important sections of the line; and the realization that electrification might well have to be adopted as a policy—came about more or less simultaneously, as explained above. As, however, the first stages of the quadrupling works were put in hand (and, in fact, were in part completed) before electrification powers were granted, the Author considers it best to review the widening and other engineering developments before turning to the initial electrification work. The latter therefore forms Chapter VIII.

Attention will first be given to the works at Victoria station; between there and Poupart's Junction; and between Balham and Windmill Bridge Junction.

At Victoria, it was virtually impossible to widen the station as it was hemmed in between the London Chatham & Dover Railway's station on the east, and Buckingham Palace Road on the west. Hence the idea was developed of, in broad terms, doubling the number of platform faces by constructing what practically amounted to a new station to the south of the existing one; the actual platforms themselves would run from one station to the other, but midway there would be connections to enable trains to and from those parts of the platforms in the existing (or north) part of the enlarged station, to get past trains standing at the new (or south) extensions to those platforms.

When Victoria station was first opened, the two roads approaching it from the bridge over the Thames, were carried along the east side of the Grosvenor Canal basin until they divided to enter the separate stations used by the L BSC Rly and the LCD Rly. As the junction into the two stations was just to the north of the remaining part of the canal basin (which had been reduced in size in order to make space for the two stations), in actual fact the two roads leading to and from the station on the east side, used by the Chatham company, continued more or less straight; and the two roads leading to and from the station on the west side, used by the Brighton company, curved sharply to the left (for incoming trains) in order to reach that station, which was, in effect, built 'behind' the canal basin. Incidentally, when the line was opened with roofing over it (see Volume II, Chapter VII) the signal-box controlling the junction was mounted in the retaining wall to the east side of the double-line approach to the station. Hence it soon became known as the 'Hole-in-the-Wall' box. When the junction and box became redundant on building the separate Chatham lines approach (Volume II, Chapter X), a new Chatham box sited somewhat similarly in a recess in the wall east of that company's new line, acquired the old name of the 'Hole-in-the-Wall'. The two boxes must not be confused.

It will be seen that, in order to build a new 'south' station, the L BSC Rly had to acquire the site of the remaining part of the Grosvenor Canal basin, this involving shortening the canal into little more than a relatively short arm off the left (or north) bank of the River Thames, upstream of Grosvenor Bridge. Only when this land had been obtained, the basin filled in, and the ground consolidated, could any railway work proper be undertaken. Hence the enlargement of Victoria station was one of the last parts of the overall widening and improvement works, to be completed.

Down Grosvenor Bank, the formation had to be widened (three more roads being needed) on the Up or west side on account of the proximity of the Chatham company's lines on the east side, but Grosvenor Bridge itself did not have to be widened: the bridge already carried three L B S C Rly roads, and space for two more roads could be found on the site of the wide platform (built as part of the 1866 bridge widening (Volume II, Chapter X), and partly resited about 1880 (Chapter V)). South of Grosvenor Bridge, past Battersea Pier Junction and as far as Battersea Park Junction, a two-road widening was needed on the Up or west side. Beyond Battersea Park, a single-road widening was needed on the Up or west side as far as Poupart's Junction, beyond which there were already four roads to Balham (Chapter V). Plate 17 shows the new bridge carrying the fourth road (which became the Up Main line) over the Low Level lines at Longhedge Junction. This new bridge, provided with three overhead stiffeners to the two main girders, is nearer to the camera than the original (1867) three-road bridge, and largely obscures the latter. The original bridge has been completely reconstructed in recent years, and now has two spans with an intermediate pier; to provide space for the latter, the layout under the two bridges has been simplified from that shown in Plate 17, the original of which was taken in 1952. More recently, the layout of the Low Level lines has been further rationalized and Longhedge box abolished.

Starting at Poupart's Junction and proceeding towards Victoria, the existing three roads as far as Grosvenor Road were being worked as follows:

Up Main
Up Local
Down

Between Grosvenor Road and Victoria, down the bank, there was only one Up road and one Down road whilst at the existing Victoria station the longer-distance traffic was handled on the east side of the station and the local traffic on the west side. In other words, the usage of the station platforms was the reverse of the usage of the two up roads, although the latter came down to a single up road for the last $\frac{1}{2}$ mile or so to the throat of the terminus. In essence, therefore, the overall position at Victoria had, since 1867, been not all that dissimilar from what had obtained at London Bridge in early days, where the London & Croydon traffic flow joined the London & Greenwich flow at Corbett's Lane Junction (the Croydon flow coming in from the west at that junction), whereas the Croydon's station at London Bridge was to the east of the Greenwich's station—see Volume I. As long as the two up roads approaching Victoria merged into one at Grosvenor Road, the working at Victoria was not affected in this respect; but as soon as two Up roads became available right in to Victoria the position would have greatly deteriorated. Hence the reconstruction and enlargement of Victoria were based on a transposition of the method of working in the terminus, the longer-distance traffic being arranged to be handled on the west side and the local traffic being dealt with on the east side. To facilitate this, the working with four roads was to be on the 'alternate' system.

Between Poupart's Junction and Battersea Park, the new (fourth) road on the Up side was to become the Up Main line, the existing Up Main line (that on the west of the original three) becoming the Down Main. The existing Up Local would remain as such, and the existing Down would become the Down Local. From Battersea Park to Battersea Pier Junction, two extra roads were to be laid on the Up or west side: the first of these, next to the existing Up Main, was to be the new Up Main, in continuation of that road from Poupart's Junction; and outside it (i.e., to the west again) there was to be an Up Carriage road.

From Battersea Pier Junction over the river to Grosvenor Road box, two new roads were laid between the existing Up Local and the existing Down line, on the site of the wide platform (see Chapter XIX). The new working was to be as shown in Figure 21.

From Grosvenor Road box, down the bank into Victoria, three new roads were to be laid on the Up or west side, as shown in Figure 22.

There is insufficient space in this account to deal with any of the works in detail, but brief mention must be made of two features.

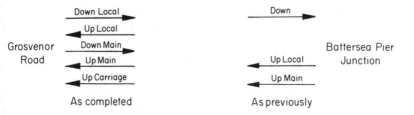

Figure 21. Widening between Grosvenor Road and Battersea Pier Junction, under 1898 Act
As completed on 10 February 1907

Figure 22. Widening between Victoria and Grosvenor Road, under 1898 Act
As completed on 10 February 1907

At Victoria, the new station was to consist of two sections, as already inferred, the North section on the site of the original station, and the South section on the site of land reclaimed from the canal basin, as already explained. Each of the three two-road bays in the North section embraced a third (middle) road in the South section, these middle roads enabling movements to and from the North section to be made while the corresponding platform roads in the South section were occupied. Loaded passenger trains going into the North section had, however, to reach the latter via the corresponding platform roads in the South section, as the middle roads in that section were equipped to deal with loaded passenger trains in the outward direction only. Due to the siting of Grosvenor Hotel, the two platforms roads on the west (or Buckingham Palace Road) side had to be made much shorter than the remainder, and hence were not long enough to hold two trains each unless both trains were short. These two platforms (the present Nos. 16 and 17) were therefore each worked as one long platform in the ordinary way, special signalling of the type already in use at London Bridge, Brighton, and Eastbourne, being introduced for those two roads.

Approaching Poupart's Junction from the Battersea Park direction, the three existing lines on one bridge, and the new Up Main line on an independent bridge, were taken over the Ludgate and West London Extension lines as follows from east to west: first, a span over formation only; then a span over the Ludgate lines; then one over the West London Extension lines; and finally one over formation only. All four spans of each bridge were slightly angled to one another as well as being on a skew over both of the two-track lines beneath them, since the Brighton company's High-Level line was on a curve. The bridge became known officially on the LBSC Rly as 'Four Span', as a result (Plate 18). Apart from Victoria itself, no station works of importance were involved in this section of the widening. Poupart's Junction Signal Box, photographed during the railway strike in August 1911, is shown in Plate 19.

Between Balham and Streatham Junction North there were already four roads, the widening having been done about 1897 (Chapter V). However, they were worked in such a way that only the middle two were available for traffic to and from Streatham Common and Selhurst; the two outer roads only communicated with Streatham Junction South, and hence onwards to Mitcham Junction or Tooting Junction. There was a down siding at Streatham Common, extending back beside the down line nearly as far as Streatham Junction North: the Southwark & Vauxhall Water Company's siding was connected to this down siding. From Streatham Common onwards there were only two roads.

The widening plan involved the rearrangement of the four roads between Balham and Streatham Junction North so that all four were available for running to and from the Selhurst direction, and similar provision was made between Streatham Junction North and Streatham Junction South[1]. The down siding from Streatham Common was to be converted into a running road, and one entirely new road provided on the Up side. From Streatham Common, two more roads were to be constructed on the down (north-east) side, into which the spur from Streatham (Chapter V) was to be slued. At Selhurst the new lines were to give access to and from Norwood Up yard and Norwood Fork, and they were also to continue, by a reverse curve and a falling gradient, until they joined the Norwood Fork-St. James's Junction line on to West Croydon, to give access to and from West Croydon. Further, connection was to be made from that line to Windmill Bridge Junction, the two junctions in the Norwood Fork-St. James's Junction line being arranged back to back.

Since the two new roads from Streatham Common onwards would be connected, both at that end and at the Selhurst end, to ordinary double-line spurs and branches, the only practicable way of working the two new roads was as a pair, down and up. This dictated the working of the whole length, and hence the alterations from Streatham Junction North towards the Croydon direction were made so that the resulting four roads were worked on the 'alternate' (down, up, down, up) system. The length from Poupart's Junction to Balham was then being worked on the 'parallel' (down, down, up, up) system, and hence at some point the method of working had to be changed. It was decided that this should be at Balham, and hence the existing four roads from there on to Streatham Junction North, as well as the widening thence to Selhurst, was all made 'alternate'. This involved a flat crossing at Balham, as shown in Figure 23 and two double-line spurs between Streatham Junction North and Streatham Junction South (Figure 24). New signal boxes were needed at Streatham Junction North, Streatham Junction South, Streatham Common South (the existing box there then becoming Streatham Common North), Thornton Heath, and Selhurst. Where the two back-to-back junctions were installed between Norwood Fork and St. James's Junction, another new box was built, and was named Gloucester Road Junction (reviving the name of a former box nearby—see Chapter V): and St. James's Junction box was abolished, its work being put on to the new Gloucester Road Junction box.

As the two new lines from Streatham Common to Selhurst were on the Down side, the site of Streatham Common goods yard had to be given up. A much larger goods yard was constructed on the Up side, on the Selhurst side of the station. Where this goods yard terminated, some hundreds of yards beyond Streatham Common Station, connections were laid between the goods yard throat and all four running roads, Streatham Common South box being built at this point. Where the west (or station) end of the yard was connected to the running

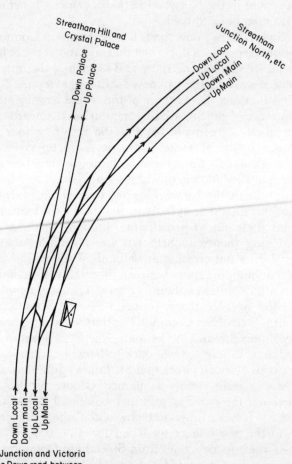

Figure 23. Balham: Altered Working on Streatham Junction North Side, August 1903

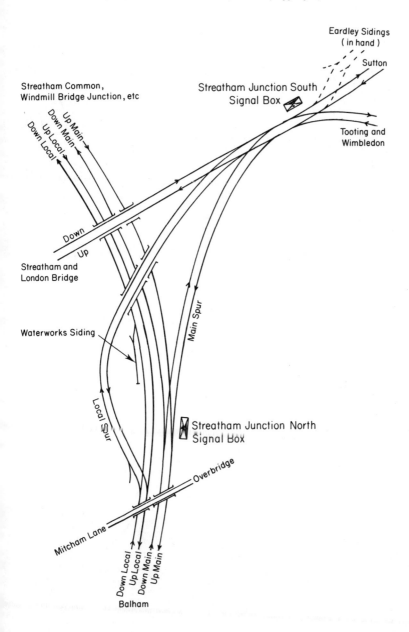

Figure 24. Streatham Junction North and Streatham Junction South, August 1903

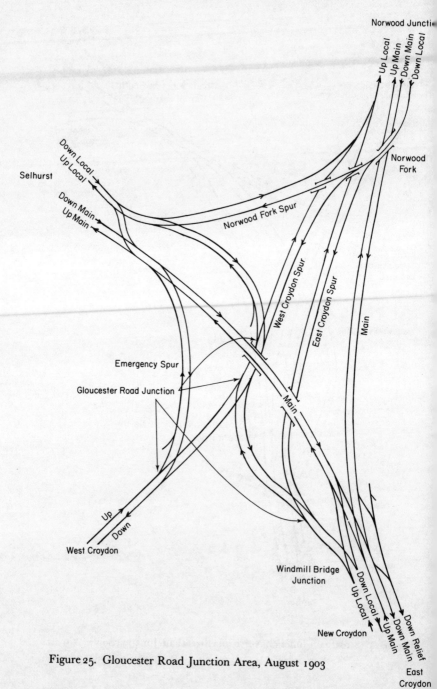

Figure 25. Gloucester Road Junction Area, August 1903

roads, a shunting box was erected, this therefore being between Streatham Common North and Streatham Common South boxes.

The rearrangement in the Gloucester Road Junction area can best be understood by reference to Figure 25, from which non-passenger lines have been omitted for simplicity. It will be seen that, apart from the double line to and from West Croydon, and the Down Relief line (i.e., the fifth running road) south of Windmill Bridge Junction, the essential feature was that the four roads north of Norwood Fork were worked on the 'parallel' system, whereas the four roads north-west of Selhurst were to be worked on the 'alternate' system with the local lines on the east (or down) side; and that both these four-track lines had to be connected to that south of Windmill Bridge Junction, which was worked on a third method—'alternate', but with the local lines on the west (or up) side. This series of connections, which exists in identical form today with the addition of a Down Relief line from north of Norwood Fork to join the fifth road at Windmill Bridge Junction, and the rearrangement of that fifth road south of Windmill Bridge Junction so as to be reversible, must have few equals in its apparent complexity but in its neatness in reality.

The works included the rebuilding of Streatham Common, Norbury, Thornton Heath, and Selhurst stations, these, as reconstructed, being spacious and a credit to the Brighton company, as compared with certain other stations on the system which were the reverse. Norbury Crossing had already been abolished and replaced by a footbridge, under section 17 of the LBSC Rly Act of 1896 (59 & 60 cap. 128, dated 20 July 1896). Plate 20 shows the new roads on the Thornton Heath side of Selhurst, before being brought into use.

The Author has yet to find the actual dates when certain sections of the foregoing works were brought into use, but the following list covers the important stages:

Reference
(a) New West Croydon spur, between Norwood Fork
and Gloucester Road Junction . . . .   28 June 1903[2]
(b) Old connections between Norwood Fork and St.
James's Junction *taken out* . . . . Week ended   4 July 1903
(c) Balham–Windmill Bridge Junction widening on
'alternate' system, and new connections between
Streatham Junction North and Streatham
Junction South . . . .   6 July 1903[3]

(d)Battersea Pier Junction–Battersea Park Junction, fourth road (on 'parallel' system) and carriage road .... ⎫

(e)Battersea Park Junction–Poupart's Junction, fourth road (on 'parallel' system) .... ⎭ c. 1905

(f)Victoria Station:

Most of new part of station (i.e., the South section) brought into use, *and existing LBSC Rly station closed for reconstruction* .... 10 June 1906

(g)Victoria station:

Most of reconstructed part of LBSC Rly station (that part henceforth known as the North section), brought into use, using Buckingham Palace Road entrance/exit (Circulating area not then completed) .... 10 February 1907

(h)Victoria–Grosvenor Road box:

Three extra roads brought into use, and 'alternate' working introduced on passenger lines .... 10 February 1907

(j)Grosvenor Road box–Battersea Pier Junction:

Two extra roads brought into use on site of wide platform situated on river bridge, this platform having been reconstructed about 1880 (see Chapter V). 'Alternate' working introduced, with both-ways working on Carriage Road .... 10 February 1907

(k)Battersea Pier Junction–Poupart's Junction and on to Clapham Junction North box:

Conversion of working from 'parallel' to 'alternate' system, with installation of flat crossing at Clapham Junction North .... 10 February 1907

(l)Grosvenor Road station: Closed .... 1 April 1907

(m)Victoria station:

Completed station formally opened .... 1 July 1908

(n)Clapham Junction South Box–Balham Junction box:

Conversion of working from 'parallel' to 'alternate' system, resulting in abolition of flat crossing of Down Main and Up Local, east of Balham Junction box and installation of similar crossing at Clapham Junction South box, west of West London Extension lines junction .... c. late 1908

It should be noted that stages (h), (j), and (k) resulted in 'alternate' working being in force from Victoria to Clapham Junction North box from 10 February 1907; and that stage (n), following stage (c), resulted in 'alternate' working being in force from Clapham Junction South box southwards all the way to

Stoat's Nest. A 'joggle' at Balham occurred where the Palace lines joined the new Local lines.

The retention of 'parallel' working between Clapham Junction North and South boxes was necessitated by the slow progress in rebuilding Clapham Junction station. The resulting hindrance to working brought about by the flat crossing at each end of the station, was not eliminated until 1910—see later in this chapter).

Attention must now be given to works away from the London area, of which the most important were those associated with the main line to Brighton, south of Earlswood. The original plans for widening south of that place were for two additional roads to be laid on the Up (or West) side right through to Preston Park, where there was already an extra Down road to the terminus at Brighton (Chapter VI); hence between Preston Park and Brighton only one extra road would be needed, which, because it would be laid on railway land, would not involve any application to Parliament. There were to be duplicate tunnels at Balcombe, Haywards Heath, Clayton, and Patcham, sited closely to the west of those existing tunnels; and the Ouse Viaduct was to be widened on the Up or west side. At Keymer Junction there was to be a left-hand double-line junction off the existing lines, with an easier radius than that existing; and a right-hand double-line junction off the new lines, leading to a rising gradient on a left-hand curve to form a flyover over the planned new lines on to Burgess Hill and Brighton, and then over the existing lines on to Burgess Hill and Brighton.

Authority for the widening works between Earlswood and the north end of Balcombe Tunnel was, as already recorded, given in 1899 under 62 & 63 Vic. cap. 205 dated 1 August, known as the LBSC Rly Various Powers Act, 1899. The next year, permission was given, under 63 & 64 Vic. cap. 30 dated 25 June 1900 (the Various Powers Act, 1900), for the purchase of a small parcel of land needed at Earlswood. In the event, much of the widening was done on both sides rather than solely on the Up (or west) side, one new road being laid on each side of the existing two roads (see later).

It was not until 21 July 1903 that authority was received for the widening works between the north end of Balcombe Tunnel and Keymer Junction. The relevant Powers were given in the LBSC Rly Act for that year, referenced 3 Edw. 7 cap. 120. Under that Act, the widening between Copyhold and the south end of Haywards Heath was to be on the Down (or east) side. From Copyhold to the north end of Haywards Heath, the widening was necessary to retain the existing facilities under which Horsted Keynes–Ardingly–Haywards Heath traffic had run alongside the existing main line since 1883 (Chapter III). The remaining parts of the widening from the north end of Balcombe Tunnel to Copyhold, and from the south end of Haywards Heath to Keymer Junction, were to be on the Up (or west) side, as planned from 1897 onwards. A partial scheme for less expensive works, involving a widening only between Balcombe and the north end of the Ouse Viaduct, was authorized in section 7 of the L BS C Rly Act of 1906, referenced 6 Edw. 7 cap. 145 and dated 4 August 1906.

In the meantime, work had been proceeding at Earlswood and south thereof. Earlswood, Horley, and Three Bridges, the three intermediate passenger stations, had to be rebuilt or extended, as well as much tipping done to widen the lengths of embankment (although many of them were low) as far as Three Bridges station. At Horley, an entirely new station was constructed some little way south of the existing one, but at Three Bridges station the widening took place solely on the Up or west side, the existing down platform and East Grinstead bay being retained without important alterations. Gatwick, the racecourse station built in 1891 between Horley and Three Bridges (Chapter VI), was already suitable for the new arrangements.

Horley new station was opened on Sunday 31 December 1905,[4] and it seems that the widening from Earlswood to Three Bridges (south end) was brought into use about 1907, as Salfords box replaced Earlswood Common in that year. The four roads were designated, from east to west, Down Fast, Up Fast, Down Slow, and Up Slow, the Down Fast and the Up Slow being the new roads (with the exception noted below) as they were laid on the widened parts of the embankment. The old Down line therefore became the Up Fast, and the old Up line became the Down Slow. The only exception to this arrangement was between Horley and Gatwick, where the Up Relief line of 1892 (Chapter VI) naturally became the Up Slow over much of its length. As the existing Down line through Three Bridges station remained unaltered (as explained above), and so became the Down Fast, the two Fast lines north of Three Bridges were out of alignment with what became those two lines through that station. The resulting 'joggle' remains today. Gatwick (race-course station) was used for ordinary passenger traffic between June and November 1907.

Five other matters of considerable importance must now be noted. The first of these arose from the need for increased siding accommodation at the London termini, for stabling coaching stock. For London Bridge, the sidings were at New Cross, where extensions had been made from time to time, including a series on the Up side north of the station that had acquired the name of Millers' Sidings (there having been two brothers, Ted Miller and George Miller, who had been foremen towards the end of the nineteenth century when the sidings had been installed). For Victoria, the sidings were conveniently sited on the Up side immediately outside that station, but were of insufficient capacity. The laying of adequate sidings to make provision for the future, anywhere near either terminus, would have been prohibitively expensive due to the cost of the land involved, and hence a large area was acquired south of Streatham in 1901, on which to lay extensive sidings. The site was east and south of Streatham Junction South, and near Eardley Road; hence the resulting yard was named Eardley Sidings (or 'Eardley', for short). Authority was given in section 11 of 1 Edw. 7 cap. 111 dated 26 July 1901 (the LBSC Rly Act, 1901). The sidings were on the east side of the line from Streatham Junction south to Mitcham Junction, which was on a falling gradient of 1 in 90 past the site; moreover, the general level of the ground was itself also tending to fall in the direction of Mitcham Junction, so that the embankment under the line at Streatham Junction South extended for about ½ mile before the Mitcham Junction line reached ground level (where the falling gradient eased and shortly the line became virtually level). To obtain a level site for Eardley Sidings, therefore, there was some excavation at the north (Streatham) end and an embankment at the south end. Hence at the north end the sidings were a relatively long way below the level of the Mitcham Junction line, but some 10-12 ft. above the latter at the south end. A double-line branch was therefore constructed on the east (or Down) side of the Mitcham Junction line, from Streatham Junction South to where the levels of the Mitcham Junction line and the sidings coincided, at which point the branch curved slightly left to enter a series of reception sidings. The embankment had of course to be widened between Streatham Junction South and the start of the reception sidings. The new Streatham Junction South box of 1903 (see earlier in this chapter) controlled entry to, and exit from, the branch, at the reception sidings end of which was a shunter's hut which, on the Engineer's plans, was called Eardley Yard signal box. Permissive working was put into force on each road between Streatham Junction South box and the shunter's hut. The hut, and therefore presumably the sidings, was brought into use in 1905.

The second matter to be reviewed here was an enlargement of Willow Walk goods depot, which had long been under discussion. Due to the proximity of Willow Walk and other streets, lateral expansion was impracticable. Hence the design finally adopted gave new shed accommodation and associated sidings on the east side of Greyhound Bridge, the existing Willow Walk goods station being west of that bridge and immediately north of the original part of the SE Rly's Bricklayers Arms station. Both the old and the new parts of Willow Walk were therefore on the Down side of the Bricklayers Arms branch. The main connections between the latter and the new part of Willow Walk were made at Mercer's Crossing box. The actual level crossing had apparently been replaced by the overbridge now carrying St. James Road, prior to the new works being undertaken. The enlarged facilities were opened on 1 June 1903.[5]

The third matter of note was the construction, at Three Bridges, of a new locomotive depot in the fork between the main line and the Horsham line. This was necessary as the site of the original depot, on the west (up) side of the main line beside the station, and at a lower level than the latter, would be taken by the extensions to the station needed by the widening works already described. Authority was granted under section 5 of the LBSC Rly Act of 1902 (2 Edw. 7 cap. 8, dated 23 June). The new depot was probably brought into use about 1904. A turntable had existed on the site from an earlier period.

The fourth event to be recorded here, of the five already referred to, was the realization about 1900 that Brighton works were becoming inadequate to cater for carriages and wagons as well as locomotives. Hence it was decided that those works should concentrate on locomotives, and that a new carriage and wagon works should be built elsewhere. A site was found at Lancing, on the south (Down) side west of the station, and authority to build the works was granted by section 5 of the LBSC Rly Act of 1902 (2 Edw. 7 cap. 8, dated 23 June)—i.e., the same section of the same Act as authorized the building of the new locomotive depot at Three Bridges. Construction proceeded slowly over a number of years, and it was not until 1912-13 that the new works began to be brought into use.[6]

The final matter which must be recorded was that the Bognor branch was doubled for the last two hundred yards, from Bersted Crossing to the terminus, on 7 April 1902, but the first $3\frac{1}{4}$ miles from Barnham (on the west coast line) to Bersted Crossing remained single. It seems likely that the decision to double this very short length of the branch, was to improve the station working. Bognor station itself had been largely destroyed twice in the nineties—having been blown down in 1897 and burnt down in 1899. In passing, it might be as well to repeat here what has earlier been stated, namely that the suffix 'Regis' was not added until Southern Railway days; in LBSC Rly times the name of the town, and therefore of the station, was (plain) Bognor.

As earlier recorded in this chapter, the LBSC Rly obtained authority in 1903 to work traffic electrically. The way that advantage was taken of these powers to initiate a trial section of working by electric traction, will be recorded in the next chapter, but the point that must be made in the present chapter is that, from about the end of 1904, the possibility of future electrification became a factor to be taken into account in the planning of a number of improvement works.

Attention must next be given to new works at a number of places.

Carshalton station, previously to the east of North Street, was resited so as to be to the west of North Street, and between there and West Street. This work was done in 1902/3.

Portsmouth Town station was rebuilt in the early 1900s to provide more terminal accommodation in what had become known as the Low Level part of the station. From 00 05 hours on Sunday 3 December 1905, until the following Saturday 11 December, all points and signals were disconnected from Portsmouth Yard box while the layout was altered, new signals erected, and the lever frame relocked. All movements were made with hand signals, and on Sunday 3rd and Monday 4th traffic was normally worked via the High Level part of the station to and from Portsmouth Harbour. Block working was maintained from a temporary ground hut, also equipped with telephones. The new work was brought into use section by section, as it was completed.[7,8]

At Groombridge and at Worthing, Up Loop lines were provided, the existing Up platforms being converted into islands. These improvements were carried out under section 4 of 6 Edw. 7 cap. 145 of 4 August 1906, and section 4 of 8 Edw. 7 cap. 183 of 1 August 1908, respectively, the L B S C Rly Acts for those years. The Author has not yet ascertained when these new loops were brought into use, but the likely date for Groombridge is 1907. That at Worthing formed part of the general scheme for modernizing the station, completed in 1911.

A new Down Relief line was provided between Norwood Junction South signal box and Windmill Bridge Junction, utilizing in part a goods line that had been put in on 4 July 1897. This Down Relief line was opened to traffic on 3 January 1908. The South Bermondsey Spur, opened in 1871 (Volume II, Chapter XII) formed a link in the Brighton's scheme for giving four roads all the way from London Bridge to Balcombe Tunnel box (and ultimately beyond), as explained earlier in this chapter. As opened it was double line only, but the viaduct on which most of it was constructed, was built for three roads. A third road was apparently laid during the Spring of 1908, and the Down Spur line is believed to have been slued into the new road at each end, thus causing the Down and Up Spur lines to be next the parapets of the viaduct, with a length of dead road between those two running roads. This dead road was destined to become the Up Main Spur. The works required a new signal box at Bricklayers Arms Junction, and this was built on the Up side and hence opposite to the existing box on the Down side. The Up Main Spur line, and Up Carriage road from New Cross to Bricklayers Arms Junction, and the new Bricklayers Arms Junction box, were brought into use on 8 August 1909.[9]

While this work was in hand, however, the electrification of the South London line was progressing and the more frequent service that was planned, on a regular basis, made it appear likely that congestion would occur on the Down South London line from London Bridge as far out as South Bermondsey. Hence, to avoid having to widen the 1866 South London part of the viaduct between London Bridge and South Bermondsey in order to take a fourth road, it was decided that the Up Main South London, the middle road of the three on that viaduct, should be made available to Down traffic, as a Down Main line, when necessary; and that this flexibility should be extended from South Bermondsey Junction along the Spur to Bricklayers Arms Junction—this being the principal reason why a new signal box had to be provided at that junction, as already recorded. The new method of working, together with a second Up Carriage road from New Cross to Bricklayers Arms Junction, came into force on 15 August 1909,[10] one week after the Up Main Spur line came into use; that line, and the existing Up Main South London line on to London Bridge, was renamed the Reversible Working Line, which was naturally soon contracted to 'the Reversible road (or line)'. Signals for both directions were of course provided for the new workings, with separate sets of Sykes lock-and-block instruments to control them. Special locking was put in to ensure that the last train in one direction over the Reversible road had arrived at London Bridge (or South Bermondsey Junction or Bricklayers Arms Junction, as the case might be), before the direction of running was changed, which was normally only done at prearranged times.[11]

The line through Sutton, Dorking, Horsham and Arundel, carried most of the Portsmouth traffic as well as an increasing volume of local traffic, particularly as far as Dorking and Horsham. There were, however, no facilities in the way of loop lines to enable fast trains to get past slower ones, except at Horsham station where there was a Down Loop with an island platform between it and the Down Main. Beyond Horsham, there was a similar loop at Ford, but nothing more. No facilities at all were provided for one up train to overtake another except for an Up Loop at Pulborough, and slower trains had therefore to be shunted into sidings, or even on to the Down road, to facilitate the daily working of up traffic. Similar shunting had also, of course, to be undertaken for down trains at places away from Horsham or Ford, using the Up road for the purpose if sidings were not available or full. Hence it was decided that there should be four roads between Sutton and Cheam, the next station to the west. A view of Cheam, about 1906, before work was started, is given in Plate 21.

Authority was granted by section 4 of the LBSC Rly Act, 1906 (i.e., 6 Edw. 7 cap. 145, dated 4 August 1906). Widening was to be carried out on both sides of the existing double line, and the work involved the complete rebuilding of Cheam station and the provision of a new goods yard on the Down side at the Sutton end of the station, in replacement of the former yard on the Up side at that same end. The quadrupling extended to the west (or Epsom) end of Cheam station, which was to be provided with side platforms to the outer roads. It was also proposed to provide a central island platform between the two middle roads, but this was never done. The widening was, as would be expected for such a relatively short length (about 1 mile), worked on the 'parallel' system, the roads being designated Down Slow, Down Fast, Up Fast, and Up Slow. Alterations to the interlocking were needed at Sutton West box to control the eastern end of the quadrupling; and a replacement signal box was required at Cheam, at the west end of the station on the up side, which controlled the western end of the quadrupling. The widening was apparently brought into use on 1 October 1911.[12]

Following the partial failure of the overall roof at Charing Cross station (SE Rly), the LBSC Rly looked into the stability of such roofs at their own stations. As a result, the two-span roof over the London side of Crystal Palace station (see Volume II, pp. 50-51) was taken down about 1906.

In the meantime, work was continuing on certain other important matters. Electric traction was brought into use on the South London line between London Bridge and Victoria on 1 December 1909, and proved a success. Hence early in the following year its extension to other routes was decided upon, as will be referred to in more detail in the next chapter.

On the quadrupled main line into Victoria, it will be remembered that 'parallel' working had to remain in force through Clapham Junction station, only, from about the end of 1908 while that station was being rebuilt. The first stage of this work was to construct a new side platform for the Up West London Extension Railway traffic (i.e., north to south, the trains hence becoming 'Down' ones when continuing beyond Clapham Junction in the direction of Balham). This was sited some way back from the existing line, and hence involved increasing the already sharp curvature for the WLE Rly through Clapham Junction station. As soon as this platform was ready, the UpWLE Rly line was slued over to run beside the west side of it. It became known as No. 12 platform, under a joint

LSW Rly/LBSC Rly system of numbering all platforms at Clapham Junction in one series, starting with No. 1 on the west side of the station; the Brighton's platform numbers started at 7. No. 12 platform and the realigned Up WLE Rly line were brought into use on 27 June 1909.[13] This enabled the new No. 11 platform, to serve the realigned Down WLE Rly line (fed by up LBSC Rly trains), to be constructed; and then that WLE Rly line to be slued over to run beside the east side of the new No. 11 platform. This was done on 7 November 1909[14] and resulted in the two WLE Rly lines being served by side platforms instead of embracing an island platform, as hitherto.

The west face of No. 11 platform, which was constructed as an island, was, when completed, then served by the diverted Down Local LBSC Rly line, the platform itself being designated No. 10. This step seems to have been completed before the end of 1909, and cleared the way for the reconstruction of the central island platform in the Brighton's part of the station (to be platforms 9 and 8). As soon as No. 9 was completed, the Up Local line was diverted to run beside that platform, thereby eliminating the flat crossings of that line with the Down Main, at each end of the station. This latter step, enabling full 'alternate' working to be introduced through the station, was carried out on Sunday 13 March 1910.[15]

The remaining new or reconstructed platforms, No. 8 for the Down Main and No. 7 for the Up Main, were brought into use when ready, which appears to have been the case by about June 1910. A new North signal box was brought into use on 5 June 1910,[16] in replacement of the previous box. The new one was 58 yds. nearer to Poupart's Junction than the one it replaced. A new frame was fitted in the South box, the signalmen henceforth having their backs to the traffic.

While the work of rebuilding Clapham Junction station was in hand, progress was continuing on the widening south of Three Bridges. The quadrupling was arranged to finish, for the time being, some 35 chains north of Balcombe Tunnel and just south of where the long straight from the Horley direction ends and the alignment curves left at 85 chains radius. At this point Balcombe Tunnel box had already been erected to control the entry into an Up Goods line that had been brought into use as far as Three Bridges somewhere about 1900. The work of widening involved heavier work than farther north, as the line was mostly in cutting. The widening was continued for a short distance south of Balcombe Tunnel signal box, so as to form the start of the widening towards the south. The Up Goods road was ultimately made the Up Slow, and the new road on the Down side became the Down Fast; the existing Down road then became the Up Fast, and the existing Up road was taken up, a new Down Slow being provided at normal '6 ft.' spacing from the Up Slow. This resulted in a 'joggle' in the Fast roads south of Three Bridges station, through which, as already noted, the original alignment for what became the Fast lines, was retained. The corresponding 'joggle' in the Fast roads at the north end of Three Bridges station, has been referred to already. Three Bridges South signal box was renamed Three Bridges Central, and an additional box, the new Three Bridges South, was erected on the Up side 744 yards south of the Central box. At the Balcombe Tunnel box end of the widening, the 'stepping over' to the Down (east) side of the Fast lines, as compared with the position of the former main lines, resulted in a slight sharpening of the start of the curve into Balcombe Tunnel itself. The widening between Three Bridges and Balcombe Tunnel box was brought into use on Sunday 22 May 1910,[17] and completed the quadrupling throughout from Earlswood. By continuing to use the 'old' line via Redhill, moreover, the Brighton therefore now had four roads from both London Bridge and Victoria, as far as Balcome Tunnel box, some $\frac{3}{5}$ of the way to Brighton.

The falling-off in passenger traffic in certain areas has already been referred to earlier in this chapter. In the inner London suburban area, it was thought that electrification would, by providing an improved service, regain some at least of the lost traffic. In other areas, it was thought that recovery of traffic would occur if passengers could, at certain places, join and leave trains between existing stations; omnibuses and tramcars, in the Edwardian period, normally stopped more or less anywhere, by request, to pick up or set down passengers; to have fixed stopping places only, was not general policy for public road transport until the period between the two World Wars.

Hence it was decided to erect simple low-cost 'halts' at certain intermediate places having good traffic potential, where there were already convenient means of public access to the line—e.g., beside over- or underbridges, or at level crossings over important roads. It was considered that such facilities, if they could be achieved with low operating costs, would probably encourage a return of some, at any rate, of the lost traffic. The 'halts' were to have a minimum of staffing, the collection of fares on the trains themselves being considered wherever practicable. Reduction of expenditure in train operation was sought by the use of lightweight railcars, whose design was based on the principle—first tried in the relatively early days of railways—of combining the locomotive and the passenger accommodation in one vehicle, which could be driven from either end.

As early as 1903 the East Southsea branch from Fratton (Chapter IV) had been selected for a trial of the railcar principle, the trial being conducted in conjunction with the London & South Western Railway who were co-owners of the East Southsea branch as part of the Portsmouth Joint Lines. That branch had for some time been losing traffic to local road-service competition, so two railcars were constructed for use on it, under the superintendence of Dugald Drummond of the LSW Rly. The first car, after preliminary tests elsewhere (including a few days between Tunbridge Wells and Eridge), was put into service on the East Southsea branch on 1 June 1903. It proved a failure there for the basic reason that it was underpowered, and the second car (which had started service a few days later) as well as the first was withdrawn after service on 9 June, both cars then being returned to Nine Elms works on the LSW Rly for modification. One of the cars, after having been improved, was returned to the East Southsea line in October 1903, and apparently gave a tolerable performance; hence the second one was similarly rebuilt and entered service on that branch about June 1904. The branch itself was singled from the running point of view, using the former 'To Southsea' road, and worked as 'one engine in steam'.

The next step was to provide two intermediate halts, at Jessie Road Bridge and Albert Road Bridge, to encourage the return of traffic. These were both opened on 1 October 1904. However, the reliability of the railcar service left something to be desired, and a single-coach ordinary train had to be used from time to time instead of the scheduled railcar. Accordingly, when the LBSC Rly was considering the introduction of similar services on lines solely in their own ownership, they did not feel that they should draw too heavily on the East Southsea branch experience.

The Brighton felt that railmotor services, with intermediate halts, would be worthwhile on the West Coast line between Brighton and Worthing, and on the East Coast line between Eastbourne and St. Leonards. For the latter it was decided to use railcars, but for the former services small locomotives each semi-permanently coupled to a single coach with driving compartment at the non-locomotive end, were to be employed. Moreover, for the East Coast line services it was decided to test the relative merits of steam-driven and petrol-driven railcars.

On the West Coast line, halts were built at Holland Road (roughly at the site of the original Hove station); at Dyke Junction, immediately east of where the Dyke branch left the West Coast line; at Fishersgate, between Portslade and Southwick; at Bungalow Town, between the west end of Shoreham Viaduct and Lancing; and at Ham Bridge, between Lancing and Worthing. The services commenced on 3 September 1905, and were successful in building up the traffic. The single-coach train units were officially known as 'motors', along with the railcars themselves, but later the apt phrase 'push and pull' began to be applied to those instances where traffic justified a coach at each end of the locomotive; and eventually that phrase also became common for single-coach units.

On the East Coast line, halts were built at Stone Cross, between Stone Cross Junction and Pevensey station; at Pevensey Bay, at Norman's Bay, at Cooden, and at Collington Wood, between Pevensey and Bexhill stations; and at Glyne Gap, between Bexhill and St. Leonards. These were all opened on Monday 11 September 1905, although the motor services did not apparently commence until 14 September—perhaps because the motors themselves were not quite ready for regular use. Services operated by the steam motors were reliable and business started to develop, but the petrol-driven motors were underpowered.

As a result of the foregoing experience, it was decided that the basic principle of such services was sound, and that the single-coach train unit was the best method of working the services. The steam cars were kept on the Eastbourne–St. Leonards services, but the petrol cars were put on the Kemp Town branch from Brighton, a halt at Hartington Road, north of Kemp Town Tunnel, being opened on 1 January 1906. Here again they were not very successful, and eventually, after various periods when

they were out of service, they took over motor services on the
Lewes–Seaford line on 6 October 1906; that line had had a
motor service for a short period already, provided by single-
coach train units, in connection with which Southease &
Rodmell halt had been opened between Southerham Junction
and Newhaven, on 1 September 1906. In the meantime,
Collington Wood Halt had been closed in August 1906.

Other halts, also served by motors, were built as follows:

HALT	BETWEEN	OPENED
West Coast Line		
Lyminster	Angmering and Ford	1 August 1907
Fishbourne	Chichester and Bosham	1 April 1906
Nutbourne }	Bosham and Emsworth	1 April 1906
Southbourne }		1 April 1906
Warblington*	Emsworth and Havant	November 1907
Bedhampton	West of Havant	1 April 1906
Oxted lines		
Hurst Green	Oxted station and Horst Green Junction	1 June 1907
Monks Lane	Hurst Green Junction and Edenbridge Town station, north of Edenbridge Tunnel	1 July 1907
High Rocks	Groombridge and Tunbridge Wells	1 June 1907
Three Bridges–Horsham line		
Lyons Crossing†	Crawley and Fay Gate	1 June 1907
Roffey Road }	Fay Gate and Horsham	(1 June 1907)
Rusper Road†}		(1 June 1907)
West Croydon–Sutton line		
Bandon	Waddon and Wallington	11 June 1906
Beeches	Wallington and Sutton	1 October 1906
Woodside and Selsdon Road Joint Line		
Bingham Road	Woodside and Coombe Lane	1 September 1906
Spencer Road	Coombe Lane and Selsdon Road	1 September 1906

*Opened as Denville
†Renamed Ifield on 6 July 1907
‡Renamed Rusper Road Crossing Halt on 1 July 1907. Again renamed
    Littlehaven Crossing Halt later in July or in August 1907, and finally
    Littlehaven Halt in January 1908.

The last four listed were the only ones in the London area provided for railcar services; Bingham Road and Spencer Road were on the line which was joint with the South Eastern Railway and which was worked alternately by the two companies. The S E Rly had also started to run railcars on some of their own lines. Brandon Halt is shown in Plate 22.

In passing, it is worth recording here that most of the above halts still remain in use, of course rebuilt to modern standards and without the suffix 'Halt'. There have been other changes of name than those specifically marked in the above list, but those changes were not made within the period covered by this book.

Various other events relating to the period 1899-1912 must now be mentioned. First must be matters relating to the line itself. The Bognor branch was doubled as between Barnham Junction and Bersted Crossing, on 30 July 1911; partly done in 1902, as recorded earlier in this chapter, this completed the doubling through to Bognor, and involved a remodelling of the layout at Barnham to incorporate a double junction immediately west of that station, to give direct running to and from the branch.

Earlier, it had been decided to reconstruct Portcreek Bridge. To give a wide enough opening for ships to pass, the new structure was designed in such a way that each track was carried on a separate swing bridge, each of the two bridges being swung about a pivot mounted near the north side of the opening. That is, each swing span was pivoted at one end instead of at, or near, its centre; and the two spans, normally parallel with one another in the closed position to enable trains to pass, could each be swung through about 90 degrees in opposite directions, to lie parallel with the north side of the navigation opening to clear the latter for shipping. Each span was of course landed on a pier on the south side of the navigation channel in its normal position, but its own weight was actually carried by tensioners from an overhead portal structure mounted over the pivots of the spans, this portal structure itself being tied back to anchors on the north shore of the opening. Hence each span was supported entirely by the tensioners and portal structure, since it was completely unbalanced by any tail on the inboard side of the span. The weight of railway traffic on the spans when the latter were closed, was of course transmitted to the landings at the outboard ends of the spans. This special bridge was designed by the L S W Rly in 1908, and the new bridge, on the west side of the original one, seems to have been brought into use about 1909-10.

The overall roof at Chichester station had been removed by 1909. The Deptford Wharf branch was doubled east of New Cross Lift Bridge, by 1906.

Until 1907, the usual width of LBSC Rly bogie stock had been 8 ft. 6 in. (sometimes less). Certain 'motors' had stock up to 8 ft. 10 in. wide, whilst one of the 1897 'Royals' was 8 ft. 9 in. wide. In 1907 new stock was built for the 08 45 Brighton–London Bridge and 17 00 London Bridge–Brighton 'City Limited' trains, the train including two vehicles 56 ft. long, one 9 ft. 2 in. wide and the other 9 ft. 6 in. These dimensions were of course acceptable on the main line, on which the stock was intended to run, and on most of the Company's other routes, but were tight at the south (or station) end of Lewes Tunnel—at which, as explained in Chapter III, the 6 ft. was somewhat reduced in order to give safe clearance for normal stock on the inside of the curve at the tunnel exit. The 'City Limited' stock could itself pass through Lewes Tunnel, but would be too close to bogie stock on the other road. Hence an instruction was issued that on any occasion when the 'City Limited' stock was worked over the Keymer line, no other train was to pass in Lewes Tunnel. This restriction remained into Southern Railway days, when alterations at Lewes necessitated the tunnel mouth being widened; and in any case the old 'City Limited' stock did not have to be catered for under electrification. There were also restrictions on the use of this stock through Crystal Palace Tunnel—see Volume II, p. 59 (general statement on that tunnel) and p. 66, Note 7 (final sentence).

Upper Warlingham & Whyteleafe station was renamed Upper Warlingham on 1 October 1900, whilst Willingdon was renamed Hampden Park on 1 July 1903. Other changes of name in the period were Box Hill, which became Box Hill & Burford Bridge in December 1904; and Shoreham, which became Shoreham Harbour in July 1906 and then Shoreham-by-Sea in October 1906. New Croydon—the Local side of East Croydon (see Volume II, p. 241)—was renamed East Croydon Local on 1 June 1909, the Main part of the station becoming East Croydon Main on the same date. Morden became Morden Halt in 1910.

In consequence of the move of Christ's Hospital School from London to a site near Stammerham Farm, on the Down side west of Horsham, a new station was built at the junction leading to the Guildford line. This station, which was provided with a Loop line on the Down side as well as the normal Down and Up Main lines, was named Christ's Hospital and was opened on 28 April 1902. The main buildings, which were large and impressive, were on the Down side, facing a large area for cabs, which was reached by an approach road. The first platform was on the 'railway' side of the buildings, and served the Down Loop. Beyond the Down Loop was an island platform, one face also serving the Down Loop and the other face serving the Down Main. A V-shaped platform served the Up Main and the Down Guildford line, and there was an island platform between that line and the Up Guildford line. That is to say, both the Down Loop and the Down Guildford lines had platform faces on either side. Up trains could also depart from the Down Loop, so that most of the scholars' trains used that line. The Down and Up Guildford lines merged into the single road of the Guildford line, beyond the island platform on that side of the new station. A goods yard was provided on the Down side South of the new station. Two new signal boxes were provided: Christ's Hospital North replaced the Stammerham Junction box of 1865, whilst Christ's Hospital South was entirely new. The latter was brought into use on 27 April 1902, and no doubt the North box was commissioned then or even a few days earlier.

New signal boxes to shorten block sections and thus facilitate traffic working, were brought into use as follows:

SIGNAL BOX	BETWEEN	DATE
Sutton & Wallington Intermediate*	Wallington and Sutton Junction boxes	1899
Holmethorpe Siding†	Merstham and Redhill No. 1 boxes	February 1900
Whyke Road	Portfield Ballast Pit and Chichester East boxes	1900
Belmont & Banstead Intermediate* (later, B Intermediate)	Belmont and Banstead boxes	1901
Sutton & Belmont Intermediate* (later, A Intermediate)	Sutton Junction and Belmont boxes	1902
Banstead & Epsom Downs Intermediate* (later, C Intermediate)	Banstead and Epsom Downs boxes	1902

Warningcamp	Amberley and Arundel boxes	1904
Tilehurst Lane	Dorking (North‡) and Lodge Farm Crossing boxes	1908
Tulse Hill Intermediate	Tulse Hill Junction and Streatham boxes	1908
Hurst Green Intermediate	Hurst Green Junction and Crowhurst Junction North boxes	c. 1908
Lingfield Intermediate	Crowhurst Junction North and Lingfield boxes	c. 1908

*Only in circuit on Epsom race days. At other times, arms and lamps were removed. In fact some of the signals, at any rate when the Author first remembers them in the early 1920s, did not have spectacles or lamps. These were unnecessary as the boxes were only used on Derby and Oaks days (end of May or early in June), the boxes being closed after the return race traffic and long before it was dusk.

†Built by the S E Rly, on that company's line, which however was still used by many LBSC Rly trains.

‡At Dorking, the signal box proper was at the north (or Leatherhead) end of the station, whilst there was a covered ground frame at the south end of the station. Originally, the box itself was called (plain) Dorking, and the ground frame was called the Shunting box. The latter gradually became known as the South box, and in 1901 this became the official designation, the station box then becoming Dorking North box.

The latter title must not be construed to imply that the station itself was then renamed Dorking North. It remained (plain) Dorking until 9 July 1923 when the newly-formed Southern Railway renamed the ex-LBSC Rly Dorking station, calling it Dorking North; at the same time the Southern Railway renamed the ex-SE Rly Dorking station, calling it Dorking Town.

Beddingham Crossing box was upgraded to a block post in 1910, and a new box was brought into use at Barnham Junction in 1911 in connection with the doubling of the Bognor branch.

It was recorded in Chapters II and III that the 1867 Agreement with the South Eastern Railway, originally effective for 10 years from date, had been extended from time to time so as to be in force in 1899. As from 1 January in that year the South Eastern Railway and the London, Chatham & Dover Railway were brought together in a Working Union, under the title of the South Eastern & Chatham Railway, but the two companies continued to exist as separate entities. The Brighton's Agreement with the South Eastern was continued, and on 5 January 1909 its validity was extended for a further period of five years.

A scheme for a light railway, based on the use of tramcars, was put forward in 1902 for a line from Eastney (east of Portsmouth) on the south-eastern corner of Portsea Island, to South Hayling. It was to cross Langstone Channel (between Portsea and Hayling Island) by a transporter bridge, and was to serve the LBSC Rly's Hayling Island station. The concern took the name of the Portsmouth and Hayling Light Railway, and was active in 1903. It never materialized.

Reference was made in Chapter V to two schemes for lines to Sutton in competition with the Brighton company's lines. The first of these was a proposal in 1882 for a line from Worcester Park, and the second was in 1888 for one from near Raynes Park, in both cases on the LSW Rly. The Metropolitan District Railway had been concerned between those dates, in attempts to reach Wimbledon and various points in Surrey, but the LSW Rly had themselves decided to build a line from the Putney area to Wimbledon to occupy that part of the territory involved. A third proposal for a competitive line to Sutton was actively pressed in 1909, and the Wimbledon and Sutton Railway obtained an Act for this purpose in the following year (10 Edw. 7 & 1 Geo. 5 cap. 47, dated 26 July 1910). The company concerned was nominally independent, but the Metropolitan District Railway was in the background and was given full running and staff powers. Section 5 of the Act gave the new company 3 years for the purchase of the necessary land, and two more for construction. An extension of time for the purchase of land was granted by 3 & 4 Geo. 5 cap. 37 of 15 August 1913, but the commencement of the First World War in 1914 caused matters to be shelved.

By the early 1900s the reliability and performance of road motor vehicles had become such that they could be seen by their devotees as becoming of ever-increasing importance as a means of transport. Hence ideas began to form that special provision should be made for motor vehicles, instead of driving them amid horse-drawn traffic, equestrian riders, cyclists, and pedestrians on the ordinary roads. As early as 1906 there was, in fact, a proposal for a 'motor way' between Thornton Heath and Brighton. Railways at this time did not, however, feel that road transport would be likely to do appreciable harm to their commercial prospects, and were certainly not alarmed at proposals for 'motor ways'.

The line to Brighton was used in an interesting experiment during the week beginning on Monday 25 July 1910, to show the practicability of telephoning from a moving train to a position on the lineside. Equipment designed by Hans von Kramer, of Birmingham was used, Mr. von Kramer travelling in the 14 03 train from London Bridge and speaking successfully to a gentleman in one of the signal boxes at Three Bridges.[18]

It will be recalled from Volume I, Chapter XIV, that several of the overbridges on the Croydon–Epsom line were constructed with a pier in the '6 ft.' space, and hence had rather limited clearances. A fatality occurred about 1908 due to a guard striking his head when looking out through a bridge of this type between Ewell and Epsom. As a result, authority was obtained to take that bridge down. Two more (carrying what are now called Anglesey Gardens and Cherry Hill Gardens/Merebank Lane on either side of Wallington) were also taken down in later years, and others were rebuilt at later dates in connection with road widening schemes. Collington Wood Halt, closed in 1906, was reopened as West Bexhill Halt on 1 June 1911. Hartington Road Halt on the Kemp Town branch was closed after that date.

The Hellingly Hospital line, in no way associated with the LBSC Rly, was built in 1899 to connect that hospital with the Heathfield line. It started from sidings on the Down side at Hellingly, and from 1903 was operated electrically.

Only one train accident during the period covered by this chapter, needs to be mentioned here. This occurred to an up train at Stoat's Nest on 29 January 1910. A wheel on a carriage axle shifted outwards towards the journal, thus making the wheelset concerned wide to gauge. Hence a derailment took place when the train was passing over switch and crossing work south of Stoat's Nest station, as the train was about to run through that station after having come via the Quarry line. The derailment caused the death of five passengers in the train and two persons on the station as well as injuries to 42 other people. Tests of increased severity on the force needed to drive wheels on to axles, were laid down to obviate the risk of further trouble of this type, whilst Stoat's Nest station was renamed Coulsdon North & Smitham Downs on 1 June 1911.

NOTES

1. The existing single-line flyover spur, forming the Down Sutton and Portsmouth line, was to be widened on the west side, so that the

original road would become a down line and the new road would become an up line. The double line thus formed ultimately became the Local spur.

The existing single-line direct spur, forming the Up Portsmouth and Sutton line, was also to be widened on the west side, so that the original road would become a down line and the new road would become an up line. The double line thus formed ultimately became the Main spur.

2. LBSC Rly Special Traffic Notice No. 27, 1903, page 11.
3. LBSC Rly notice No. 135, dated 2 July 1903.
4. LBSC Rly Notice No. 142, dated 27 December 1905.
5. A good description of the facilities (well known to the Author in later days) appears in *The Railway News*, LXXIX (23 May 1903), 814.
6. *The Railway News*, 99 (29 March 1913), 708.
7. Portsmouth Joint Line Notice No. 140, issued by the LBSC Rly and hence headed LBSC Rly and LSW Rly and dated November 1905 (actually issued on 30 November).
8. *Ibid.*, Notice No. 141, also issued by the LBSC Rly and hence similarly headed, and dated December 1905.
9. LBSC Rly Notice No. 156, dated 5 August 1909.
10. LBSC Rly Notice No. 157, dated 12 August 1909.
11. Details will be found in *The Railway Engineer*, XXXI, 177–181. The information in that article was also issued separately in the form of a pamphlet, by Messrs. McKenzie & Holland Ltd., the signal engineering firm who were involved in the work and who utilized Sykes gear for actual working. The pamphlet is entitled 'The Reversible Line'.
12. Date of alterations to locking in Sutton West box and of new Cheam signal box.
13. West London Extension Railway Notice, dated 20 June 1909.
14. West London Extension Railway Notice, dated 4 November 1909.
15. LBSC Rly and WLE Rly Notice No. 161, dated 10 March 1910.
16. LBSC Rly and WLE Rly Notice No. 164, dated 31 May 1910.
17. LBSC Rly Notice No. 163, dated 10 May 1910.
18. *News of the World*, Sunday 31 July 1910, 13.

Note: The Times, in an article contributed by a correspondent and entitled 'Forgotten Inventions', which was printed on 22 July 1960, stated that the trial had been made in June 1910.

The contemporary account in *News of the World* is probably correct as regards the date, as compared with an account written 50 years later. News of what, in 1910, was a novelty would hardly have been delayed for a month before being published.

CHAPTER EIGHT

Electrification
(1903-1912)

ELECTRIC TRACTION on railways had become practicable many years before it began to be thought of as a real alternative to steam.

Prior to the building of railways, people had generally walked between their homes and their places of work in cities and large towns. The speed and comfort of travelling even relatively short distances by railway were, however, such that it became worthwhile to many to walk from home to the nearest station; then to travel by train to the station closest to the factory or office at which they were employed; and finally to walk between that station and their place of work. With the development of public road services by omnibuses and street tramways, large numbers of people began to find that it was more convenient to use them than to wait for trains, and in addition the lengths of walks at each end of the bus or tram journey were often less than those to and from railway stations. Various railway companies saw electrification of their local services, with more frequent regular-interval services than they were providing with steam locomotives, as the most likely way to recapture lost traffic. There was no real incentive to consider electrification of main-line services, as the traffic was virtually immune from road-service competition.

Reference has already been made to the steps which led up to the LBSC Rly's decision to seek Parliamentary authority to work trains electrically, including Major Cardew's assessment that considerable advantages could be secured by the electrification of the Brighton's longer-distance services. The necessary general powers for electrification were given in 1903, and the LBSC Rly board then retained Philip Dawson in a consultative capacity to report to them on the practicability and most suitable method of converting their suburban system to electrical working. In particular, he was asked to look, in the first instance, at the question of electrifying the South London line.

Philip Dawson, when making his investigations, would naturally have taken account of the January 1902 report to the Brighton board, by Charles Morgan, the Brighton's Chief Engineer. In that report, Morgan had drawn attention to the disadvantages from the LBSC Rly viewpoint, of the third rail system that he (Morgan) had seen in operation in Italy during his visit there in 1901 (see Chapter VII).

Dawson's report was passed to the directors in July 1904, and advised them that the South London line should be electrified, and that if the results were as Dawson anticipated, they would be justified in carrying out his (Dawson's) recommendation that the whole of the suburban system should be converted. His advice that the alternating-current single-phase 'overhead' system should be adopted was strongly influenced by the need to adopt a system that would be satisfactory for long-distance electrification as well as for purely suburban lines, should there ever be any thought of such extensions (see also Chapter XI).

The Brighton board generally accepted Philip Dawson's recommendations, and as a result asked him to prepare specifications, and to invite tenders, for the plain section of the South London line between Peckham Rye and Battersea Park. The tenders were received in April 1905, and the contract was awarded to the Allgemeine Elektricitäts-Gesellschaft of Berlin, who sub-contracted the overhead line work, including feeders and switchgear, to Messrs. R. W. Blackwell & Company of Westminster, London.[1] Shortly after the main contract was awarded, the LBSC Rly decided to extend electrification from Peckham Rye into London Bridge, and from Battersea Park into Victoria, so that through working could be achieved between the two London termini. These extensions were covered by a second contract with A.E.G., which was signed on 30 March 1906; Messrs. R. W. Blackwell & Company[1] were again the sub-contractors for the overhead line work, including feeders and switchgear. The rolling stock was built by the Metropolitan Amalgamated Carriage and Wagon Company.

There is insufficient space in the present account to give extended technical descriptions of the system or of its constructional features. However, it must be recorded that the supply was at 6700 volts 25 hertz, the feed coming direct to Queens Road Peckham from the London Electric Supply Corporation generating station at Deptford. The overhead conductor was supported by two catenaries side-by-side, each catenary being normally carried on insulators mounted on top of steel structures. Except in certain instances (e.g. under low bridges) this arrangement was carried out throughout. The use of two catenaries was to enable the insulators to be mounted away from the centre-line of the track concerned, so as to miss the blast from engine funnels; but it also made for a stiffer configuration. The normal height of the conductor was 16 ft. above rail level, but it was reduced in height as necessary beneath overbridges. At London Bridge and Victoria the conductor was raised to 19 ft. 9 in. above rail level, so that there would be adequate clearance for men to stand on the roofs of vehicles, in order to lamp oil-lit steam stock or to light non-bypass lamps on gas-lit steam stock. Bow collectors were employed, being arranged in pairs so that one collector of each pair could be raised in the opposite direction to that of the second collector of that pair. As pairs of collectors were mounted at each end of each train unit, the collectors actually in use at the front and rear of the train unit were of course those that 'trailed' with respect to the direction of travel at the time. The conductor wires were staggered to a distance of up to 9 in. on each side of the centre-line of the track, to avoid the occurrence of slotted bows.

The stock, all newly built, was formed into 9 coach units, the end motor vehicles of which each had driving compartments at their outer ends. Behind each driving compartment was a guard's compartment, the remainder of the two end vehicles of each 3-coach unit each making provision for 66 third-class seats [these would nowadays be designated second class]. No provision was made for second class when three classes were still normal practice. The middle vehicle of each 3-coach unit seated 56 first-class passengers. All passenger accommodation was in compartments, with individual doors to facilitate quick loading and unloading. Each vehicle had an open side passage way to facilitate train working by assisting passengers to find seats The motor coaches each had four 115-h.p. single-phase motors (the largest then available). The stock was 63- ft. 7 in. long by 9 ft. 3 in. wide (Plate 23).

At London Bridge, four platform roads on the South London side of the station were equipped for electric working (in Southern Railway days these finally became Nos. 19-22 before the recent reconstruction of the entire terminus). Between London Bridge and Peckham Rye, the two outer South London Line roads were electrified (the unelectrified middle road being reversible between London Bridge and South Bermondsey Junction, as explained in Chapter VII), whilst between Peckham Rye and Battersea Park the two roads used by LBSC Rly trains were of course equipped. From the junction at Battersea Park to Victoria, the Up Local and the Down Local roads, only, were electrified, as the layout was such that South London line trains had to use those roads. In Victoria station five platform roads were equipped through the South Section into the North Section (these latter became the present Nos. 9-13). Repair shops for the rolling stock were built at Peckham Rye in the fork between the South London and the Tulse Hill lines.

The work of installing the overhead structures (Plate 24), and of fitting up the catenaries and conductors, was as far as possible done at nights or on Sundays between trains, with the minimum number of possessions. Hence completion of the work was a lengthy business. The first trial run took place on 17 January 1909,[2] between Battersea Park and East Brixton, and was followed by others (Plate 25). The public opening between London Bridge and Victoria took place on 1 December 1909. Technical details have been published elsewhere.[3,4,5,6]

Electrical operation was a commercial success. Before the falling-off of traffic already referred to, some 8,000,000 passengers used the South London line each year; by 1908 the figure had fallen to 3,000,000. Within the first month the traffic had increased by nearly 55 per cent, and by April 1910 the number of passengers using the line had doubled. The rate of increase continued, and eventually the line was being used by more people than before the fall-off started. For publicity purposes the LBSC Rly named it 'The Elevated Electric' (much of the South London line was above ground level, so that the word 'elevated' had two meanings in the Brighton's advertising).

The success of the South London electrification fully supported Philip Dawson's expectations, and early in 1910 it was decided to extend this system of working to the Crystal Palace from Victoria, the new work therefore starting at Battersea Park and covering the line via Clapham Junction, Balham, and Streatham Hill. As the same main and sub-contractors were to be employed, and similar equipment was to be used for the static work, the only features of interest were associated with physical limitations at certain points to the erection of normal structures to carry the catenaries. The main places concerned were through Leigham Court and Crystal Palace Tunnels; and between Poupart's Junction and Clapham Junction due to the proximity of the LSW Rly and the Transfer Siding.

In the tunnels, the catenaries were supported by steel beams carried on brackets let into the tunnel arch, the insulators being mounted on top of the beams. Between Poupart's Junction and Clapham Junction there was insufficient space for any upright members between the LBSC Rly's Up Main line or the Transfer Siding, and the LSW Rly's Down Main Local line. Hence on this section long cantilevers were carried from 'outside' (i.e. to the east of) the LBSC Rly's Down Local line, reaching over all four of the Brighton's roads to cover possible future requirements. The length of these cantilevers necessitated supports with the uprights spaced well apart; hence they were so designed that a fifth road could be taken through the framework of the upright should it ever be necessary (Plate 26). This facility for a widening of the existing four roads was never required, but the elevation presented by the long cantilever carried on a wide support was the reason why, in the First World War, these structures became colloquially known as 'guns'. One, near Poupart's Junction, was left as a structure for Poupart's Junction Up Home signals, when these were resited after the single-phase electrification was done away with in Southern Railway days. This structure was later used to carry colour-light signals, which duty it still performs in 1978.

In other places various designs of supporting structure for the catenaries were needed, but none of them was of sufficient importance to warrant reference in this account.

Between Battersea Park and Clapham Junction South, only the two Local lines were electrified, as an extension of the South London line electrification between Victoria and Battersea Park. Between the south end of Clapham Junction and the south end of Balham, however, all four roads were equipped in order to give passing facilities if necessary (Plate 27). Beyond Balham there was, of course, only a double track to be equipped as far as the junction at the west end of Crystal Palace station, from which point the two roads into the 'London' side of the station were electrified. The electrification in fact extended some little way towards Sydenham in order to provide facilities for trains to reach the Pit Roads between the two 'London' platforms, those roads being used as sidings for electric stock and being equipped accordingly. At Clapham Junction, one of the three Pig Hill Sidings was electrified, with a facing lead off the Up Local and a trailing connection on to the Down Local, to enable up trains to be turned back at Clapham Junction if need be. At Streatham Hill, electrification was applied to a dead-end bay on the Up side so that down trains could be turned back there, and also to two down sidings.

Experience on the South London service had shown that the all-first-class middle vehicle in the 3-coach units provided an unnecessary amount of accommodation in that class, and that a 3-coach formation was not satisfactory as a standard: it was insufficient at peak periods, and too lavish in slack hours. Additionally, the development of 150 h.p. single-phase motors made if possible to have improved train formations. The reformed South London trains consisted of 2-coach units, a motor third and a control-trailer composite, the motor coach having two 150 h.p. motors. In slack hours one unit was adequate, but two units were coupled together to form a 4-coach train for peak periods. For the Crystal Palace services, stock was limited to 57 ft. 7 in. by 8 ft. because of clearances in Crystal Palace tunnel (Volume II, p. 52 (general statement on that tunnel) and p. 66, Note 7 (final sentence)), and the trains were made up of 3-coach units each consisting of a control-trailer composite, a motor third, and a control-trailer composite. Two such units were coupled together to form a 6-coach train for peak perids. The motor thirds each had two 150 h.p. motors. Messrs. Metropolitan Amalgamated Carriage and Wagon Company again built the new rolling stock, and in addition there were some ex-steam vehicles converted. Again there was no provision for second class as then understood.

Whilst work was in the planning stage on the line between Battersea Park and Crystal Palace, it was decided to make further extensions. These were, in essence, to cover two new routes in association with the Crystal Palace. The first was the line from that station to Norwood Junction and Selhurst, and the erection of carriage sheds and repair shops at Selhurst; the second was the line from Peckham Rye to Tulse Hill, and the two spurs from the latter up to the Crystal Palace line at Leigham Junction and West Norwood Junction respectively. The first of these lines was the more interesting in that, by requiring electrification of the down and up connections between Bromley Junction and Norwood Junction, and the Norwood Fork Spur the works involved the use of a considerable number of structures to carry one conductor wire only, over appreciable lengths of single track. A light form of construction, using a single pole and arm, was employed. Electrification from Crystal Palace to Norwood Junction was in fact primarily to enable the sheds and shops to be sited where land was readily available)i.e., on the west side) and the extension to Selhurst (which actually went a short way north of that station, towards Thornton Heath) was to enable the sheds and shops to be reached from that end since there was no convenient method of getting into them from the down side at the Norwood Junction end. Electrification between Peckham Rye and Tulse Hill, and the Leigham and West Norwood Spurs, involved Knight's Hill Tunnel, through which the same method of supporting the catenaries was adopted as was being used through Leigham Court and Crystal Palace Tunnels.

Apart from the normal two roads, additional work was involved. The middle road was electrified between London Bridge and Peckham Rye (this was reversible as far out as South Bermondsey Junction for South London line trains, as already explained), and two further roads were equipped in London Bridge station (in later Southern Railway days, Nos. 17 and 18). At Crystal Palace, the three 'Croydon' bays were electrified, as well as the up siding at the Norwood Junction end of the station. At Norwood Junction, the Down Relief road was equipped as well as the Down Local, whilst 10 roads in the shed, shops, and adjacent sidings, were also electrified.

The line from Battersea Park to Crystal Palace ('London') side was electrified on 12 May 1911, in time to participate in the working of the heavy traffic in connection with the Festival of Empire held at Crystal Palace and opened on that date by King George V. The extension to Norwood Junction and Selhurst was also used in connection with this working. Although the work on the Tulse Hill lines was ready in 1911, it could not be brought into use until the power was available. A coal strike early in 1912 did not help matters, and eventually some electric services were started via Tulse Hill to and from Crystal Palace, continuing to Norwood Junction and Selhurst, on 3 March 1912, as a means of economizing in the use of locomotive coal. Opening of the Tulse Hill and Norwood Junction lines, and the Leigham and West Norwood Spurs, to regular traffic took place on 1 June 1912.

Steam workings over the East London line, to and from Peckham Rye, ceased after 31 May 1911, as the need to run round at Peckham Rye was a source of delay to the LBSC Rly's electric services.

NOTES

1. Messrs. Blackwell sub-let the cabling to Siemens Bros. and to Johnston & Philips, and the switchgear to British Thomson-Houston.
2. Austin, Edwin, *Single-Phase Electric Railways*, Constable & Co., London, 1915, 4.
3. Dawson, Philip, *Electric Traction on Railways*, The Electrician Printing and Publishing Company, London, 1909.
4. Dawson, Philip, *The Electrification of a Portion of the Suburban System of the London, Brighton and South Coast Railway*, Excerpt Minutes of Proceedings Inst. C.E., CLXXXVI, 1911.
5. Long, Montagne F. *The Electrification of the LBSC Rly Suburban System*, Ninth Paper of Transactions, Inst. Loco. E., Session 1912, 12.
6. Austin, Edwin, *Single-Phase Electric Railways*, Constable & Co., London, 1915.

CHAPTER NINE

Miscellaneous matters and Train Service summary (1870-1912)

REFERENCE WAS made in Volume II to some of the principal appointments in the LBSC Rly up to 1869. The following summary brings the position up to 1912.

Samuel Laing, the Chairman, retired on 2 June 1896 and was succeeded by Lord Cottesloe from 24 June, who, as Hon. T. F. Fremantle, had joined the board in 1868 (see Volume II). Lord Cottesloe retired from the Chairmanship on 5 February 1908, and was succeeded by the Earl of Bessborough from that date.

J. P. Knight, the General Manager, died on 20 October 1886, and was succeeded by Allen Sarle, the Secretary since 1867. Sarle also retained that office, until he retired in December 1897. The combined position was then again split, the new General Manager from 8 December 1897 being J. F. S. Gooday, the Continental Traffic Manager of the Great Eastern Railway, whilst the new Secretary from 26 January 1898 was J. J. Brewer, the Chief Assistant Solicitor.

Gooday was with the LBSC Rly for less than two years, because in September 1899 he returned to the GE Rly as General Manager of that Company. He had to give up that post on account of ill-health, and on 25 May 1910 joined the LBSC Rly board. When Gooday left the Brighton he was succeeded by William Forbes, formerly Traffic Manager on the London Chatham & Dover Railway and a nephew of J. S. Forbes, the latter company's Chairman. William Forbes' appointment as the Brighton's General Manager dated from 30 May 1899, although Gooday did not actually leave until the September.

F. D. Banister, the Engineer, resigned in 1895, and was succeeded by C. L. Morgan from the GE Rly, on 29 November of that year.

William Stroudley, who had been appointed Locomotive Superintendent on 1 February 1870 (see Volume II) died, as a result of illness, on 20 December 1889. He was succeeded by R. J. Billinton, chief locomotive draughtsman of the Midland Railway who had, however, until 1872, been on the Brighton, latterly under Stroudley, in a similar position to that which he vacated from Derby. Billinton died on 7 November 1904, and was succeeded on 1 January 1905 by D. Earle Marsh from the Great Northern Railway. Earle Marsh retired late in 1911, and was succeeded by L. B. Billinton, R. J. Billinton's son.

David Greenwood, the Superintendent of the Line, retired on 30 June 1907, and was succeeded by F. Finlay Scott.

By 1879 most Departmental offices had been established in the London area, in contrast to the number at Brighton at an earlier period (see Volume II, Chapter XV). Only the Locomotive, Rolling Stock, and Marine Engineering offices still remained on the coast.

Although, as will be seen from the above, vacancies at the highest levels were often filled from outside, appointments to other senior positions more directly concerned with the day-to-day running of the railway were, as usual with railways in the 'company' days, made from those already with the Brighton. This custom was of course the foundation of the 'railway families', where younger people were proud to follow in their elders' footsteps, habitually joining (and staying with) the railway with which the family connection had originally started. In this connection the author has pleasure in showing, in Plate 28, a portrait of Mr. H. W. B. Eastland, taken about 1918 when he was Station Master at West Croydon. He started at Norwood Junction in 1876 and, after becoming Station Master at Carshalton, Mitcham Junction, and Penge, went on promotion to Leatherhead; thence again on promotion to Crystal Palace where he was responsible for the local arrangements for dealing with the Festival of Empire held at the Palace in 1911, and with the introduction of the electric train services just prior to that event. In October 1911 Mr. Eastland was again promoted to West Croydon, from which he retired in 1924. His son, Mr. F. H. Eastland, was in the Auditor's Department, and went overseas in 1914; and his granddaughter, Miss Joan Eastland, who was born in the station house at West Croydon (Volume I, Plate 2) and who served the successors to the L B S C

Rly for 37 years, has become the Author's research partner. Miss Eastland's grandmother, Miss Frances Mary Roach, was a telegraph clerk at Plumpton, and another member of the Roach family became Station Master at Brighton in 1923.

Staff welfare was always well to the fore on the LBSC Rly. The company established a superannuation fund early in 1872, which was approved by the shareholders on 24 January of that year and was authorized by section 18 of the LBSC Rly Act, 1874. Not all classes of those employed by the company were then eligible for superannuation, but a new scheme was set up in 1898 and was authorized by the LBSC Rly (Pensions) Act, 1899 (referenced 62 & 63 Vic. cap. 54), so as to enable the old fund to be amalgamated into the new, overall, fund and so to cater for all employees.

The disfiguring of rolling stock by rude sketches and words as long ago as 1847, was noted in Volume II, and vandalism occurred from time to time. For example, on Wednesday 19 December 1888, an obstruction was placed on the up line between Ashtead and Epsom (joint LBSC Rly/LSW Rly line);[1] whilst it was discovered on Sunday 13 March 1892 that seats had been slashed in carriage stock in sidings at Norwood Junction.[2] Damage to railway property is obviously not a problem of recent date.

In the limited space available in this Volume, it is impossible to give any lengthy review of the train services on the LBSC Rly during the period covered by this chapter. However, on the following pages are given examples of typical freight services in March 1875,[3] and typical passenger services in the winter of 1904-05 and in the summer of 1912.

The 19 23 Battersea to Portsmouth ran via Mitcham Junction. There were other freight trains on the routes concerned which did not go as far as the Coast—e.g., at 00 50 from Battersea Yard, at 19 00 from Battersea Yard, and at 22 00 from New Cross, all to Redhill; at 14 26 from Battersea to Horsham via Three Bridges (25 minutes allowed at Three Bridges as there was no through running connection on to the Horsham line in 1875); and at 19 05 from New Cross to Horsham via Sutton.

Up services were to a similar pattern and there were local freight services in connection with the above through workings. All freight trains normally ran on Sundays as well as on other days, but some did not run on Mondays. Certain cattle trains on the West Coast line and associated lines (e.g., the Steyning and the Midhurst lines) also conveyed passengers—probably in connection with markets, etc.

TYPICAL FREIGHT SERVICES FROM LONDON TO THE SOUTH COAST
(MARCH 1875)

Depart	From	To	Remarks
00 05	Bricklayers Arms[4]	Brighton	Conveyed mailbags to Redhill and Brighton.
00 15	Lillie Bridge (Kensington)	Brighton	Conveyed (inter alia) trucks of beer from Redhill, ex Reading, to Brighton on Mondays, Wednesdays, and Fridays.
00 30	New Cross	Eastbourne	—
00 50	Bricklayers Arms[4]	Newhaven	—
01 05	Bricklayers Arms[4]	Littlehampton	—
01 35	Bricklayers Arms[4]	Seaford	—
02 10	Bricklayers Arms[4]	Brighton	—
12 15	Battersea Wharf	Eastbourne	—
17 05	Bricklayers Arms[4]	Brighton	—
19 23	Battersea	Portsmouth	—
21 00	Bricklayers Arms[4]	Brighton	Conveyed Wimbledon Line traffic as far as Norwood Junction.
22 30	New Cross	Brighton	—
23 30	Bricklayers Arms[4]	Portsmouth	Conveyed mailbags to Arundel (bags thrown out while train passed station at reduced speed).
23 45	Bricklayers Arms[4]	Hastings	—

To show typical branch-line passenger services in the winter of 1904-05, the Author has selected the Dyke branch. Rail-motor services had not then been started (except on the Southsea branch, jointly with the LSW Rly). On weekdays and Sundays there were four trains each way between Brighton and The Dyke, the first leaving Brighton on weekdays at 10 25 and the last leaving The Dyke at 17 10; on Sundays the corresponding times were 10 00 and 17 15. The journey time, including a stop at Hove, was 20 minutes to The Dyke, and 18 or 19 minutes from there back to Brighton. The morning weekday service (10 25 Brighton) and its return working at 11 15 from The Dyke, also conveyed freight. For the latter purpose there was a siding serving the outer end of the east side of the single platform at The Dyke, the platform therefore acting as a dock. The Sunday service of four trains each way also ran on Christmas Day—one wonders how many Christmas-day travellers made use of this facility, even allowing for the fact that the Dyke station served the villages of Fulking and Poynings.

Second-class fares were discontinued in 1911–1912 except on the Newhaven boat train services.

By 1912, LBSC Rly train services had probably reached their zenith. What were, for the period, good services were provided, and there were a number of through workings to and from other companies. Pullman cars, first class only, had been run in trains to and from Brighton since 1875, and the use of these vehicles was gradually extended. In the summer of 1912, there were Pullman services to and from Eastbourne and also to and from Worthing, in addition to the Brighton services. The usual timing from Victoria to Brighton was 65 minutes, sometimes fast but otherwise with a stop at Clapham Junction to pick up, or at East Croydon. There were two return 60-minute trips by 'The Southern Belle', formed of Pullman cars only, between Victoria and Brighton. There was also a 60-minute trip each way between Brighton and London Bridge, leaving Brighton at 08 45 and returning from London Bridge at 17 00; this service was popularly known as 'The City Limited', and included Pullman facilities. To and from Eastbourne apart from the use of Pullman cars on weekdays, there was an all-Pullman service on Sundays, taking 90 minutes for the journey.

'The Sunny South Special' ran from Liverpool (Lime Street) at 11 00 and from Manchester (London Road—now Piccadilly) at 11 20, the two portions being united at Crewe and then running via Birmingham to Kensington where the service was handed over by the London & North Western Railway to the LBSC Rly. The train was booked to leave Kensington at 15 35, and, after calling at Clapham Junction and East Croydon, to reach Brighton at 17 05. After reversal, the train then called at Lewes en route to Eastbourne, where the booked arrival was 18 00. The LNW Rly provided side-corridor gangwayed stock, with a restaurant car, for the service, which ran every weekday; two sets of stock were needed, as the south to north working left Eastbourne at 11 35. En route from Brighton to Eastbourne, this train was prohibited from being put into the loop road at Lewes on account of tight clearances.

Many cheap fares were in operation, and by specified trains it was possible to travel from London Bridge or Victoria to Brighton for 8s 6d (42½p) first class return, and from 5s 9d (28½p) third class (would now be designated second class). An annual season ticket between London and Brighton, available at intermediate stations, cost £43 first class and £27 10s (£27.50) third class (now second class).

Excellent services were provided in the London suburban area, with good season ticket facilities. For example, a three-month first-class season ticket between Epsom and London Bridge and Victoria, cost £4 15s (£4.75)—in passing, it may be noted that, even in Southern Railways days up to 1941, the corresponding rate was still only £7 9s 9d (£7.48) for facilities increased to cover Epsom Downs as well as Epsom, and all S Rly London termini.

The LBSC Rly served a number of racecourses, and these, and other events, provided good traffic and usually necessitated extra trains. The build-up of such extra traffic, over and above the steadily increasing ordinary traffic, was the reason why a number of intermediate signal boxes were opened at various places, as explained in earlier chapters.

NOTES

1. Notice issued in January 1889.
2. Notice issued in March 1892.
3. LBSC Rly Time Tables for Goods, Coal, and Cattle Trains, March 1875 and until further notice.
4. LBSC Rly freight depot at Willow Walk.

CHAPTER TEN

Summary of Signalling and Traffic-working Developments up to 1912

CERTAIN SPECIFIC steps relating to the above subjects have already been noted in chronological order in this three-volume account, but a number of important matters, affecting the system as a whole, have only received, at best, passing mention. Within the strict limits of space available to the Author, it is impossible to do more than note certain developments which were especially applicable to the Brighton. For completeness, reference is also made to various matters relevant to the earlier years of the company. The overall outline is given in summary style.

Semaphore signals

The idea for signals of this type for use on railways has commonly been credited to Mr. C. Hutton Gregory when he was Engineer to the London & Croydon Railway. However, Gregory was not the originator of the idea, since Mr. J. U. Rastrick proposed the type to Mr. Gregory when he (Rastrick) was Engineer to the London & Brighton Railway;[1] and, having seen semaphore signals working successfully on the Croydon, proposed on 29 August 1842 that this type should be used on the Brighton in lieu of the latter Company's disc pattern.[1]

By about 1844 the London & Brighton had established semaphores as their standard pattern of signals.

Distinguishing between distant and stop signals

In 1846 the London & Brighton introduced a double-disc 'turnover' signal for distants (then commonly called 'auxiliaries') to make them clearly distinguishable by day from stop signals (standardized to the semaphore pattern).[2]

In 1872, Mr. W. J. Williams, the Outdoor Superintendent, recommended that distant signals should be of the semaphore type (instead of the double-disc 'turnover' pattern), and that, to distinguish them by day from stop signals, the distants should have fishtailed ends to their arms. The first use of such arms was at Norwood Junction in August 1872, but it seems that the change from double-disc 'turnover' distants to semaphore distants was not, for two or three years, always accompanied by 'fishtailing'. For example, the diagram for Burgess Hill signal box in 1874 (see Figure 20), and others of that period, show square-ended semaphore distants to replace double-disc 'turnovers', and the earliest Notices that the Author has so far traced which show fishtailed distants are dated 1875.

The 'turnover' distants continued to exist in some places until at least 1880.

The foregoing methods of distinguishing distant from stop signals, were of course only of value by day, and for night working reliance continued to be placed on drivers' knowledge of the road. In the early 1900s the LBSC Rly decided to adopt the Coligny-Welch reflector which, by means of a special system of mirrors, showed an illuminated > beside the signal lamp and hence displayed that sign to the right of the signal spectacle. It had the advantage that the sign was visible regardless of whether the signal was 'on' or 'off', and so at all times showed that the signal was a distant. When properly cleaned and focused, the > sign could be seen a long way before reaching the signal on a clear night.

The LSW Rly and the SEC Rly (the working organization to run the SE Rly and the LCD Rly) also adopted the Coligny-Welch reflector, and it was also used elsewhere. The LBSC Rly seems to have been fully equipped by about 1911.

Development of semaphore signals

With Messrs. Saxby & Farmer regularly supplying mechanical signalling equipment to the LBSC Rly (Volume II (Chapter XV)), the firm's standard patterns were used on that company. Signal arms were carried in slots in the posts, these slots being long enough for signal arms to drop vertically and so be virtually invisible to drivers. Apparently because of fears that a glass carried in a spectacle might drop out (with the result that, if it were a red glass which fell out, a white (or 'proceed') light would be shown)), it was decided that coloured glasses should be mounted around the periphery of a rotatable disc, which was carried on a vertical spindle in the lampcase. By turning the disc, either a red, or a green, or a white, light could therefore be shown through a clear glass lens in the lampcase, as the disc was rotated through either 45 or 90 degrees about the actual lamp. By arranging two such rotatable discs, one above the other and with the lower one of larger diameter than the upper one, a single lampcase could be used to give night signals for two semaphore arms reading in opposite directions (e.g., an up and a down signal on the same post). The rotatable discs were turned by mechanical linkage off the down rods of the signal arms. The 'all right' position (arm vertical, with white light) was abolished on the Brighton in 1882.[3]

This design was used consistently on the LBSC Rly up to the 1880s, but was finally abandoned in 1897 after more than one untoward incident concerning the lamps, and a design in which the night indication was given by a spectacle moving in front of the lens of the lampcase, was adopted. At the same time, new signals were given arms mounted on the fronts of the signal posts, instead of working in slots in the posts.

Until the 'nineties', Messrs. Saxby & Farmer adopted the practice of painting a black stripe across the face of the arm, instead of a white one as was generally the case. It is probable that the reason for this was the continued use of a light, slightly orange-tinted, red instead of the darker red usually adopted.

Signal-box equipment

Mention was made in Volume II, Chapter XV, of the general use of Tyer's two-position needle block instruments, and reference was made in Chapter III of this Volume to the adoption, on one length, of Hodgson's block instruments interlocked with the signal frames in the boxes concerned. Later, much use was made of Harper's instruments which gave three indications to the 'accepting' signalman but which otherwise looked like Tyer's two-position instruments; Harper's instruments could in fact be worked with Tyer's, and in certain places were so worked.

Sykes lock-and-block began to be used in some boxes from about 1880, and gradually considerable stretches of main line were equipped as well as the London suburban area. Details of the types of instrument used in LBSC Rly boxes, exist in the Author's records, but there is quite insufficient space to publish this information.

Various types of lever frames were used, but here again space precludes publication of details.

Interlocking between levers, to the standards then customary, was carried out by the 1870s, and was made obligatory in the U.K. by an Act of 1889.

Indication of type of train, and destination or route

To enable an approaching train to be identified by signalmen and station staff, nearly all railway companies developed a system which showed what was considered to be essential information in this respect. Most companies decided that the most important thing was the type of train (e.g. express passenger, ordinary passenger, through freight, pick-up freight, etc), signalmen at junctions and other important points working to their timetables and running the traffic accordingly. The LBSC Rly, together with the LSW Rly, SE Rly, and LCD Rly, decided that, with their conditions and alternative routes, it was more important to define the destination or route of each train, rather than its type.

Hence, whilst most companies arranged locomotive head-codes on the basis of the type of train, the LBSC Rly based their system on the route to be followed, and made no distinction between, for example, passenger and freight trains on the same route. This resulted in the need for various types and colours of discs and boards by day, displayed in various positions on the locomotives, and on the use of combinations of coloured lights at night. The LSW Rly, the SE Rly, and the LCD Rly adopted similar principles but, perhaps inevitably, with different shapes and colours of headboards.

Many of the night codes involved the use of green lights, generally in combination with white ones, but from 1917 only white lights were used on the LBSC Rly in order to avoid the risk of a green headlight, perhaps 11 ft. above rail level if carried at the foot of the chimney of the locomotive, from being mistaken for a clear signal by a train travelling in the opposite direction. To achieve this simplification to only white lights, sometimes involved the use of additional positions in which lamps at night, and discs or boards by day, could be displayed.

Train describers between signal boxes, to give signalmen advice on the route (and sometimes the type of train as well) of trains that were coming to them, were also introduced. The LBSC Rly normally used Walker's pattern describers.

Brakes

A number of designs of what came to be called 'continuous' brakes, were developed by different railways, following various inventions. The word 'continuous' meant that the brakes were capable of being applied more or less simultaneously on every vehicle of the train equipped with the necessary apparatus. The presence in the train of any vehicles not so equipped resulted in a gap in the continuity of the brake. That is to say, control by the driver only extended as far as the last vehicle equipped with the necessary brake apparatus. If, for example, the front four vehicles of his train were so equipped, but the fifth was not, the driver's control ended at the fourth vehicle; even if the sixth vehicle and all behind it were equipped, the brakes on those vehicles could not be operated by the driver, or by a guard riding in one of the first four vehicles. Even if the brake were normally capable of being operated by a guard without the need for locomotive, the guard's control was of course still limited to vehicles whose braking system could be, and was, coupled to the guard's own vehicle.

As a result of trials and evaluations, the LBSC Rly adopted the Westinghouse 'automatic' compressed-air brake, the word 'automatic' in this context meaning not only that the brake system was continuous as explained above, but that it would act automatically on both parts of a train which became accidentally divided.

The Act of 1889 already mentioned as requiring signal frames to be properly interlocked, also required the use of automatic continuous brakes on all U.K. passenger trains, with certain relatively unimportant exceptions.

By late Victorian times non-passenger-carrying coaching vehicles (e.g. horse boxes, milk vans, etc.) were also being equipped with continuous brakes to facilitate train working and marshalling, and the practice soon spread to certain types of freight vehicles.

Passenger communication

Following various incidents, including some involving assaults on passengers in the days when ordinary non-corridor compartment stock was customary, individual companies adopted various means by which passengers could attract the attention of the train crew. The usual method was based on a cord led through eyelets along the fascia boards of carriage stock, with connectors from one vehicle to the next, and at the far end coupled to a loud-sounding bell or gong adjacent to the guard's position, or on the engine. Hence any passenger feeling it essential that the train should be stopped, had to open the window of the compartment in which he or she was riding, and then reach for and pull the cord (a considerable length of which might have to be pulled in to take up the slack in a long train, before the bell or gong was actuated).

The LBSC Rly adopted, in the late 1870s, an electrical system, actuated by pulling a knob in the compartment concerned. Electric cables in each vehicle, with couplers between vehicles, completed the circuit from a battery to an electric bell. This system was invented by one of the company's own staff, Inspector S. Rusbridge.

Slip carriages

The LBSC Rly early made use of slip carriages, which were detached from trains 'in speed' (the Brighton's official term) at various stations to give improved services to certain towns. Such services were obviously 'one-way' only, as trains in the opposite direction still had to call at what were commonly called 'slipping stations', in order not only to provide suitable train services but to enable vehicles that had been slipped to be added for return to their starting point.

Slip carriages, one of which had to be the leading vehicle of those that were to be slipped, were provided with a special form of coupling at the front end. A guard who rode in the relevant guard's compartment operated a lever which uncoupled the slip portion from the main train, at a pre-determined point on the approach to the station at which the slip portion was to stop. Depending on the type of automatic continuous brake used on the railway concerned, arrangements were provided for preventing the detachment of the slip portion from automatically braking both portions of the train, as would otherwise be the case. Special tail signals were needed on each part of the train.

Slipping was widely used by a considerable number of railway companies as well as by the LBSC Rly. It required extra care on the part of all concerned, over and above that needed for normal operation, since once the slip was made, the main train had to keep going until it was at least clear of the station at which the slip portion was booked to stop. Moreover, the signalman at that station could only send 'train out of section' (or equivalent) to the box in the rear, when the slip portion, as well as the main train, was clear.

Each slip carriage itself was provided with storage reservoirs which gave an excellent reserve of brake power for emergency use by the slip guard, if circumstances became such that he had to make a quick stop. Normally, however, the slip guard had to stop the detached portion (which could of course be formed of ordinary stock behind the slip carriage) by means of his hand brake.

Level crossings

Reference has been made in all three Volumes, where appropriate, to the necessity for level crossings at certain places, over roads of various descriptions. With the increase of traffic and the higher speeds of trains, as compared with what was usual when the lines concerned were originally being planned and built, some of these crossings began to become a nuisance to road users on account of the frequency with which the gates had to be shut in order that trains could run. Additionally, there were occasional accidents.

The LBSC Rly, in common with other railway companies, therefore, took opportunities that arose from time to time to seek authority to 'stop up and close' certain crossings. Certain instances (e.g., the abolition of Norbury Crossing, authorized in 1896—see Chapter V) have been noted, but space is insufficient to give details. Where crossings could not be closed, fixed signals were often installed and were worked by gate boxes. Some of these (e.g., Beddingham Crossing) were later upgraded to block signal boxes in order to increase line capacity by shortening block sections.

The end of the Victorian period marked the end of an era for virtually all U.K. Railways. Not only were the main principles of signalling and train working established; they had been enforced by the 1889 Act. Later developments, up to the end of the period covered by this chapter (i.e. 1912), and in fact beyond it up to the end of the L BS C Rly's life as a separate company on 31st December, 1922, were more in the nature of improvements than of basic changes.

It was not until after the Brighton had lost its individual identity, that certain changes of a more fundamental nature were made (e.g., the adoption of colour-light signalling on a wide scale and the widespread use of track circuits, as well as different methods of identifying trains, both to station staff and to signalmen). Hence any consideration of such matters falls outside the scope of this account.

NOTES

1. Included in a Report dated 29 August 1842 by Mr. Rastrick to the board of the London & Brighton Railway. The relevant portion of that Report reads as follows:

> I have committed to inform you that Mr. Statham [Resident Engineer at Brighton] having stated to me that the signals made use of on the Brighton Railway were a perpetual source of Expense to keep them even in tolerable working order, I determined to go upon the Croydon Railway and examine the signals put up by Mr. Gregory on that line which were put up on a plan I had some time ago (and before our Brighton Line was opened to the Public) made out and communicated to Mr. Gregory.
>
> These Signals I consider by far the most complete of any that I have seen and with such improvements as I find I can make to them I believe they would not if ever be liable to be out of order and at several of our intermediate Stations the signal erected at the Centre of the Station would answer the purpose of the two that are there made use of.
>
> The Expense of the New Work for these Signals would be about fifteen pounds each, as all the signal lamps, at present attached to the signals now in use would be made use of to be applied to the new Signals now recommended to you.
>
> By this change the Signals would then be uniform all through with the Croydon.

  See also Volume I, pages 166 and 187.

2. Volume I, page 187.

3. L BS C Rly Appendix for October 1882, page 76.

CHAPTER ELEVEN

The Last Years
(1912-1922)

A LTHOUGH THE system had been completed as a whole by 1899, extensive improvements and modernization were necessary during the succeeding years up to 1912 in order to make provision for increasing traffic to and from places outside the inner London area, as recorded in Chapter VII. In certain districts, however, notably in the inner London area and along the East and West Coast lines, there had been a falling-off in passenger traffic on account of competition from public road services. The company had sought to combat this by one of two means.

Where it appeared that more frequent train services, with additional intermediate stops at places where there seemed to be good traffic potential, would be successful in arresting the decline, rail-motor services had been introduced with cheaply-constructed halts (involving low costs in manning) between certain existing stations. Where, however, the fall-off in traffic was heavy and where it would have been extremely costly to have built such halts, apart from operation being in any case expensive, the company had adopted a policy of electrification.

Although the rail-motors originally introduced had been successful in regaining traffic, experience had shown that, as originally conceived, they were not powerful enough to be strengthened with extra stock when necessary to cater for improved traffic. The use of small existing locomotives pulling or propelling one or more vehicles, as mainly used on the West Coast lines, avoided this disadvantage, but the capacity of such rail-motors was in any case inadequate for the inner London area.

Electrification on the South London line had, however, been

so immediately successful in regaining traffic at reduced operating costs that, as explained in Chapter VIII, it was at once clear to the Brighton's board that lines associated with the Crystal Palace should also be electrified. By mid-1912 the Palace electric services were in full operation, and their success fully justified expectations.

Hence, in presenting their half-yearly report for the period 31 December 1912, the Brighton's directors announced the decision that the remaining London suburban services were to be electrified, and that it was to be anticipated that the whole of the work would be completed within four years of its commencement. The report went on to say that the work would be done in sections, electrical working being established on each section as it was ready.[1]

In summarizing the report, *The Railway News* drew attention to the fact that contemporary experience in Germany and in the United States favoured the single-phase system of electrification for long-distance traffic (it was, of course, with such possibilities in mind that Philip Dawson had originally recommended that, in the then state of knowledge of the art, single-phase alternating-current working should be adopted). *The Railway News* went on to suggest that 'it is now evidently only a question of time for the Brighton company to extend electrical working to its seaside resorts',[2] and subsequently averred that the board's opinion was that electric working to Brighton and Eastbourne would be necessary.[3]

The lines to be electrified in order to complete the suburban system were as follows:

(a) London Bridge–Norwood Junction–Windmill Bridge Junction–East Croydon–Coulsdon North.

(b) Sydenham–Crystal Palace.

(c) Norwood Fork–West Croydon–Sutton–Cheam.

(d) Tulse Hill–Streatham–Mitcham Junction–Sutton.

(e) Balham–Windmill Bridge Junction and to the West Croydon line.

(f) Streatham–Streatham Common.

(g) Streatham Junction North–Streatham Junction South.

It will be noted that (b) would complete electrification to Crystal Palace, and that (c), (d), (e), and (g) would cover all routes to Sutton from both London Bridge and Victoria. Although Cheam (the next station west of Sutton) was a good residential area which was steadily growing and was very close to Sutton, the main reason why electrification was to be taken as far as Cheam under (c) was because of the impracticability of having adequate turn-round facilities at Sutton. The quadrupling from Sutton West box to Cheam (Chapter VII) and the availability there of land for sidings provided the capacity which Sutton lacked. Figure 26 shows the London area, with the newly authorized electrification extensions.

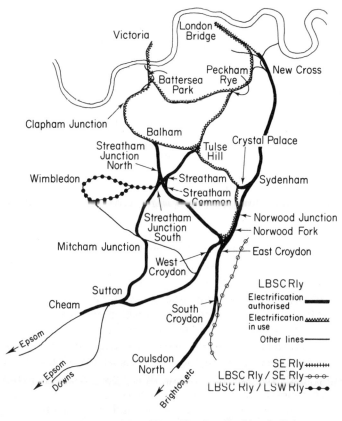

Figure 26. LBSC Rly Electrification: Position in July 1912

Detailed designs and costings would obviously have been prepared before the directors had taken the step to announce what was, until it had been agreed by the shareholders, only a recommendation. Hence contracts were able to go ahead quickly, again on the basis of A.E.G. (Berlin) for the static work and the Metropolitan Carriage Company for the rolling stock, which was to be of a different pattern from either of the basic designs already in use. First priority was given to the line from Norwood Fork through West Croydon, forming (c) of the above list. When completed, this would enable electric working to be established between Victoria and West Croydon via Crystal Palace. The population of Croydon, already 134,037 in 1901, had risen to 170,165 in 1911 and was still increasing rapidly, so that there was every likelihood of good train loadings to and from West Croydon.

Traffic potential was also good at Waddon and at Wallington, so it was considered that some up trains should start from the latter. Hence it was decided to provide a centre reversing siding at Wallington, immediately west of the station. This would involve sluing over the Down road beyond the Sutton end of the Down platform, to join a length of new road laid for some 250 yds. 'outside' the existing Down road, and converting the old Down line into the reversing siding; the new Down road resuming its original alignment beyond the stops of the reversing siding.

At Sutton the existing layout consisted, in essence, of two ordinary double-line junctions laid back to back. At the London end, the route via Mitcham Junction joined that via West Croydon, and immediately west of that junction the Epsom Downs branch left the main line on to Cheam and Epsom by means of a left-hand curve. To facilitate working, a Down Loop line had been provided many years earlier to enable trains off the West Croydon line to reach the Downs Branch without fouling the Mitcham Junction–Cheam–Epsom line. To improve the working still further under electric traction, it was decided that the layout at Sutton should be altered so that both Down and Up West Croydon lines would make direct connections with the Epsom Downs line, clear of the Mitcham Junction–Cheam–Epsom line. A new Sutton Junction signal box would be needed. Consideration had been given to such improvements at Sutton at an earlier date, but the electrification decision brought matters to a head.

Additional carriage siding accommodation would be needed when extra routes were electrified, and as both London Bridge and Victoria were involved, a site was chosen west of Streatham Hill. This was easily accessible to London Bridge via Leigham Junction, at once through Tulse Hill and later, under the overall scheme, through Crystal Palace; and also to Victoria via Balham. The works were authorized by the LBSC Rly Act 1914, referenced 4 & 5 Geo. 5 cap. 102 and dated 31 July 1914, and involved widenings to underbridges as well as tipping and levelling of ground. Some sidings had been in existence on the site as early as 1904.

Work on the Streatham Hill scheme was started in anticipation of the Act, but the work at Sutton was not started seriously by the end of July 1914. Apart from these positive statements, the Author is unable to state the exact position which the electrification works on the West Croydon line had reached by the summer of 1914. This is because he has not so far been able to find any reliable documentary evidence.

Hence the following summary has been built up from approximately-dated photographs, from the clear recollections of a former signalman (employed as a box boy at Sutton in 1914), and from the personal memories of the Author and an old friend of conditions about 1919-1920. It is therefore subject to revision should any reliable evidence to the contrary be found. It seems that by the summer of 1914

(i) At Wallington, the centre reversing siding was well forward, but had not been completed;

(ii) Between Norwood Fork and Sutton Home signals the anchorages for the overhead structures were prepared; and

(iii) Between West Croydon and Sutton Home signals the overhead structures were erected and the catenaries and conductor wires were installed; but

(iv) No overhead work was installed between Norwood Fork and West Croydon.

The reason why no work was undertaken at this stage beyond Sutton Home signals was, of course, because of the pending alterations over the junctions at Sutton—in the event, that work was not undertaken for another 10 years, until 1924/25 and after the LBSC Rly had ceased to exist as a separate entity. A reason why the overhead structures were apparently not installed between Norwood Fork and West Croydon by the summer of 1914 may, it is thought by the Author, have been because of the need for non-standard equipment in the area of Gloucester Road Junction, whereas most of the rest of the route only involved routine work. Be that as it may, the following statement was published in April 1914:[4]

> The extension of electrification on the Brighton Railway is being pushed on. It is hoped that the section between Victoria, West Croydon and Wallington, on which a good deal of work is in progress, will be opened about the summer of next year [1915]. The electrification through to Epsom has not yet been undertaken.

The first part of the statement might be read as implying that work was actively in hand on section (e)—i.e., that between Balham and Windmill Bridge Junction/the West Croydon line—but this was not so, and in fact that route was not taken in hand until about 1922, as will be explained later. The final sentence of the above statement, referring to an extension to Epsom, was of course not in the plan then being executed.

Attention must now be directed elsewhere. As noted in Chapter VI, powers had been granted to quadruple the main line to Brighton as far as Preston Park (beyond which the work could be done on land already in railway ownership); and the Slow lines had been opened as far south as Balcombe Tunnel signal box (north of that tunnel) on 22 May 1910 (Chapter VII). An extension of time for the works south of that box, had been granted under the LBSC Rly Act 1911 (2 Geo. 5 cap. 60 dated 18 August 1911), but the 1912 decision to complete the London suburban electrification must have pointed the way to the desirability of taking another look at the need for further quadrupling of the main line to Brighton. This resulted in a decision not to undertake very expensive works until the need was again proven.

In July 1914 events in Europe moved rapidly towards the start of World War I, in which the U.K. was involved from 4 August 1914 as a result of declaring war against Germany. Since the main contractors for the LBSC Rly's electrification works were a German firm, the outbreak of war very soon brought work on the Norwood Fork-West Croydon-Sutton line to a standstill, by stopping material and equipment already ordered from being delivered. Moreover, no work could be started on any of the other routes scheduled to be done. Disorganization after the war also prevented an early resumption of electrification, and it was apparently not until about 1920 that activities were resumed on the West Croydon line. However, in anticipation of making a station to replace Beeches Halt, a new signal box was built on the down side just west of Beeches Avenue overbridge, in December 1916, but this was not then brought into use. It was to replace Sutton and Wallington Intermediate box (Chapter VII).

While electrification itself was the most important feature in the immediate pre-war years, certain other matters which relate to that period must now be recorded. Further, attention must be given to certain works during the War.

It has already been explained that one of the advantages of electrification was that improved train services could be run. To facilitate this, it was decided to build a number of new signal boxes, which would give additional block sections along the most heavily worked sections. These were, in order,

Wandsworth Common North, on the Up side on the New Wandsworth side of Bellevue Road Bridge. (The existing Wandsworth Common box, on the Up side south of the station, was to be renamed Wandsworth Common South.)

Balham North, on the Down side west of the bridge over Balham High Road.

Norbury Manor, on the Down side about midway between Norbury and Thornton Heath stations.

Whitehorse Road, on the Down side about midway between Thornton Heath and Selhurst stations.

The signal-box structures were all erected by the early summer of 1914, but the Author is uncertain whether or not any or all of the lever frames had actually been installed. The Sykes Lock-and-Block apparatus had all been made and was awaiting delivery.[5] Work on these boxes was stopped on the outbreak of war, and was never resumed, but the box structures remained intact until well into Southern Railway days. The Author remembers them well.

Certain matters of importance concerning the East London Railway must now be chronicled. The most important from the LBSC Rly's point of view was probably that the double line between Deptford Road Junction and Old Kent Road Junction (on the Brighton's South London line), from which passenger services had been withdrawn after 31 May 1911 (Chapter VII), was closed altogether early in 1913. This meant that all movements between the LBSC Rly and the East London had henceforth to be made via New Cross. Following this, the East London line was electrified on the 4th rail system, with Metropolitan Railway trains, and was equipped with automatic and semi-automatic signalling between Shoreditch and Canal Junction (where the East London divided to reach New Cross LBSC Rly and New Cross SEC Rly). This was brought into use on Monday 31 March 1913,[6] and with it there ceased regular through workings of passenger trains between the LBSC Rly and the Great Eastern Railway. The GE Rly continued to operate a freight inter-change service to New Cross LBSC Rly, and to Hither Green Sidings via New Cross SEC Rly. Earlier, on 17 July 1911, Deptford Road station on the East London line had been renamed Surrey Docks; but the signal box at Deptford Road Junction, where the Up Side connection from New Cross LBSC Rly joined the East London line, retained that name although reduced in status to a ground frame (only opened when it was necessary to use the Up Side connection for a through working).

A number of new works completed just before the First World War must next receive mention. At Norwood Junction, an additional down line was laid between the Down Crystal Palace line off Bromley Junction, and the Down Goods which turned out of the Down Local. The Down Goods was also upgraded to Down Relief, and hence enabled additional down passenger facilities to start at Norwood Junction North instead of at the

South box, from which the extra road already extended as the Down Relief as far as South Croydon Junction. By means of the new connection off the Down Crystal Palace line, three down parallel moves could be made simultaneously—Down Main, Down Local, and Down Crystal Palace to Down Relief. The Author has not yet ascertained the date at which this work was carried out, but it seems to have been in 1914.

Further out, what was previously referred to as the Withyham Spur was at last brought into use. As explained in Chapter III, this spur, connecting the East Grinstead-Groombridge-Tunbridge Wells line with the Uckfield-Eridge-Groombridge line, had been authorized in 1878 but not built, and the 1881 Oxted and Groombridge line was to join the East Grinstead-Groombridge line west of the west end of the spur. Hence when the spur was built, through running would be possible between both the East Grinstead and the Oxted lines, and Eridge, both for Uckfield and for Hailsham-Polegate (authorized in 1876 after earlier authority for a local line—Chapter II). The spur was constructed and the two tracks were laid on it by 1888, but the line was not brought into use when that from Oxted and Edenbridge was opened to Ashurst Junction on 1 October 1888. Instead, the two roads on it were used as sidings, entered at the Ashurst Junction end, and were utilized for holding locomotives (and probably rolling stock) that either awaited repairs or had been condemned. To prepare the spur for opening, the layout at Ashurst Junction had to be completed and a new junction had to be laid in at the Eridge end, which was named Birchden Junction (in the 1881 Table of Distances, the notional point of junction was called Eridge Junction—see Chapter III and Note 5 therein).

Birchden Junction signal box, which was on the west side of the junction, and the spur, were brought into use on Sunday 7 June 1914,[7] the new line being named the Ashurst Spur.

Another event of some historical importance was the abolition of what became known as Courtrai Road bridge, a short way north of Honor Oak Park station. This had been one of the six bridges of the type illustrated on page 55 of Volume I, and had been built by the London & Croydon Railway. It had been modified, as described therein, but its principal characteristics had not been altered. Camberwell Borough Council gave up all rights to the bridge on 30 December 1913, and demolition took place early in 1914.

One other matter of some interest concerned Tooting Junction, on the joint LBSC Rly/LSW Rly lines to Wimbledon. The main train service ran via the 'Lower' loop, serving Merton Abbey and Merton Park, and hence somewhere about 1910/11 the 'Upper' loop serving Haydons Road was worked by push-and-pull trains of the two companies (known as 'motors' on the LBSC Rly).

In this connection, the Author was advised that the Brighton's engines came from New Cross and were away from their depot for about 19 hours at a time. In order that the ash-pans could be raked out, an engine pit was therefore constructed in 1912 in each road of the 'Upper' loop, clear of the junction and hence not far from the original (pre-1894) station on the 'Upper' loop. Engines of freight trains working to and from Tooting Junction no doubt also used the pits.[8]

Bandon Halt, between Waddon and Wallington was closed on 7 June, 1914.

Finally, a number of signal box alterations were made in order to facilitate traffic working, as follow:

Adversane box, on the down side south of Adversane Crossing, between Billingshurst and Cray Lane boxes, was opened on 19 August, 1912.

Thorndell box, on the up side between Hardham Junction and Amberley, was opened in August, 1912, in replacement of a temporary hut that had been erected there in June 1911. It was 1 mile 1370 yds. south of Hardham Junction box and 2 miles 348 yds. north of Amberley box.

Hamsey Crossing, previously only a gate box, was upgraded to a block post on 28 May 1913 to divide the section between Cooksbridge and Lewes West, and so to facilitate the working at Lewes.

Burpham box, on the down side between Amberley and Arundel, was opened on 15 March 1914. It was 1 mile 1373 yds. south of Amberley box, and 1 mile 1386 yds. north of Arundel box. It replaced Warningcamp box at the level crossing of that name only some ¾ mile north of Arundel station, and hence about 1 mile south of the site of the new Burpham box (which almost exactly divided the

Amberley–Arundel block section). Warningcamp box was abolished on 27 February 1914 and the timber structure re-used for Burpham box.

Langhurst box, on the down side between Hurst Green Junction and Edenbridge Town, was apparently opened about 26 June 1914. It was 1 mile 877 yds. south of Hurst Green Junction; and 2 miles 1211 yds. north of Edenbridge Town Box.

Farlington Intermediate box, on the up side between Bedhampton Mill and Farlington Junction boxes, was brought into use on 17 November 1914. It replaced Bedhampton Mill Intermediate.

The Brighton's 1867 Agreement with the South Eastern had, as already noted in Chapters II, III, and VII, been extended from time to time. The 5-year continuation of that Agreement on 5 January 1909 therefore fell due for review towards the latter part of 1913. Negotiations between the two companies were, in fact, still in progress at the start of the First World War, in which the United Kingdom became involved on and from 4 August 1914. It had already been decided that, in such an event, the Government would take control of all the railways in the United Kingdom. Hence, under such conditions, there was no call for any further extensions of such inter-company Agreements.

Newhaven became one of the main South Coast ports for the support of the armies in France, and hence expansion of the existing facilities were needed to deal with the greatly increased traffic. The main alteration was the construction of a set of 10 down reception roads, land for which was taken on the north (or Lewes) side of the level crossing north of Newhaven Town station. Entry to these reception roads, and exit from two up departure roads, was controlled by a new signal box on the up side, 1021 yds. north of the existing Newhaven Town box. The new box was named Newhaven Town North and the existing one renamed Newhaven Town South. The work was probably done in 1915.

A halt at Salfords, between Earlswood and Horley, with side platforms on the Slow lines only, was opened on 8 October, 1915, for staff in an adjacent works. It was built to the north of the sidings adjacent to the Up Slow line, and hence well to the north of the existing signal box (opened in 1907—see Chapter

VII). It will be recalled that earlier there had been local agitation for a station to be provided at Salfords.

Sidings for war-time traffic were constructed at Hilsea, at the north end of Portsea Island, late in 1915, and were entered through a facing connection in the Up road, worked from Green Lanes Crossing box. They appear to have been brought into use shortly after 12 November.[9]

West Croydon North box was renewed in 1915, the new box being on girders across all tracks, and brought into use on 16 May.

A siding to serve the National Aircraft Factory near Waddon was brought into use in May 1918. This factory was constructed adjacent to the then Croydon Aerodrome, and to reach it the siding, which formed a trailing connection with the Down road between Waddon and Wallington, had to curve to the right until it was virtually at right angles to the running road. It then crossed Stafford Road (equipped with an electric tramway) on the level to enter the factory area. The connection left the Down road some distance on the Wallington side of Waddon station, and a ground frame was provided at the site.[10]

Action was in hand to divide the Waddon–Wallington block section by the provision of an intermediate box, but this was not finished when the Aircraft Factory siding was brought into use. Hence temporary arrangements were made for the siding ground frame to be unlocked by a key from Waddon box, which had to be taken to the ground frame by the guard of the train that was to work the siding. The whole train had to be put away at the siding, and, after the work there was finished and the ground frame again locked, the key had to be taken forward to Wallington box. This could be done six times, after which the electric lineman had to transfer all six keys back to Waddon box again. To enable a running move to be made while the train working the siding was 'inside', the key had to be taken back by hand to Waddon, and collected again from there to let the train in the siding come out and proceed to Wallington.[11]

The foregoing was, of course, basically normal procedure, but some delays can hardly have been avoided if the siding had to be worked by day among a regular passenger service. Bandon signal box, on the down side, 1438 yds. west of Waddon box and 1409 yds. east of Wallington box, was brought into use on 25

May 1918. It directly controlled the Aircraft Factory siding ground frame, enabling the key locking to be abolished.[12]

The middle siding at Wallington was brought into use on 6 February 1916.

Cliftonville Tunnel, between Preston Park and Hove, was blocked during the War,[13] but the Author has not yet ascertained details.

A number of stations and halts were closed to passenger traffic during the War period, and most were never re-opened. The following list is believed to be complete:

STATION OR HALT	CLOSED	RE-OPENED
Albert Road Bridge Halt	8 August 1914	No
Bingham Road Halt	15 March 1915	(1935)[14]
Coombe Lane	1 January 1917	(1935)[15]
East Southsea	8 August 1914	No
Glyne Gap Halt	1 October 1915	No
Haydons Road	1 January 1917	(1923)[15]
Jessie Road Bridge Halt	8 August 1914	No
Lyminster Halt	In or soon after September 1914	No
Merton Abbey	1 January 1917	(1923)[15]
Old Kent Road & Hatcham	1 January 1917	No
Spencer Road Halt	15 March 1915	(1935)[14]
Tooting Junction	1 January 1917	(1923)[15]

In addition, the following closures on other companies' lines must be recorded here:

STATION	COMPANY	CLOSED	RE-OPENED
Brockley Lane	SEC Rly	1 January 1917	No
Clapham[16]	(LCD Rly)	3 April 1916	No
Stokes Bay (Portsmouth area)	LSW Rly	1 November 1915	No
Tattenham Corner[17]	SEC Rly	September 1914	(1928)[15]
Wandsworth Road[16]	SEC Rly (LCD Rly)	3 April 1916	No

At the close of hostilities, during which the railways of the United Kingdom had been under Government control through the Railway Executive Committee, it was clear that there would never be a return to pre-1914 conditions. The future of the railways was not rosy, and their days of virtual monopoly in the field of land transport were past. This was undoubtedly appreciated, perhaps not quite in that way, by the Government, but it was certainly not understood by many railwaymen and members of the public.

Consideration was, in fact, given by the Government to nationalization of the railway system, but this was finally dropped in favour of Grouping arrangements under an Act of 1921. That Act required most of the railway companies to be formed into four large Groups. The LBSC Rly was to form part of the Southern Railway, along with the LSW Rly, the SE Rly, and the LCD Rly (managed jointly since 1899 under the title of the SEC Rly), and certain smaller companies. The effective date of the Grouping was to be 1 January 1923, so that none of the existing companies had any period of real independence between the outbreak of war in August 1914 and the start of Grouping.

Hence the LBSC Rly was not alone in being unable to make any worthwhile plans for the future, since the Grouped companies might proceed along different courses from those of the individual companies. Virtually all that could be done, in fact, was to resume activity, as far as possible and when practicable, on works that were already in hand in 1914. Among these was the bringing into use of the new carriage sidings at Streatham Hill, on which work had commenced before the War (see earlier in this chapter). The Author has not so far ascertained the date when these sidings were opened to traffic, but considers that it was probably about 1920. The Down-side widening from Balham, to provide reception roads onwards to Streatham Hill, was however never completed; evidence of what was intended may still be seen in the unfinished extensions to underbridges.

The main project which the Brighton had in hand in 1914 was electrification of the remaining sections of the London suburban area, and it seems that the gap between the section already in use north of Norwood Fork Junction, and the section between West Croydon and Sutton Home signals, was completed about 1920 by the erection of supports, catenaries, and conductor wires.[18] Late in 1920 the LBSC Rly board submitted to the then Ministry of Transport a comprehensive scheme for electrification of the main line to Brighton,[19] and on 28 February 1921 Sir William Forbes, the General Manager, stated, in a discussion on railway electrification, that 'he was just about to forward a voluminous report on the subject to the Minister of Transport'.[20] Nothing came of these proposals, no doubt because of the forthcoming Grouping.

However, the company announced in August 1922 that electrification to Purley and Coulsdon 'will be rapidly proceeded with' and that 'it is anticipated that the work will be completed next year. The progress of the scheme was interrupted by the War.'[21] It would seem that the supports were erected on the Balham–Gloucester Road Junction and associated lengths by about the end of 1922 or early in 1923, and that they reached Coulsdon North late in 1923.[18] There was, however, an interval before the catenaries and conductors were erected, and it may well have been the autumn of 1924 (i.e. nearly two years after the LBSC Rly had lost its separate identity in the Southern Railway) before that part of the work was complete as far as Coulsdon.[18] At the 1921 census, the population of Croydon had risen to 233,032.[22]

Electrification had also been started south of Tulse Hill through Streatham as far as Streatham Common and Streatham Junction South, and the supports had been erected and the beams had been placed in position in Leigham and Streatham Tunnels.[23] The catenaries and conductors may well also have been erected on all this length, but the Author cannot recollect this sufficiently clearly to be certain. The probability is that the Local and Main spurs between Streatham Junction North and Streatham Junction South had also been done, but here again the Author cannot be certain. Incidentally, the beams were not taken out of Leigham and Streatham Tunnels until some 15–20 years ago, and were of course clearly seen from the footplate;[23] the special supports for the insulators under Streatham High Road overbridge, across Streatham station, lasted until even more recent years.[23] The work south of Tulse Hill was, of course, part of section (d) of the general works, explained in the earlier part of this chapter. The Author has not so far come across any documentary evidence of when the work south of Tulse Hill was done, but it was probably during 1914 when the complete scheme as a whole was being actively pursued. His own personal memories of the 'Elevated Electric' go back to about 1919 on the South London and Crystal Palace services, where it it was generally colloquially known as 'The Overhead'.

As already explained, electrification had so far ceased at Sutton Home signals on the West Croydon line, in anticipation of the improved layout which was to be installed at the east end of Sutton station. This work, too, was badly held up, and the new Junction signal box, erected about 10 yds. on the London (or east) side of the existing Junction box, was not brought into use until 4 January 1925.[24] The necessary alterations to the layout took place in stages, of which the principal ones were on 18 January[25] and 8 February.[26] Hence it was not until later in 1925 that the supports and wires could be taken from Sutton West Croydon line Home signals, over the junctions and into the Epsom Downs platforms; the supports were actually continued for some 200-250 yds. beyond Sutton station, in the direction of Belmont, in order that down electric trains could run forward out of the station sufficiently far to be able to cross to the Up Epsom Downs line so as to start back from there—although there were facilities for starting back from the Down Epsom Downs line. The catenaries and conductors were probably put up early in March, and the work completed soon afterwards. Electrification in part of the old station at West Croydon is shown in Plate 29.

Single-phase electric working was instituted to Coulsdon North and to Sutton on 1 April 1925, but the length south of Tulse Hill was never used for any regular service, and may not have been supplied with power. The rolling stock for the Coulsdon North and Sutton services was of a different type from that hitherto used for the workings previously operated. Instead of power bogies being fitted under passenger-carrying vehicles, separate motor vehicles were employed in conjunction with driving trailers, and the usual formation was a five-car unit consisting of a driving trailer third; a driving trailer composite; a motor van (with accommodation for guard and luggage); a trailer composite; and a driving trailer third. The motor van itself had a driving cab at each end. The vehicles were built by the Metropolitan Carriage Wagon & Finance Company at Birmingham, the electrical equipment being supplied by the General Electric Company. Each motor van was fitted with four 250 h.p. single-phase motors. As the vehicles were screw-coupled into units, alterations to the formation of units could readily be made. Two units could be run in multiple to cater for peak traffic.

Beeches Halt was rebuilt as a station as part of the works, and Carshalton Beeches box was brought into use in replacement of Sutton and Wallington Intermediate, on 29 March 1925. The station was opened on 1 April 1925. Plate 30 shows the arrival of the inaugural electric train at Carshalton Beeches on 31 March 1925, en route for Sutton.

The events which occurred in the period 1923-1925 and which are outlined above, of course actually took place under the control of the Southern Railway, but as they formed a part of the scheme conceived, and approved in principle, by the L B S C Rly, it has been essential to make brief reference to them in this account.

Among the Author's many clear recollections of 'The Overhead', from regular travelling and from observations, are that signals could not always be seen as easily as they ought to have been; and that, perhaps because of the 'triangle' made by the two catenaries and the conductors, smoke and steam seemed to hang around, particularly in foggy weather, more than was the case on non-electrified lines.

Note must now be taken of certain other events during the period between the end of the first World War and the Grouping. Dealing first with purely L B S C Rly lines, occasional slips continued to occur in the sides of the deep cuttings south of New Cross. The soil was clay, and the cuttings were through ground in the vicinity of the former Croydon Canal (Volume I). In most cases the slips were readily contained but a more serious one apparently occurred about 1921 on the Down side some 300-400 yds. south of New Cross station; this is supposed to have covered a siding which ran beside the Down Local line, beyond where the three existing sidings now end. In this event is supposed to lie the old-time title of 'under the Bank' for these sidings, but the Author lacks documentary evidence.

Itchingfield Junction signal box on the Up side, was replaced by a new box in the fork of the junction, on 24th October, 1920.

Crystal Palace Bank signal box, on the Down side between Sydenham and Crystal Palace, was abolished in 1921. About 1920, a new group of sidings was laid in on the south (New Cross) side of the Surrey Canal, and to the east of Wharf Road Down side. These sidings were entered from the Lift Bridge end, and were intended to hold empty wagons for Deptford Wharf, to supplement the Ballarat Sidings on the Up side beside (but at a lower level than) New Cross station and sidings (see Chapter V). Because the additional facilities near the Lift Bridge were alongside the premises of the Mazawattee Tea Company, they were generally known as the Mazawattee Sidings; but to the New Cross men they were simply the New Sidings. At Eardley sidings a proper ground frame was installed, and was known as Eardley Scissors Crossing box. Walker's describers were fitted between the new box and Streatham Junction South box. The new facilities were brought into use on 5 July 1922.

On 1 July 1921, the Metropolitan Railway took over the management of the East London Railway on behalf of the Joint Committee for that line, and on and from 1 January 1924 the Metropolitan took over maintenance of the East London. From 1 July 1885, as explained in Chapter V, it had been done by the SE Rly; and, after 1 January 1899, by the SEC Rly; hence the Southern Railway, into which the SEC Rly was Grouped on 1 January 1923, undertook maintenance for the year 1923, before the Metropolitan took this responsibility over. For the record it may be noted that the Southern Railway, as representing the largest single interest in the East London after the Grouping, assumed ownership from the beginning of 1925 until the formation of the London Passenger Transport Board in 1933.

At various times proposals had been made for railways to serve the area to the south-east of Croydon and eastwards towards Orpington. The Southern Heights Light Railway eventually obtained powers to construct such a line, but, despite the granting of extra time in 1921, nothing came of the scheme.

Only three accidents which occurred during the period 1912-1922 need be referred to here. The first was at Streatham Junction South on 3 November 1919, the second was at Heathfield on 19 April 1920, and the third was at Littlehampton on 4 August 1920.

Streatham Junction South

This was a sidelong collision at night between the engine of a train running under clear signals, and a light engine which was standing foul, but the circumstances were such that some explanation is essential. A light engine from Eardley Sidings to Battersea was, due to a telephonic misunderstanding, taken by Streatham Junction South as being for New Cross. Hence the signalman pulled off for it to run up to his advanced starter to await acceptance by Streatham box. The driver saw that the wrong road had been set for him, but he apparently passed what would in later days be called the home signals (but were then called the starters) and the facing lead on to the Up Main Spur leading to Streatham Junction North, before he stopped his engine and eventually went to the box. The signalman, having been acquainted of the position, keyed out the Sykes backlock on the signal for the Streatham direction (the engine not having reached the treadle), and then arranged with the signalman in Streatham Junction North box that the latter would take the engine instead of empties (which he had accepted from the South Junction and which were coming from the Mitcham Junction direction).

Having made these arrangements, the South Junction signalman proceeded to change the road and then pulled off for the engine to run on the Up Main Spur, without appreciating that the engine was already ahead of the points concerned and so could not make the move he had signalled for it. The driver, having returned to his engine and knowing what was intended, then started forward but at once realized that he was not on the Up Main Spur, and stopped again but with the rear of his engine foul of the Down Main Spur.

The South Junction signalman had by now taken on, received acceptance for, and pulled off for, a train on the Down Main Spur, again without realizing that that road was not clear.

In the resulting collision 40 passengers in the down train complained of injury

The Inspecting Officer placed the blame jointly on the driver of the light engine for running past a signal that was wrongly off for him, and for failing to realize where he had stopped, and on the signalman for failing to see where the engine was, before he changed the road. The Inspecting Officer also thought that there was a case for track-circuiting at Streatham Junction South.

Heathfield

This was a low-speed derailment at a facing connection leading into a safety siding, under clear signals. The points had earlier been run through and the tips of the switches, and other components, had been damaged, but this had not affected the facing-point-lock mechanism or detection.

Two passengers complained of shock.

Littlehampton
This was a buffer-stop collision due to brake pipes not having been properly connected and failure to make proper brake tests. A total of 13 passengers complained of minor injuries or shock.

The final day of the L B S C Rly's separate existence was Sunday 31 December 1922. On and from Monday 1 January 1923 the company formed part of the newly-constituted Southern Railway, but a meeting of the Brighton company's shareholders was held in 1923 in connection with the final half-yearly report. The following figures[27] give a general picture of the size of the L B S C Rly (shown in Figure 27) in its last year, and statistics of the traffic handled and of the locomotives, rolling stock, and ancillary equipment used for the purpose. The overall outline financial position is also given:

ROUTE MILEAGE		miles	chains
Owned		431	2
Share of Joint Lines		17	11
Leased or Worked		8	14
Share of Jointly Leased or Worked		—	75
	Total	457	22

TRAFFIC STATISTICS
Passenger (numbers)

First Class		1,328,474
Second Class*		100,483
Third Class†		40,123,702
Workmen‡		14,968,313
	Total	56,520,972

*Only in Continental trains to and from Newhaven.
†Would now be designated Second class.
‡Would not be included in Second-class totals.

Freight originated

		tons
Merchandize		911,821
Coal, Coke, and Patent fuel		313,417
Other Minerals		570,975
	Total	1,796,213
Head of Livestock originated		205,383

TRAFFIC MILEAGE	*miles*
Steam Coaching	7,659,449
Electric Coaching	1,194,040
Steam Freight	1,184,318
Steam Shunting	1,748,662

LOCOMOTIVES AND ROLLING STOCK	
Steam Locomotives	615
Rail Motor Cars (Jointly owned)	2
Coaching Vehicles	2,604
Freight Vehicles	10,357
Service Vehicles	684
Electric Motor Cars	50
Electric Trailer Cars	84

ROAD TRAFFIC VEHICLES	
Motor Driven	11
Horse Drawn	360
	(336 horses)

SHUNTING HORSES	14

FINANCIAL SUMMARY	
	£
Capital Issued (including nominal additions)	29,700,658
Receipts in respect of Railway Working and of certain Separate Businesses	7,750,421
Expenditure	6,622,103
Net Receipts	1,128,318
Miscellaneous Receipts (net)	215,938
Total Net Income	1,344,256
Proportion of Amount Recoverable from Government under Section II of Railways Act, 1921	205,000

Dividend for Year:	
Undivided Ordinary Stock	5¼ per cent
Preferred Ordinary Stock	6 per cent
Deferred Ordinary Stock	4½ per cent

The London Brighton & South Coast was not a large railway in comparison with those companies whose routes connected London with cities and towns to the west of the Capital, and to the north-west, north, and north-east. One of these other companies (the Great Western) had over 3000 route miles in 1922, two (the London & North Western and the Midland) had over 2000 route miles, and three others (the Great

Eastern, the Great Northern, and the London & South Western) had over 1000 route miles. Even the North Eastern Railway, without any line to London, had over 1700 route miles.

Since London lies in the south-east part of England, a railway system serving only the counties of Surrey and Sussex, and small areas of Hampshire and Kent, would naturally be on a more limited scale than systems (such as the London & North Western and the Midland) that stretched to the border of Scotland. In fact, the existence of a route mileage as high as that of the LBSC Rly in such a relatively limited area, is a good indication of the complexity of the system.

As will be noted from the foregoing statistics, a considerable quantity of freight traffic originated within its own system or was brought into it at Deptford Wharf or from the Continent. This was of course supplemented by a substantial traffic (e.g. in coal) which originated on other companies and was handed over to the Brighton. Nevertheless the LBSC Rly was essentially a 'passenger' line, and had a very heavy regular traffic from what were then called season-ticket holders but who are nowadays referred to as commutors. Brighton in particular, and other South Coast towns to a lesser extent (as well as certain other inland centres), provided a regular all-the-year-round traffic apart from a very large seasonal traffic (mainly holiday makers), in addition to heavy suburban traffic. It was, of course, the fact that there was such a year-in, year-out, traffic, that enabled the capital expenditure on the Crystal Palace electrification to be justified after the worth of electric working had been demonstrated by the immediate results from the South London line; and it was the results of electric working to and from Crystal Palace that made the Brighton's directors decide to electrify the remainder of the suburban system and, later, to propose that the main line to Brighton should also be converted.

When Philip Dawson was preparing his initial report to the Brighton directors on the advantages of electrifying the suburban lines, he had no doubt taken note, as already mentioned, of the earlier review of the Brighton's Chief Engineer when the latter reported against the use of conductor rails on the LBSC Rly (see Chapters VII and VIII). Seen in that light, Dawson really had no alternative but to have his proposals based on the use of an overhead conductor. To keep the weight of this down to a practicable figure, the current drawn by the trains had to be limited, and this meant the use of what in those days was a fairly high voltage. This in turn meant that, on the one hand, the basic method could also be attractive for longer-distance traffic as well as for suburban work and that, on the other hand, the use of single-phase traction motors instead of direct-current traction motors, would save the weight of rotary converters carried on the trains themselves.

Experience elsewhere that had accumulated over the years, however, had shown that the advantages of a simple conductor-rail system, hitherto vetoed by the Brighton directors on the initial report by Charles Morgan (the LBSC Rly Chief Engineer), might perhaps have been given insufficient weight. It is, in fact, at least possible that had a further eight or 10 years elapsed before the Brighton had been forced to consider electrification under the powers granted to them in 1903, improvements in d.c. traction motors might have resulted in matters proceeding along a somewhat different path to that actually followed by the Brighton company.

Be that as it may, the LBSC Rly was satisfied with its method of electrification, and there is little doubt that, if the first World War had not intervened and brought about, as an aftermath, the Grouping, a considerable portion of the Brighton system would ultimately have been electrified on the 'overhead' system. The LBSC Rly pressed on with electrification as soon as possible after World War I, using material contracted for before that War (Plate 31), but orders for the material needed to electrify the remaining London suburban lines, were not placed as matters were by then in the hands of the Southern Railway.

The Southern decided that the third-rail system was to be adopted for all further electrification schemes on the S. Rly. Further, existing 'Overhead' electrification on ex-LBSC Rly lines was in due course to be done away with in favour of the third-rail system. Hence the Coulsdon and Sutton project only had a life of some $4\frac{1}{2}$ years, being finally put out of use in September 1929.

The LBSC Rly was not a very popular line in the 1890s, as explained in an earlier chapter. The great improvements brought about in the early years of the present century, in the way of widening works and rebuilding of stations, enabled greatly improved services to be arranged, and this eventually largely eradicated the sometimes not very complimentary views of regular users of the line. The company entered the Southern Railway with the considerable esprit-de-corps that had existed for a long time among its staff, and hence was in a position to contribute much valuable experience to the corporate whole of the new Southern Group.

As a tailpiece, the Author has included Plate 32, showing Littlehampton about 1930, with a 'motor' approaching the station.

The LBSC Rly had much of interest to show, and the Author is personally very glad that his memories of it go back to about 1917 and that he often travelled on it, and observed it at first hand, in the last two or three years before the Grouping of 1923. He is also very glad that he began to know it intimately from as early as 1925/26 when it was still virtually unchanged—as he did for all sections of the Southern Railway.

NOTES

1. *The Railway News*, XCIX (25 January 1913), 183-185.
2. *Ibid.*, 185.
3. *Ibid.*, (1 February 1913), 239.
4. *The Railway Gazette*, XX (2 January-26 June 1914), 503.
5. Verbal statement to the Author many years ago by his close friend the late Mr. T. S. Lascelles, who had spent nearly all his professional life with the W. R. Sykes Interlocking Signal Company, and who was the firm's Managing Director when he died.
6. East London Railway Notice dated March 1913.
7. *The Railway News*, CI (13 June 1914), 1205.
8. Private communication many years ago to the Author from his old friend the late Mr. J. Pelham Maitland, who not only informed him of the origin of the engine pits, but added that in his (Pelham Maitland's) opinion the engines of LSW Rly push-and-pull trains did not use these pits, which were therefore solely used by LBSC Rly engines.
9. LSW Rly and LBSC Rly Portsmouth Joint Line Notice, Instruction No. 29, 1915, dated 12 November 1915.
10. The opening notice for the siding gave the distance from Waddon station as 'about ½ mile'. That distance was repeated in a further notice one week later, and it was also given on page 275 of the LBSC Rly Appendix for August 1922. Additionally, various Southern Railway Signal Instructions relating to Waddon and issued in connection with the repositioning of certain signals at various dates

following the siding being taken out of use in 1924, gave distances which imply that the siding connection had been at a position which accorded with the above-quoted distance from Waddon.

Important evidence to the contrary has, however, only recently been brought to the Author's attention. This consists of an Engineer's Department plan dated 30 September 1920, showing the National Aircraft Factory Siding and including a proposed siding connected thereto. That plan must therefore be accepted as depicting the Aircraft Factory Siding as it actually was, and cannot be regarded in any sense as being only a scheme for a proposed resiting of the Aircraft Factory Siding itself. From the scale of this plan, the Aircraft Factory Siding made connection with the Down road only some 550–575 yds. on the Wallington side of Waddon box (which was, until its demolition in recent years, only a few yards on the east or west Croydon side of milepost 11). That is to say, the Aircraft Factory Siding connection must have been only a relatively short distance beyond milepost $11\frac{1}{4}$, and not in the vicinity of milepost $11\frac{1}{2}$ as implied by all the Operating and Traffic Department notices and Instructions referred to in the first paragraph above.

The recollection of the Author, supported by those of his research partner and certain of his colleagues, is that the siding passed through an orchard as it curved away from the running lines, but he is not disposed to attempt to explain the marked discrepancy in its actual position as revealed above.

11. LBSC Rly Weekly Notice No. 21 for week ending 25 May 1918.
12. LBSC Rly Weekly Notice No. 22 for week ending 1 June 1918.
13. Dendy Marshall, C. F., *A History of the Southern Railway*, Southern Railway, 1936, 308. Also 2nd Edition, revised by Kidner, R. W. Ian Allan, 1963. Vol. I., 226.
14. By the Southern Railway, after reconstruction as station.
15. By the Southern Railway.
16. SEC Rly (LCD Rly) side only; the LBSC Rly side remained open.
17. Infrequent public service withdrawn, but racecourse traffic continued. Clark, R. H., *A Southern Region Chronology and Record, 1803–1965*, The Oakwood Press, 1964, 88.

Tattenham Corner station was also used until after the First World War for ambulance trains.
18. Recollections of a local member of the LBSC Rly staff who was employed in the area from 1914 onwards, together with those of an interested outside observer during the same period. Opinion supported by the reasoned views of certain ex-S Rly staff, and by the Author's own recollections (unfortunately not as clear on this point as on many others).

19. *The Railway Gazette*, XXXIII (3 December 1920), 748.
20. *Ibid.*, XXXIV (4 March 1921), 333.
21. *Ibid.*, XXXVII (11 August 1922), 210.
22. *Croydon: the Story of 100 Years*, Croydon Natural History & Scientific Society, Croydon, 1970, 60.
23. Personal observations by the Author.
24. S Rly Signal Instruction No. 1, 1925, dated 30 December 1924.
25. *Ibid.*, No. 2, 1925, dated 13 January 1925.
26. *Ibid.*, No. 3 1925, dated 3 February 1925.
    Note: Due to some error, there were two separate Signal Instructions No. 3—that dated 3 February and referenced above, and an earlier one dated 20 January and having no relevance to Sutton.
27. Taken from the *Railway Yearbook, 1922*, Railway Publishing Company, London 212-213.

Locomotives and Rolling Stock from the Traffic Point of View

IN A book dealing with the London, Brighton & South Coast Railway from the overall point of view, the most important matters are those concerned with the build-up of the system and the engineering works involved, together with the development of safe methods of working. To give full particulars of the accommodation provided at individual stations, and of the locomotives, rolling stock, and ships, would introduce a measure of detail which would be out of place. Various accounts giving details of the locomotives, in particular, have already in any case been published elsewhere.[1,2] There are, however, certain matters concerning locomotives and rolling stock from the traffic point of view which must be mentioned in this account. These matters have therefore been brought together in this Annex to the three volumes.

Virtually from the start of the London & Brighton Railway, locomotives were assessed as a means of moving traffic (this, of course, is what they are provided for), since as early as September 1840 the directors were informed that one of the engines on the Shoreham branch had become unsafe to use (see Volume I, page 161). Two years later, in a Report dated 29 August 1842 to the directors of the London & Brighton Railway, J. U. Rastrick, the company's Resident Engineer, said '... I have had the steam up in the Locomotive Engines for our luggage trains and I find the work about the Engine very good but I have ordered several alterations and additions to be made to them which I expect will make them very complete and in the course of Ten Days, or a fortnight the first Engine will be ready to send off and if possible I will return from the north to have it tried with a good load of goods behind it.'[3]

When the LBSC Rly system began to expand as a result of the building of lines to serve untapped districts, each of those lines was, in general, built to connect the district concerned with a town of some local importance. That is to say, most services on the 'new' lines tended to be self-contained and through working was uncommon (in the general absence of facing points on main lines, through working on to branch lines was in any case not facilitated). Hence the then Locomotive Superintendent, J. C. Craven, began to produce locomotives that were individually designed to meet the characteristics and traffic working requirements of the lines concerned. This policy, perhaps at first sight laudable enough at the time, was carried to the extent that even minor details were designed 'from scratch' on many occasions—this naturally leading to waste of design effort, waste of maintenance effort, extra costs, and hence, ultimately to waste of the shareholders' money.

When William Stroudley took over from Craven, in 1870, the Brighton was still suffering from the aftermath of the financial crisis of 1867. The new Locomotive Superintendent soon introduced a fresh approach, using a strictly limited number of classes of locomotives, each class normally being suitable for general use throughout the system for work of a particular nature. Additionally, parts were, if practicable, used in more than one class of locomotive, thereby simplifying maintenance and hence reducing costs, naturally to the shareholders' advantage. This policy has always, by implication, been credited directly to Stroudley, but, seen in perspective, there seems little doubt that the LBSC Rly board must have given guidelines to Stroudley to the effect that maintenance costs had to be reduced as well as day-to-day operation improved. It is, in fact, not impossible that Stroudley's own leanings in this direction may have been one of the factors which led to his appointment to his Brighton post.

The locomotive policies which were established in Stroudley's time were continued for the rest of the LBSC Rly's separate existence. They were of course also followed in principle by the other major railway companies, who had developed them independently. In earlier times light axle-loadings were a hampering feature on certain routes (e.g., the South London Line), but these variations were gradually overcome in most cases and latterly it was only a number of branches on which there were restrictions on the use of certain classes of locomotives.

As the Brighton's routes were all relatively short (none was as long as 100 miles), the company made considerable use of tank engines. The standard length of turntable was for many years 42 ft., but later 45 ft. was adopted. This was adequate for all Stroudley engines and was undoubtedly a factor in retarding the introduction of 4-4-0 classes; and when these were introduced by R. J. Billinton the 45 ft. tables had to be fitted with extension gear in order that the 4-4-40s could turn on them. The introduction of 4-4-2 locomotives in 1905 necessitated the provision of 55 ft. tables at those places to which those engines were regularly worked, whilst where space was limited 50 ft. tables were provided for the K class 2-6-0s, although 4-4-2s could not turn on them as they needed 52 ft. Finally, 60 ft. turntables were fitted at Brighton (two), Eastbourne, Newhaven, Three Bridges, and Victoria.

The short runs pointed the way to the development of large tank engines, and a number of through workings over the main lines, including the 60-minute 'Southern Belle' trains to and from Brighton, were often entrusted to such locomotives. As even at the end of the LBSC Rly's separate existence, there were only eleven 4-4-2 tender engines, two 4-6-2 tanks, and seven 4-6-4 tanks, they were naturally mainly used on routes that had the hardest workings.

Despite the difficulties of the Portsmouth route, particularly via Sutton and Dorking, the train weights were not normally such that other classes of locomotives had difficulty in timing the trains. Hence it was not usual for locomotives of class J (4-6-2-T) or L (4-6-4T), in particular, to be used on the Mid-Sussex line or (for that matter) on the West Coast Line trains. They were not, however, prohibited from running on those lines.[4]

The LBSC Rly made fairly extensive use of Pullman Cars. First introduced on to the Brighton in 1875, they soon became popular with travellers between London and Brighton, and eventually they became something of an institution on the LBSC Rly. For over 30 years the cars were assembled in England (first at Derby and later at Brighton itself), from components made in the United States of America. The wheels and brakes, and the buffing and drawgear, were of LBSC Rly pattern for the cars run on that line. From 1908 onwards the cars were built in England, and eventually more features of British practice were introduced. The cars were operated by the Pullman Car Company (a British concern) from 1915 (previously to 1908, the cars had been operated by a British-based concern owing allegiance to the main Pullman organization in America). The LBSC Rly was responsible for running the cars in selected trains, and for the maintenance of their running gear. The Pullman Company was responsible for the maintenance of the car bodies and for staffing them in traffic, as well as for catering where applicable. Fares from travellers went to the railway company, but supplements were charged to passengers who decided to use the cars, and such supplements were retained by the Pullman Company; the latter also, as already noted, took receipts from catering in the cars.

Up to the outbreak of the First World War in 1914, Pullman cars were for first-class passengers only, but six American-built cars were refitted as third-class cars from 1915 onwards, and later second-class cars were introduced in the Newhaven Boat trains, whilst further thirds were built new (as already noted second class was retained in the Newhaven Boat trains after it had been abolished elsewhere on the Brighton Company's system). Up to the late 1890s, all Pullman cars on the LBSC Rly were carried on 4-wheel bogies, but with increases in length 6-wheel bogies were fitted to keep the inner axles of the two bogies within the lengths of mechanical fouling bars.

Although bogie stock had been built by the LBSC Rly for a considerable period, it was only about 1898 that the company decided that all future main-line stock should be bogie vehicles. Large numbers of six-wheeled passenger-carrying vehicles continued in use, however, and appeared on main-line workings as loose stock mixed with bogie vehicles. A number of seven-coach bogie train units had been formed, electrically lit and with the lighting of the unit under the control of the guard. These were the forerunners of other, longer, sets used in circuit working on various routes. Otherwise, stock was mainly 'loose', trains being formed as required.

Where Pullman cars were run, they were normally included in trains of set formation, the necessary lighting controls for electrically-lit stock being taken through the Pullman cars—although the lights in those cars themselves were controlled by the Pullman staff carried in the cars. On occasions, the regular set of vehicles including the Pullman car(s) might not be available for some reason (for example, by late running or if it were shut in by a derailment), and emergency arrangements had to be made. In such an event, perhaps one of the ordinary bogie train units might be all that was available and in that case a Pullman car taken from the small pool of spares, or from a 'stopped' regular set, was attached to the train unit. The latter thus ran with the Pullman car as either the leading vehicle or the last one. This arrangement was also sometimes followed when extra trains were needed, and only a bogie train unit was available to cover a service advertised to have Pullman facilities. This practice, which continued occasionally well into Southern Railway days, was a well-known sight to the Author, but seems not to have been understood by observers not familiar with the circumstances.

Some details of LBSC Rly coaching stock have been published elsewhere.[5]

The commercial requirements of the area served by the company did not, in general, call for freight vehicles of the types necessary in industrial areas and hence owned by railways whose business was closely involved with the industries concerned. Of the traffic originating on the LBSC Rly system, probably the largest individual items were tree trunks, conveyed more particularly from stations in the Wealden area. Single-bolster wagons were normally employed for such loads, being marshalled in rakes of two, three, or four depending on the lengths of the trunks concerned.

The LBSC Rly required the maximum dimensions of stock to travel generally over its lines, to be as follows:[6]

Width (above a height of 3 ft. 6 in. above rail level)	9 ft. 0 in.
Height in centre (above rail level)	13 ft. 6 in.
Height at side (above rail level)	12 ft. 0 in.

Below 3 ft. 6 in. above rail level, the width was limited to 8 ft. 10 in.; and below 1 ft. 3 in. it was limited to 8 ft. 8 in.

NOTES

1. *Locomotives of the LBSCR*, by D. L. Bradley, The Railway Correspondence and Travel Society, London. Parts 1, 2, and 3, published in 1969, 1972, and 1974 respectively.
2. *e.g.*, *The Locomotives of the LBSC Rly*, The Locomotive Publishing Company, 1903; and *The Locomotives of the LBSC Rly, 1903-1923*. *Ibid.*, 1928. Also, *The Locomotives of the LBSC Rly*, Tilling, W. G., various editions.
3. Original held by Public Records Office under reference LBR 3/12.
4. The impression appears to have been held in certain quarters that Class L locomotives, in particular, were not allowed to pass over Ford Bridge.

   The Author has found no evidence to justify such an impression. Ford Bridge had been strengthened in the 1890s and was capable of taking all classes of LBSC Rly locomotives.

   After the Brighton had become part of the Southern Railway in 1923, matters were reviewed and the then Chief Engineer came to the conclusion that REGULAR use of class L engines over Ford Bridge was undesirable. This, however, did not really affect matters —engines of that class had never run regularly over that bridge in any case.

   The occasional use of classes J and L on the Sutton-Horsham-Mid Sussex line and over Ford Bridge continued until at least the late 1920s, the Author still having notes made at the time of his personal observations some 50 years ago.
5. *e.g.*, Newbury, P. J., *Carriage Stock of the LBSCR*, The Oakwood Press, 1976.
6. LBSC Rly Appendix for August 1922, p. 178.

COMPREHENSIVE INDEX TO VOLUMES I, II, AND III

§ Not to be confused with SE Rly station of that name (now Addiscombe), a long way east of East Croydon station.

SUPPLEMENTARY INDEX No. 1
Bridges and Viaducts Actually Built

General References: I, 47, 49–52, 54, 124, 129, 209, 219, 220, 226, 227, 229, 230, 233, 237, 245; II, 53, 70, 77, 90, 92, 105, 107, 112, 129, 142, 147, 155, 156, 158, 173, 207–208, 217; III, 4, 9, 25, 26, 29, 33, 50, 57, 61, 65, 76, 78, 114, 115, 117, 118, 169, 197

Individual Structures by name:

Name	Between or At	Volume and Page
Addiscombe Road Bridge[1]	Immediately south of East Croydon stn	II, 242
Adur Bridge	Southwater and West Grinstead	II, 93
Adur Estuary Bridge	(see Shoreham Viaduct)	
Adur Viaduct	Bramber and Shoreham Jct	II, 95
Anerley Road Bridge	Immediately south of Anerley station	I, 51
Arun Bridge (later rebuilt and soon after renamed Ford Bridge)	Littlehampton and Arundel (first station) (now Ford)	I, 209, 210–211, Plate 14; II, xi, 98–99, 134, 135–137, Plate 7, xiv–xv, Plates 8, 9, and 10; III, xi, 68, 224 (Note 4)
Arundel Road Bridge	Immediately north of present Arundel stn	II, 104
Ashcombe Bridge	Falmer and Kingston Tunnel	I, 219
Balham High Road Bridge	Immediately east of original Balham Hill stn, and immediately west of present Balham stn	II, 53, 238; III, 82
Battersea Bridge	Over River Thames, between Chelsea and Battersea, on WLE Rly	II, 130
Battersea Park Bridge	Immediately south of Battersea Park stn, on High-Level line to Poupart's Jct	II, Plate 12
Battersea Rise Bridge[2]	28 Chains south of Clapham Jct stn	II, 59, 238; III, 82
Beckenham Hill Bridge	Immediately north of Penge (West) stn (see also Penge High Street Bridge)	I, 51
Bedford Road Bridge	Immediately east of present Balham stn	II, 238
Beehive Bridge (Commonside Road East)	On Streatham Jct. South-Mitcham Jct. line, at 9 m 43 ch.	II, 210; III, 79
Bellevue Road Bridge	Immediately on London side of present Wandsworth Common stn	II, 53; III, 82
Bepton Road Bridge	Midhurst LBSC Rly and Midhurst LSW Rly	II, 92; III, 58

Name	Between or At	Volume and Page
Woldingham Road Viaduct	Upper Warlingham and Oxted Tunnel; with the building of Woldingham (originally Marden Park) station, now situated between Upper Warlingham and Woldingham stations	III, 29
Woodplace Lane Bridge (original)	Coulsdon (now Coulsdon South) and first Merstham Tunnel	I, 125, 127

NOTES FOR SUPPLEMENTARY INDEX No. 1

1. Not referred to by name on II, 242.
2. Sometimes colloquially referred to as Freemason's Bridge. The latter name is only officially applied to the overbridge carrying Battersea Rise over the L S W Rly Main lines, immediately to the west of the L B S C Rly in this vicinity. Freemason's Bridge (over the L S W Rly) is therefore immediately west of Battersea Rise Bridge (over the L B S C Rly).
3. Not referred to by name on II, 104.
4. Not referred to by name on II, 108, but actually over one of the roads to Norbury Park Estate.
5. Official name is Brockley Way Bridge.
6. Informal name only. Bridge officially designated by position only (i.e. 6 miles 77 chains).
7. Informal name only. Bridge officially designated as High Street Bridge at 7 miles 11 chains.
8. Brockley station later built at site where what is now Endwell Road crosses over the railway.
9. Extent of viaduct covered in this account. The viaduct actually extends south of Corbett's Lane Jct., as far as Greenwich.
10. Official name is Dunton Road Bridge.
11. Not referred to by name on II, 159.
12. Bridge built to carry road over railway opened in 1839. Honor Oak Park stn not opened until 1886.
13. Now officially designated Hill Place Viaduct.
14. Name later given to this bridge, which was originally designated New England Road Underbridge.
15. Not referred to by name on II, 211.
16. Not referred to by name on II, 159.
17. Not referred to by name on II, 194.
18. Not referred to by name on II, 194.
19. Name not apparently in use until about 1850.
20. Not referred to by name on II, 76.
21. Not referred to by name on II, 76.
22. Not referred to by name on II, 104.
23. Modern name and not given on II, 122.
24. Not referred to by name on II, 94.
25. Down Line bridge brought into use about 1897. Up Line bridge brought into use in 1903.

SUPPLEMENTARY INDEX No. 2
Level Crossings[1] (All Types)

General References: I, 125-126, 129-130, 209-210, 220, 225, 230, 233, 237; II, 64, 70, 77, 92, 107, 112, 142, 147, 155, 173, 214; III, 4, 9, 25, 26, 29, 33, 57, 61, 65.

Individual Crossings by name:

Name	Between or At	Volume and Page
Adams Well	Groombridge and Tunbridge Wells	II, 155
Adversane	Billingshurst and Rats Bottom Crossings	II, 90
Alfred Road[2]	Edinburgh Road Crossing and Unicorn Gates	III, 51
Anchor	Isfield and Barcombe Mills	II, 76; III, 41
Anchor Gates[3]	Unicorn Gates and R.N. Dockyard itself	III, 51
Angmering Road	Immediately west of Angmering stn	I, 210
Arundel (Ford)	East of Arundel (Ford) stn[4]	I, 210
Arundel Road	Immediately west of original (later closed) Littlehampton stn on West Coast line	I, 210
Ashtead	Immediately east of Ashtead stn	II, 73
Ashurst	Spatham Lane Crossing and Plumpton stn	I, 226
Balcombe Tunnel	North of Balcombe Tunnel	I, 120
Barcombe Mills	Immediately north of Barcombe Mills stn	II, 75
Barns Green	Itchingfield Jct and Billingshurst	II, 90
Basin Road	At east approach to Chichester stn	I, 210
Baynards	Immediately at Horsham end of Baynards stn	II, 145, 147
Beddingham	Southerham Jct and Glynde	I, 220
Beddington	Immediately east of Beddington Lane	II, 64
Bedelands (Bodelands or Bedelwood)	Haywards Heath and Wivelsfield	I, 126
Bedhampton	Stockheath Crossing and Bedhampton Mill Crossing	I, 237
Bedhampton Mill	Bedhampton Crossing and Farlington Jct	I, 237
Bee Brook	(see Brook Lane Crossing, west of Angmering)	

Name	Between or At	Volume and Page
Bersted	North of Bognor	II, 142; III, 155, 164
Berwick	Immediately east of Berwick stn	I, 220
Billingshurst	Immediately west of Billingshurst stn	II, 90
Black Boy Lane	New Fishbourne Crossing and Brook Lane Crossing, east of Bosham stn	I, 237
Blackfriars Road	East of Portsmouth	I, 237; III, 49, 56
Bosham	Immediately west of Bosham	I, 237
Braggs Lane	West of Bexhill	I, 220
Brambletye	East Grinstead and Forest Row	II, 158
Bramley	Immediately on Horsham side of Bramley & Wonersh stn	II, 146, 147
Brickfield	West of original Portslade stn, itself west of present stn	I, 129
Brighton Road, Croydon	Norwood (Jolly Sailor) and West Croydon (now an overbridge south of Gloucester Road Jct area)	I, 56
Broad Road	Drift Lane Crossing and Inlands Road Crossing, and the fifth road crossing west of Bosham	I, 237
Broadwater Road	West of original Worthing stn	I, 210
Brook Lane	Angmering and original (later closed) Littlehampton stn	I, 210
Brook Lane	Just east of Bosham stn	I, 237
Buckingham Road	Immediately west of Shoreham (now Shoreham-by-Sea) stn	I, 209
California	Immediately south of California (now Belmont) stn	II, 217
Carshalton Road	About ½ mile east of Mitcham stn, on West Croydon–Wimbledon line[5]	II, 64, 213
Castle Lane	Steyning and Bramber	II, 95
Cemetery	Portcreek Jct and Portsmouth	I, 237
Chapel No. 1	East of Plumpton	I, 226
Chapel No. 2	East of Plumpton	I, 226
Chesswood	East of Worthing	I, 210
Clay Lane	West of Fishbourne Crossing	I, 237
Cold Blow	New Cross (Gate) stn, and New Cross Lift Bridge, on Incline Road	III, 73
Compasses	Three Bridges and Rowfant	II, 70
Cooksbridge	Immediately east of Cooksbridge stn	I, 225
Copnor	Portcreek Jct and Portsmouth, as line was built	I, 237
Copyhold	North of Haywards Heath stn	I, 125
Cosham	Immediately w of Cosham stn	I, 237

Name	Between or At	Volume and Page
Cow	Ranscombe Crossing and Beddingham Crossing, east of Southerham Jct	I, 220
Crawley	Immediately west of original Crawley stn	I, 233
Cray Lane	Frogshole Crossing and Pulborough	II, 90
Dartmouth Arms	Immediately north of original Dartmouth Arms stn	I, 56, 184; III, 92
Daux	15 chains east of Billingshurst stn	II, 91
Dell Quay	East of Chichester stn	I, 210
Dene Farm	Earlswood and Horley	I, 125
Denehurst	Earlswood and Horley	I, 125
Denton	Immediately north of Newhaven Town stn	I, 227
Ditton Farm	Polegate and Stone Cross Jct	I, 220
'To Dockyard'[6]	Immediately west of Portsmouth Town (now Portsmouth & Southsea) stn	III, 48, 51
Dorset Road	Second Crossing eastwards of Bexhill stn	I, 220
Drayton	Immediately east of Drayton stn	I, 210
Drift Lane	Fourth Crossing west of Bosham stn	I, 237
Dundonald Road[7]	Morden and Wimbledon; with the building of the Merton Park stn, Dundonald Road crossing now situated between Merton Park and Wimbledon	II, 64
Dutton's Lane (Straight Lane)	Portcreek Jct and Portsmouth	I, 237
East Chiltington	Plumpton and Cooksbridge	I, 225
Edinburgh Road[8]	Portsmouth High Level and Alfred Road Crossing	III, 51, 52
Elm Grove	Second Crossing east of Goring stn	I, 210
Emsworth	Immediately east of Emsworth stn	I, 237
Farm	North of Wivelsfield stn	I, 126
Faygate	Immediately east of Faygate stn	I, 233
Ferring	West of Goring stn	I, 210
Fishbourne	About ¾ mile west of Chichester stn	I, 237; III, 58, 59
Five Bell Lane	North of New Cross stn	I, 56
Forge	Horley and Three Bridges	I, 125
Forge Farm	Birchden Jct and Eridge	II, 155
Fratton	East of Fratton stn over East Southsea line	III, 57

Name	Between or At	Volume and Page
Frogshole	Rats Bottom Crossing and Cray Lane Crossing (north of Pulborough)	II, 91
Funtington	West of Bosham Crossing, the latter being immediately west of Bosham stn	I, 237
Gallops Homestead	East of Spatham Lane Crossing, the latter being east of Keymer Jct on the Lewes line	I, 225–226
Gardner's	Second Crossing west of Portslade Crossing	I, 129
Gilham Wood	Sixth Crossing east of Pevensey	I, 220
Goring Road	Immediately west of Goring stn	I, 210
Gossops Green (Goffs Lane)	Crawley and Faygate	I, 233
Grange Road	Immediately east of Grange Road stn	II, 70
Green Lane	West of Funtington Crossing, between Bosham and Emsworth	I, 237
Green Lanes	Second crossing south of Portcreek Jct, on way to Portsmouth	I, 237
Grovers Field	Fifth crossing east of Pevensey	I, 220
Hamsey	¾ mile east of Cooksbridge	I, 225
Harbour Station	Public entrance to Portsmouth Harbour stn, over Watering Island (later South Railway Jetty) line	III, 50
Hardham	68 chains south of Pulborough	II, 91
Hassocks Gate	South of Hassocks Gate stn	I, 125
Havensmouth	Third crossing east of Pevensey	I, 220
Henty's	Goring and Angmering	II, 22
Holmethorpe	Merstham and Redhill	I, 225
Horley (Two)	Immediately north of original Horley stn, and immediately south of that stn, respectively	I, 125
Horsham Road	Short distance west of Crawley Crossing	I, 233
Hour Glass	Balcombe Tunnel and Balcombe stn	I, 126
Humphrey Farm (Maiden Bower)	North of Balcombe Tunnel Jct	I, 125
Ifield (Lions Farm)	Crawley and Faygate	I, 233
Inlands Road	Fifth crossing west of Bosham Crossing, the latter being immediately west of Bosham stn	I, 237

NOTES FOR SUPPLEMENTARY INDEX No. 2

1.Not all the level crossings listed below still exist:
>Some were either replaced by bridges or were abolished during the life of the LBSC Rly (i.e. up to the end of 1922), as referred to in the three volumes of the present account and hence indexed below.
>Further crossings were either replaced by bridges or were abolished from 1923 onwards. These changes are *NOT* covered in the present account and hence are *NOT* indexed below.
>Yet further crossings have disappeared as such, due to the railway lines concerned having been closed in relatively recent years.

2.First Crossing of North Dockyard line inside outer periphery of R.N. Dockyard at Portsmouth.
3.Third (and last) Crossing of North Dockyard line inside outer periphery of R.N. Dockyard at Portsmouth.
4.Station renamed Ford in 1863.
5.Site of level crossing represented by overbridge immediately west of present Mitcham Jct station, not built until 1868.
6.Official name of crossing not known to Author.
7.'Modern' name when area commenced to be built up.
8.Entrance of North Dockyard line to outer periphery of R.N. Dockyard at Portsmouth.
9.Merton Park station (originally named Lower Merton) was built in 1868 immediately on the Morden (south-east) side of Kingston Road Crossing.
10.Sometimes shown as Lyon's Farm Crossing.
11.Site of level crossing represented by overbridge east of Morden Halt.
12. Site of level crossing represented by footbridge.
13.Present Portslade station built in 1881, on Brighton side of Crossing. When originally built, Portslade station was on Shoreham side of crossing, which was therefore *east* of the original station.
14,15.The authorised route through Shipley was dropped without any constructional work having been done, and a new route was authorised to start from Itchingfield Jct nearer to Horsham than the route from Barns Green—see II, 86. Adoption of this new route meant that Shipley Crossing was never made.
16.Public thoroughfare renamed Eastfields Road in recent years, and level crossing now known by that name.
17.Second crossing of North Dockyard line inside outer periphery of R.N. Dockyard at Portsmouth.
18.Site of level crossing represented by overbridge some 400 yds west of present Mitcham Jct station (not built until 1868), and on line to Wimbledon.

SUPPLEMENTARY INDEX No. 3
Tunnels[1]

General References: I, Chapters Five and Six (schemes for railways between London & Brighton), and pp. 141–142.

Individual Tunnels by name:

Name	Between or At	Volume and Page
Argos Hill[2]	Rotherfield and Mayfield	III, 9
Balcombe	Balcombe Tunnel Jct and Balcombe stn	I, 120, 123, 133, 141, 142; II, 280; III, 151
Betchworth	Dorking and Holmwood	II, 109; III, 66
Bo-Peep[3]	Bo-Peep Jct and St. Leonards (Warrior Square) stn	III, 41
Brighton[4]	Under Brighton stn, between line to Shoreham and the (Lower) Goods Yard	I, 128, Plate 8; II, 233
Cane Hill Covered Way[5]	Coulsdon North and Merstham New (now Quarry) Tunnel	III, 115–116
Cinder Hill	Newick & Chailey and Barcombe	III, 23
Clayton	Hassocks stn and Patcham Tunnel	I, 122, 123, 131, 133, 141; III, 151
Cliftonville	Preston Park and Hove[6]	III, 106, 205
Cocking	Cocking stn and Singleton Tunnel	III, 60–61
Coombe Lane[7]	Park Hill Tunnel and Coombe Lane stn	III, 76
Crowborough[8]	Crowborough stn[8] and Sleeches Viaduct, on line to Buxted	II, 155
Crystal Palace	Crystal Palace and Gipsy Hill (just west of Crystal Palace stn)	II, 52; III, 165, 176, 177
Denmark Hill[9]	Peckham Rye and Denmark Hill (just east of Denmark Hill stn)	II, 195–196
Denmark Hill	Denmark Hill and East Brixton (just west of Denmark Hill stn)	II, 195–196
Ditchling Road	London Road (Brighton) and Kemp Town Jct	I, 216, 219
East Grinstead No. 1	East Grinstead stn and East Grinstead No. 2 Tunnel	II, 158
East Grinstead No. 2	East Grinstead No. 1 Tunnel and Forest Row stn	II, 158

NOTES FOR SUPPLEMENTARY INDEX No.3

1. In addition to tunnels on purely L B S C Rly lines, Supplementary Index No. 3 takes account of tunnels on lines where the L B S C Rly was joint owner, and also of tunnels on lines over which the L B S C Rly constantly exercised running powers.
2. Not included in L B S C Rly list of tunnels.
3. Tunnel owned and maintained by S E Rly (by S E C Rly from 1899).
4. Tunnel taken out of use for traffic purposes about 1852—see II, 233.
5. Not included in L B S C Rly list of tunnels although 411⅔ yds. long (L B S C Rly Notice), as this structure had been built by the Cut-and-Cover method.
6. Hove station bore the name Cliftonville when the line from Preston Park through Cliftonville Tunnel, was brought into use.
7. Tunnel on Woodside & South Croydon Rly, owned jointly by L B S C Rly and S E Rly (S E C Rly from 1899), but maintained by S E Rly (S E C Rly from 1899).
8. Crowborough Tunnel and Crowborough station were named Rotherfield Tunnel and Rotherfield station, respectively, until 31 July 1880.
9. This Denmark Hill Tunnel was renamed Grove Tunnel by the Southern Railway after 1923.

Under its new (and present) name, it must not be confused with Grove Tunnel at Tunbridge Wells.

10. Only called Littlebrown Tunnel (or Little Brown's Tunnel) in recent years. The LBSC Rly official name was Edenbridge Tunnel.

11. Falmer station was originally built at the east (or Lewes) end of Falmer Tunnel—see I, 217. That tunnel was then situated between Ditchling Road Tunnel and Falmer station. That station was itself resited on the west (or Brighton) side of Falmer Tunnel on 1 August 1865 (see I, 217, and II, 245), and thereafter Falmer Tunnel was situated between Falmer station and Kingston Tunnel, as stated in the tabular part of this Index.

12. Not to be confused with the tunnel now also so named, and situated just east of Denmark Hill station—see Note 9 above.

13. Still correct identification of the situation of Hove Tunnel, despite closure of original (1840) station named Hove and the ultimate re-use of the name Hove for the station originally built in 1865 as Cliftonville.

14. Since Falmer station was originally east of Falmer Tunnel, the initial identification of the situation of Kingston Tunnel was that it was between Falmer station and Lewes station. As explained in Note 11 above, Falmer station was resited on the west (or Brighton) side of Falmer Tunnel on 1 August 1865, and thereafter identification of the situation of Kingston Tunnel was as stated in the tabular part of this Index.

15. Streatham Hill station was originally called (plain) Streatham when the Crystal Palace & West End of London Rly's line was opened in 1856 (see II, 53). The station was renamed in 1869.

16. West Norwood station was originally called Lower Norwood (see II, 52).

17. Owned and maintained by SE Rly (SEC Rly from 1899).

18. Present name of station.

19. Tunnel was on portion of Croydon, Oxted & East Grinstead line, owned jointly by LBSC Rly and SE Rly (SEC Rly from 1899) as far south as Crowhurst Jct North. Oxted Tunnel was on that part of the line maintained by the LBSC Rly.

20. Woldingham station was opened as Marden Park on 1 July 1885, and was renamed Woldingham on 1 January 1894. Prior to 1 July 1885, the site of Oxted Tunnel was between Upper Warlingham and Oxted.

21. Tunnel was on portion of Croydon, Oxted & East Grinstead line, owned jointly by LBSC Rly and SE Rly (SEC Rly from 1899) as far south as Crowhurst Jct North. Riddlesdown Tunnel was on that part of the line maintained by the SE Rly (SEC Rly from 1899).

22. Tunnel on the Isle of Wight and Ryde Pier Rly, owned jointly by LBSC Rly and LSW Rly.

SUPPLEMENTARY INDEX No. 4

Proposed Lines for which no Important Construction was Undertaken